How to Do Everything with

Phot Elements® 2

David Plotkin

McGraw-Hill/Osborne

New York   Chicago   San Francisco   Lisbon
London   Madrid   Mexico City   Milan   New Delhi
San Juan   Seoul   Singapore   Sydney   Toronto

McGraw-Hill/Osborne
2600 Tenth Street
Berkeley, California 94710
U.S.A.

To arrange bulk purchase discounts for sales promotions, premiums, or fund-raisers, please contact **McGraw-Hill**/Osborne at the above address. For information on translations or book distributors outside the U.S.A., please see the International Contact Information page immediately following the index of this book.

How to Do Everything with Photoshop® Elements® 2

1234567890 CUS CUS 0198765432

ISBN 0-07-222638-2

Publisher	**Project Manager**	**Proofreaders**
Brandon A. Nordin	Laurie Stewart,	Kelly Marshall,
	Happenstance Type-O-Rama	K.J. Malkovich
Vice President &		
Associate Publisher	**Copy Editors**	**Indexer**
Scott Rogers	Sachi Guzman,	Jack Lewis
	Lunaea Weatherstone	
Editorial Director		**Series Designer**
Roger Stewart	**Compositor**	Mickey Galicia
	Kate Kaminski,	
Acquisitions Editor	Happenstance Type-O-Rama	**Cover Series Design**
Megg Morin		Dodie Shoemaker
	Computer Designer	
Senior Project Editor	Chris Gillespie,	**Cover Design**
Madhu Prasher	Happenstance Type-O-Rama	Greg Scott
Acquisitions Coordinator	**Illustrators**	**Cover Illustration**
Tana Allen	Michael Mueller,	Tom Willis
	Lyssa Wald	
Technical Editor		
Bill Bruns		

This book was composed with QuarkXPress™.

Dedication

This book is dedicated to my mother, Nathalie Plotkin. She first encouraged my interest in photography (and later in writing), helped me to set up my first darkroom, and taught me to use a camera as more than just a "snapshot machine." She raised three sons (our pictures are sprinkled through the book, as is hers)—a doctor and two engineers—and instilled in all of us a strong sense of values that has served us well. Good job, Mom!

About the Author

David Plotkin is the Manager of Data Administration for Longs Drug Stores and holds a Masters degree in Chemical Engineering from UC Berkeley. He designs computer systems and databases for a living, and is a self-taught web-building tool user—and the author of *How to Do Everything with FrontPage 2002*. He has been a photographer since the age of 12, and has done extensive semi-pro and action photo work. He has his own darkroom and created camp yearbooks long before the days of computers. He has extensive experience with digital photography, including cameras, scanners, printers, and software. David maintains web sites for various non-profit and charitable organizations, and has written several other computer books on database topics and graphics. He lives in Walnut Creek, California, with his wife Marisa, a successful writer of children's books (see www.MarisaMontes.com).

Contents

Acknowledgments

Many people contribute to a book, and this is especially true of a book that includes many photographs. This book would have been much harder to write had it not been for the efforts of the following people:

- Michael and Robin Crahan, whose little girl Erin appears in many photos (the "Starbucks Coffee Cup" girl). Thanks for allowing me to use their photos and their likenesses.

- Albert and Christine Course, whose son Ryan also appears in this book. Admittedly, using pictures of toddlers is kind of like cheating, since they are so cute—and Ryan is cuter than most.

- My parents, Norman and Nathalie Plotkin, for allowing me to use them as the subject of many pictures. Most were taken on their 50th anniversary—now, *that* is longevity!

- My brother Fred (the doctor) whose likeness appears in many images—and got removed from one of them just because I could!

- My brother Larry (the engineer). Most of the outdoor scenes and European buildings were from Larry's collection, and he graciously allowed me to use them. He is the most artistic of the three brothers, and it really shows in his photos.

- My wife Marisa, not only for allowing me to use her portraits, but for putting up with the brutal schedule that goes along with writing a book. Fortunately, she is a writer herself (children's books), so she understands just how hard it is to write a book.

- My brother-in-law, Ruben Montes (another doctor!). His likeness—along with the first baby he ever delivered—appears in this book.

- The friendly people of Sydney, Australia. You folks should recognize your skyline in the Photomerge chapter. My advice to anyone who has not visited Sydney: Go!

Of course, the other "batch" of people who made this book a reality are the hard-working folks at McGraw-Hill/Osborne. These include my acquisitions editor Megg Morin, acquisitions coordinator Tana Allen (really delightful lady), and the best tech editor you can hope for—Bill Bruns, who also did *How to Do Everything with FrontPage 2002* for me.

Lastly, there was Laurie Stewart and her hard-working editorial and production teams—Sachi Guzman and Lunaea Weatherstone, copyeditors; Kate Kaminski, compositor; Chris Gillespie, computer designer; and Kelly Marshall and K.J. Malkovich, proofreaders. When the publisher moved up the publish date by three weeks, they went into overdrive, working nights and weekends to get everything edited and laid out. A book like this one is harder than most because of the large number of images, but they pulled it off, and even managed to keep a sense of humor about the whole thing.

Introduction

The fact that you bought this book—or are considering buying it—means you are ready to join the large number of people who have discovered the wonders of digitally editing photographs. Whether you get your photos into digital form by using a digital camera, scanning your snapshots or negatives, or having the corner drugstore put them on a CD for you (yes, they do that now—at least many do), the wonders of what you can achieve with your photos are only beginning. In front of you is a whole book on how to use one of the premier digital editing packages. Think of this book as a way to explore this fascinating new world.

What Is this Book About?

Significant advances on the hardware front have made digital photography more and more accessible. Cameras that cost under $1,000 now produce images that rival film quality. Color inkjet printers that cost between $150 and $400 produce beautiful prints on glossy paper, and scanners that cost less than $200 produce scans with resolutions of over 2400 dots per inch.

And yet, the real opportunity provided by digital photography (beyond seeing your pictures immediately on that tiny screen on the back of the camera) is to fix pictures that are less than perfect. Maybe the exposure or color was a little off, or a busy background distracts from the main subject. With regular film, you'd need a darkroom, an enlarger, a bunch of nasty chemicals, and considerable expertise (trust me, I know) to correct some of these items—and some you could never fix. For example, you can't add a person to a photograph who isn't there.

In other words, the real opportunity with digital photography is in the software. Software like Adobe Photoshop Elements 2. You can continue to take film pictures if you wish, but with a scanner or a handy digital photo lab at the drugstore, you can digitize the images—and that is where the fun begins. You don't need the darkroom, the enlarger, or the nasty chemicals. What you *still* need is the considerable expertise. And *that* is what this book provides. It teaches you to use Adobe Photoshop Elements to modify your digital photographs, using the power of the built-in tools. With a little care and some hard drive space, nothing you do is irreversible—you can always start over from the original. And you don't have to commit the image to paper until you are truly satisfied with it.

How Is this Book Organized?

This book is divided into five parts:

- Part I, "Get to Know Photoshop Elements"
- Part II, "Make Simple Adjustments to Your Images"
- Part III, "Apply Changes to Specific Parts of Your Images"
- Part IV, "Use Effects, Filters, and Text to Go Beyond the Darkroom"
- Part V, "Share Your Images with Others"

Part I, "Get to Know Photoshop Elements," introduces the various parts of the software, including navigation, the desktop, palettes, and the toolbar. It shows you how to set the software up the way you like, open and save images, and use the various tools to view images.

Part II, "Make Simple Adjustments to Your Images," teaches you to make general corrections to the overall image, such as adjusting brightness, contrast, and color. It also shows you how to use the Brush and other toolbox tools to modify an image, sharpening and blurring the image, as well as other effects. With the Dodge and Burn tools, you can simulate old photography techniques for lightening and darkening specific portions of the image. Finally, this section shows you exactly how to repair cracked and faded photos.

Part III, "Apply Changes to Specific Parts of Your Images," teaches you to select the portion of your photo you want to work with, including all areas of a certain color. Of course, once you have selected an area, you can apply changes limited to just that area, such as a gradient fill or a blur. This section also introduces layers, which enable you to stack up changes and modifications without changing the base image. You can apply fills and adjustments (like color or brightness) to layers, adjusting the amount of the effect by changing the layer opacity, and masking the effect of the layer in portions of the image. You can apply styles to a layer, modifying the contents of the layer. With the transform tools, you can flip, rotate, skew, distort, and make other transformations to selected objects. You can add objects that weren't there, remove objects that were, and modify the background of an image—or replace it altogether. You can also change images by adding simple vector shapes to it.

Part IV, "Use Effects, Filters, and Text to Go Beyond the Darkroom," introduces filters, powerful tools that can change the look of your image with very little effort. You can add texture, make the image look like it was created in alternative media (such as watercolors or color pencils), add special lighting, and even create a three-dimensional look for boxes, cylinders, and spheres. You can add text to an image and modify how the text looks, even creating a mask in the shape of text to describe an image. Finally, Photoshop Elements can automatically paste together pictures that contain overlapping images into a panoramic—handy for city skylines.

Part V, "Share Your Images with Others, " teaches you how to create a Web Photo Gallery and a PDF (Adobe Acrobat) photo presentation. It also shows you how to print your images, both one at a time and as an optimized layout to maximize the use of photo paper. Finally, you'll learn how to do batch conversions to change the file type, size, and name of a set of image files.

Who Is this Book Written For?

This book is written primarily for people who want to learn how to use Photoshop Elements to manipulate digital photographs. There are many features of Photoshop Elements that you won't use when working with photos, and these are not covered because there simply isn't room to cover everything this powerful package can do. This book does not assume you are an expert photographer, but it focuses on the software, and so does not teach you to become an accomplished photographer. It assumes you know how to either create digital photos or convert film images/slides/negatives to digital form. It presents information in a logical, step-by-step format, so you can read the book through to learn what Photoshop Elements can do—and then refer to it later as you need to refresh your memory on a particular technique.

So, enjoy the experience! There is nothing quite like taking a so-so photo and turning it into a work of art. Working with digital photos and Adobe Photoshop Elements is fun and rewarding. And the first time you restore a damaged (and possibly irreplaceable) photo for someone, you'll know a real feeling of satisfaction.

Part I

Get to Know Photoshop Elements

Chapter 1

Navigate in Photoshop Elements

How to...

■ Work with the interface

■ Get help in more ways than one

■ Use the QuickStart screen

■ Rearrange the Photoshop Elements desktop

■ Set the preferences to suit you

As with any software program, you must find your way around the interface if you hope to use the features effectively. The Photoshop Elements interface is busier than most—in fact, much of the screen is filled up with toolbars, help windows, palettes, and other tools to help you edit your images. The time you spend understanding the interface will allow you to use Photoshop Elements the most efficiently.

Understand the Interface

Figure 1-1 displays the Photoshop Elements desktop in its default configuration.

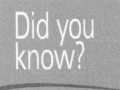 You can turn the options bar, shortcuts bar, status bar, toolbox, and all the palettes on and off by using the Window menu. The entries in the Window menu are toggles—selecting an item that is unchecked makes what you've selected visible in the work area and adds a check mark to the item. Selecting an item that is already checked (and therefore visible in the work area) hides that item and clears the check mark.

 Your default configuration may look different from what is pictured in Figure 1-1, especially if your monitor is configured to display a different resolution from the one in the figure (1028 × 768). Adobe recommends that you use this as the minimum resolution. If you use a resolution of 800 × 600, it will be very difficult to work with the palette well and the palettes themselves because of the amount of overlap you will see.

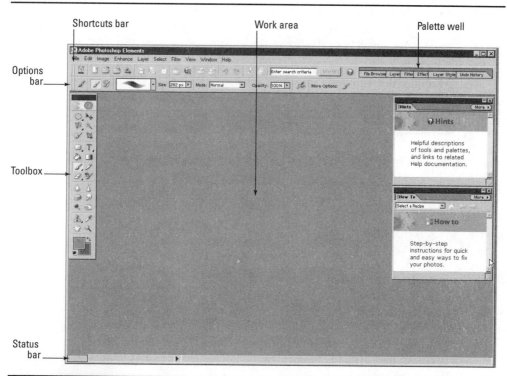

FIGURE 1-1   Working with Photoshop Elements requires that you understand the tools.

View the Work Area

The work area is the entire screen below the options bar and is where you open your images to work on them, as discussed in Chapter 3. Your open images share this area with the toolbox and any palettes you have opened.

You can open multiple images at one time. Each image appears in its own window in the work area. Once you have one or more images open in the work area, you can perform the following operations on the image windows:

Move the window   To move a window containing an image, simply click and drag the window title bar.

Resize the window To resize a window containing an image, move the mouse over a border or a corner of the window. Once the mouse pointer turns into a double-headed arrow, click and drag the border or corner. Only the window is resized; the size of the image inside the window remains unchanged.

Minimize the window You can minimize the window containing an image if you need to move it out of your way, while still leaving the image open. To do so, click the *minimize* button (the button with the dash in the upper-right corner of the window). The window will minimize down to the title bar in the lower-left corner of the work area:

Maximize the window You can maximize the window to occupy the entire work area. This is an excellent way to work when you want to see as much of a single image as possible. To maximize the window, click the *maximize* button (the button containing the single rectangle in the upper-right corner of the window). Once you have maximized the window, the control buttons (minimize, restore, and close) appear in the upper-right corner of the Photoshop Elements window on the same line as the menus.

Restore the window After you have either minimized or maximized a window containing an image, you can restore the window to its previous size by clicking the *restore* button (the button containing two rectangles in the upper-right corner of the window).

Close the window Once you are done working with an image, you can remove it from the work area by clicking the *close* button (the button with the × in the upper-right corner of the window). This performs the same function as selecting File | Close.

You can quickly maximize the work area by pressing TAB to hide all open palettes, the options bar, the shortcuts bar, and the toolbox. Pressing TAB again redisplays all these items. Pressing SHIFT-TAB hides or displays just the palettes.

View the Shortcuts Bar

The shortcuts bar contains commonly used tools, such as buttons for opening and saving files, printing, undoing, searching, getting help, and the palette well. You can turn the shortcuts bar on and off by toggling (selecting) Window | Shortcuts. When this menu option displays a check mark next to it, the shortcuts bar is visible.

By default, the shortcuts bar is "docked" at the top of the screen. To undock the shortcuts bar and move it into the work area, click the gripper bar (two vertical lines) at the left end of the shortcuts bar and drag it:

Once you have undocked the shortcuts bar, the gripper bar is replaced by a vertical title bar at the left end of the shortcuts bar. To move the shortcuts bar, click and drag this title bar. To re-dock the shortcuts bar, click the title bar and drag the shortcuts bar back to the top of the screen.

Unlike many other programs with toolbars, in Photoshop Elements you cannot dock the shortcuts bar (or any other toolbar) in any place other than at the top of the screen. Also, you cannot customize the contents of the shortcuts bar by turning individual tool buttons on and off. So don't even try.

View the Options Bar

As you make modifications to images in Photoshop Elements, you will choose tools from the toolbox (see "View the Toolbox," later in this chapter). Once you have done so, the icon for the currently selected tool appears at the left end of the options bar, along with the most commonly used options for that tool. You can use these options to configure how the tool works. In addition, a button for additional options (if there are any) appears at the right end of the options bar. For example, if you select the Paintbrush tool, the options bar enables you to set the brush style, size, blending mode, opacity, and whether to use the brush as an airbrush, as shown previously in Figure 1-1.

If the options you need are *not* available in the options bar, click the More Options button to display a dialog box of additional options:

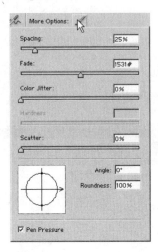

You can turn the options bar on and off by toggling (selecting) Window | Options. When this menu option displays a check mark next to it, the shortcuts bar is visible. As with the shortcuts bar, you can dock, undock, and move the options bar.

View the Toolbox

The toolbox appears at the left edge of the work area by default. You can move the toolbox by clicking on the title bar and dragging the toolbox to a new location.

As shown in Figure 1-2, the toolbox contains buttons that activate many of the tools you'll use to customize your images. To choose a tool, click the button in the toolbox or press the key for the tool keyboard shortcut. The keyboard shortcut key appears in a tool tip when you hover the mouse over a toolbox button.

Some of the buttons listed in Figure 1-2 display a small arrow in the lower-right corner:

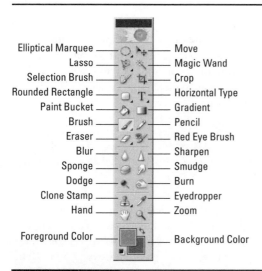

Elliptical Marquee ———— Move
Lasso ———— Magic Wand
Selection Brush ———— Crop
Rounded Rectangle ———— Horizontal Type
Paint Bucket ———— Gradient
Brush ———— Pencil
Eraser ———— Red Eye Brush
Blur ———— Sharpen
Sponge ———— Smudge
Dodge ———— Burn
Clone Stamp ———— Eyedropper
Hand ———— Zoom

Foreground Color ———— Background Color

FIGURE 1-2   The Photoshop Elements toolbar makes most of the tools available at the click of a mouse.

You use these buttons to choose one of several related tools. To select the tool currently displayed by the button, click the button. To select one of the other related tools, click the button and hold it down to display a menu of other tools:

Select one of the tools from the menu. You can cycle through the hidden tools available by pressing SHIFT and the keyboard shortcut.

The bottom of the toolbox contains the color selection boxes for choosing the foreground and background colors, and is covered in detail in Chapter 5.

View the Status Bar

The status bar runs along the bottom of the screen, and displays three types of information. At the far left end of the status bar is the zoom level—the level of magnification for the currently active image. As you change the zoom level using the Zoom tool or the View menu, the zoom level in the status bar changes to match. You can change the magnification by clicking the zoom level in the status bar and typing in a new value.

You can type in any zoom level up to 1600%. The minimum zoom level depends on the screen resolution, varying from .08% at 1600 × 1280 to 0.35% at 1024 × 768. Do not type any symbol other than a percent sign (%) when setting a zoom level or Photoshop Elements will display an error.

The right end of the status bar displays hints and tips related to the current toolbox tool. It also displays a progress bar to help you monitor operations that take a while to complete.

Just to the right of the zoom level is an area that displays information you can choose. By default, this area shows the size of the image you are working on. However, you can click the small arrowhead to display a pop-up menu from which you can select other types of information, as shown here:

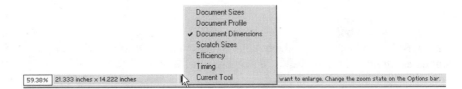

The options you can select are:

Document Sizes   Indicates the size of the current file. The number is displayed in kilobytes (K) if the image is under 1 megabyte in size; otherwise the size is displayed in megabyte (M). The first number is the size of the file without any layers (see Chapter 9). The second number is the size of the file with all layers intact. Note that file sizes are for the Photoshop Elements format even if the file is actually in another format (such as JPEG).

Document Profile   The active color profile for the current file, including Untagged RGB and sRGB IEC61966-21.

Document Dimensions   Displays the length and width dimensions of the current file. You can change the unit of measure (inches, centimeters, pixels, and so on) by setting the appropriate preferences (Edit | Preferences | Units & Rulers) as discussed in "Set Your Own Preferences," in Chapter 2.

Scratch Sizes   Displays the RAM used to process an image. The number on the left is the total amount of memory being used to process all images; the number on the right is the total amount of memory available. If you open several large images, the first number can exceed the second number, indicating that you don't have enough memory for storing all images you want to open, and that Photoshop Elements must use your hard drive to store part of an image (the scratch disk).

Efficiency Indicates the percent of time that Photoshop Elements is able to process the image from memory versus having to read and write to the disk drive. If this value is below 100%, it means that Photoshop Elements is having to use the physical hard drive (as a scratch disk), which slows operations *considerably*. If this happens, you may want to consider increasing the RAM installed in your computer. You can also allocate more of your RAM to Photoshop Elements. Choose Edit | Preferences | Memory & Image Cache. By default, Photoshop Elements uses only 50% of your available memory as a maximum. However, you can increase the amount of memory you make available for use. To do so, increase the percentage in the Maximum Used By Photoshop Elements field.

Timing Shows the amount of time (in seconds) Photoshop Elements needed to complete the last operation.

Current Tool Displays the name of the currently active tool.

View and Work with the Palette Well

The palette well appears at the right end of the shortcuts bar. The purpose of the palette well is to efficiently store the palettes that provide you with powerful functionality. Each of the palettes will be covered later in the book, but Table 1-1 briefly describes each palette, along with the number of the chapter where it is covered in detail.

Palette Name	Description	Chapter
File Browser	Displays thumbnails of your images, and enables you to open an image.	3
Filters	Displays thumbnails of the effect of each filter, and enables you to select the filter you want to use.	14 and 15
Effects	Displays thumbnails of the available special effects, and enables you to select which effect you want to use.	15
Layer Styles	Displays the available layer styles so you can choose one and apply it to a layer.	10
Swatches	Displays a list of color choices so you can pick a foreground or background color.	5
Navigator	Displays a thumbnail of an image. You can scroll around an image or change the zoom level.	3

TABLE 1-1   Palettes Available in Photoshop Elements

Palette Name	Description	Chapter
Info	Displays information about an image.	1
Hints	Displays details of the currently selected tool or palette.	1
How To (Recipes)	Displays step-by-step instructions for performing complex tasks.	1
Undo History	Displays a list of all the changes you have made to an image. Allows you to return to an earlier state of the image if you need.	1
Layers	The primary tool for displaying layers, creating and deleting layers, and adjusting layer properties.	9

TABLE 1-1   Palettes Available in Photoshop Elements *(continued)*

You can use the palette well to do the following:

Display the contents of a palette   To display the contents of a palette that is stored in the palette well, simply select the tab containing the name of the palette. You can then make your choice from the palette, as described later in this book. Once you are done using the palette, you can hide the contents of the palette by either selecting the tab containing the palette name again, or clicking elsewhere in the work area.

Rearrange the palette order   To rearrange the order of palettes in the palette well, click a palette tab and drag it to its new location in the well. You can right-click a palette tab and choose the direction in which you want to move the palette by choosing Move to Left or Move to Right. You can also choose to move the palette to the right end of the palette well (choose Move to End) or to the left end of the palette well (choose Move to Beginning).

Drag palettes out of the palette well   To move a palette out of the palette well and keep it open in the work area, click the palette title tab and drag it out of the palette well:

1

Place a palette in the palette well   To move a palette into the palette well (allowing more space in the work area), select the palette title tab and drag the palette into the palette well. Move the mouse over the title tab of the palette that will appear to the right of the palette you are dragging, and release the mouse button.

Get Started with the Welcome Screen

When you first open Photoshop Elements, it presents you with the Welcome screen:

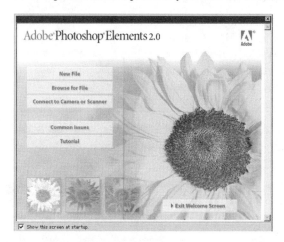

This screen presents a quick way to get started by allowing you to choose from these commands and perform the following tasks:

New File   Create a new document.

Browse for File   Open an existing document.

Connect to Camera or Scanner   Acquire a document from a scanner or digital camera.

Common Issues   Set the Recipe (How To) palette to a list of common issues.

Tutorial   Run a Photoshop Elements tutorial.

All of these commands are also available from the Photoshop Elements menus, so it is not necessary to use the Welcome screen if you don't want to. To keep the Welcome screen from appearing each time you start Photoshop Elements, clear the Show This Screen At Startup check box.

To redisplay the Welcome screen from inside Photoshop Elements, choose Welcome from the Window menu.

Obtain Help from Photoshop Elements

Photoshop Elements is a complex, powerful program, and if you are new to image manipulation programs, the power can be overwhelming. Fortunately, Photoshop Elements contains a considerable amount of help, including Photoshop Elements Help, Search, a Glossary, the Hints palette, and the Recipe (How To) palette.

Get Help from the Main Help Facilities

You can access Photoshop Elements' main help facility by choosing Help | Photoshop Element Help or by clicking the Help Contents button in the shortcuts bar (just to the left of the palette well). Either way, Help opens in your default browser, as shown in Figure 1-3. The left side of the browser window displays general help categories, and the details of each help subject appear on the right side.

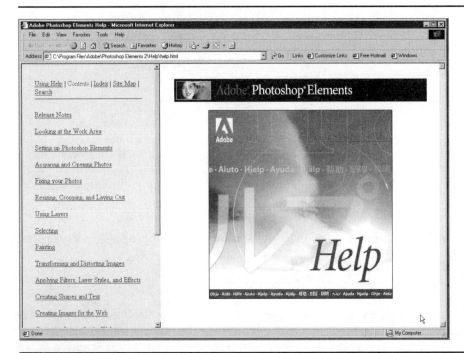

FIGURE 1-3   Get help from Photoshop Elements with the main help facility.

Find Definitions in the Glossary

If you're new to digital imaging programs, there are many terms you won't understand. The Photoshop Elements Glossary will come in handy here. It lists terms and their definitions. As with the main help facility, the Glossary opens in your browser window. You can access the Glossary either by choosing Glossary from the list of help categories on the left side of the Help browser window, or by choosing Help | Glossary of Terms from the menu.

Search for Help

If you just want to search for help on a particular word or phrase, type the search term in the Search field in the shortcuts bar, and press ENTER or click the Search button (it looks like a magnifying glass) alongside the Search field. If Photoshop Elements finds any matching results, it displays the list of help topics in the Search Results palette.

Two types of search results may be available for a search term: Results for Recipes and Results for Help. Selecting one of the Results for Recipes search results opens that topic in the How To (Recipes) palette. Selecting one of the Results for Help search results opens that topic in the Help browser.

You can choose to view only the Results for Recipes or Results for Help by selecting the type of search result from the drop-down list at the top-left corner of the Search Results palette.

View Hints in the Hints Palette

The Hints palette appears by default at the right side of the screen:

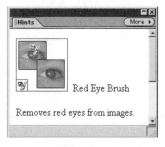

As you move the mouse, the Hints palette displays additional information about the toolbox tool or palette whose name tab appears under the mouse.

Follow a Recipe

The Recipe (How To) palette provides step-by-step instructions for making corrections to your images:

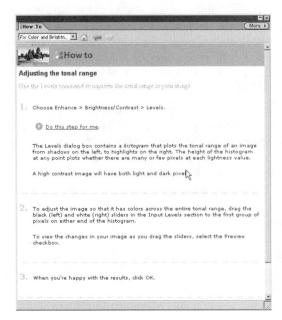

To follow a recipe, follow these steps:

1. Choose a recipe category from the drop-down list just below the tab.

2. From the list of recipes, select the recipe you want to use by clicking it.

3. Follow the instructions in the recipe to make your corrections.

Both Adobe and third-party software vendors will have additional recipes available to help you. To get additional recipes, connect to the Internet and select Download New Adobe Recipes from the drop-down list in the Recipes palette. Then follow the prompts in the resulting dialog box to download new recipes and any available program updates.

Get Important Data from the Info Palette

Strictly speaking, the Info palette (see Figure 1-4) isn't part of the help system. However, it provides valuable information as you use the tools in the toolbox. The Info palette is divided into four quadrants, each of which displays different information depending on which tool you have selected. For example, if you select the Eyedropper tool, the Info palette shows the RGB color under the tool in the two upper quadrants (the upper-right quadrant displays the color value in hexadecimal; the upper-left quadrant displays the color value in decimal), and the location (x and y coordinates) of the tool in the lower-left quadrant. However, if you select the Marquee selection tool and then drag a rectangle, the Info palette switches to show the color under the tool (upper-left), the tool's anchor point (upper-right), the current location of the tool (lower-left), and the height and width of the dragged rectangle (lower-right).

FIGURE 1-4   Use the Info palette to display location and color information about the currently selected toolbox tool.

Rearrange the Photoshop Elements Work Area to Suit You

How someone arranges the Photoshop Elements work area is very much a matter of personal taste. One person may prefer to have frequently used palettes open (which takes up some of the work area), while someone else may be willing to live with the inconvenience of keeping the palettes in the palette well in favor of having a larger area to work in. In fact, your own preferences may change as you become more experienced with Photoshop Elements and no longer need "help" palettes such as Hints or Recipes (How To).

Photoshop Elements enables you to organize your palettes to suit your current needs easily. You can move and resize palettes, dock or group them together, collapse a palette to hide its contents, and close a palette when you don't need it any longer.

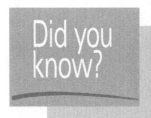

You can reset the palette locations to their factory defaults by choosing Window | Reset Palette Locations. This can be handy if you have made a real mess of your palettes by resizing, docking, and grouping them—or if you want to quickly clean up the work area by replacing palettes in the palette well in one easy step.

Move and Resize Palettes

To move a palette in the work area, click the title bar and drag the palette to a new location. Note that if you drag one palette on top of another, you may inadvertently dock or group the palettes together.

To resize a palette, move the mouse pointer over an edge or corner of the palette until it turns into a double-headed arrow. Click and drag the edge or corner to change its size.

The Info palette cannot be resized.

Dock and Undock Palettes

When you dock palettes together, you are essentially creating a mini palette well. The title tabs of the docked palettes appear alongside each other, and you can view only one palette at a time.

To view one of the other docked palettes, click the title tab of the palette whose contents you want to see. As with grouped palettes (see the next section), you move docked palettes together by clicking and dragging the common title bar.

To dock two palettes together, click the title tab of an undocked palette and drag it over the main area of another palette (or set of docked palettes) until a rectangle appears.

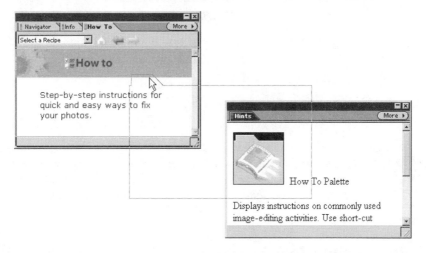

Release the mouse button and the palettes are docked together.

As with the palette well, you can rearrange the order of the palettes in a docked set by clicking and dragging a palette title bar to the right or left of other title bars in the docked set.

To undock a palette from a docked set, click and drag the palette title bar out of the docked set.

Group and Ungroup Palettes

To group two palettes together, click the title tab of an ungrouped palette and drag it over another palette (or a grouped set of palettes) until the mouse pointer is adjacent to the title tab of the palette you want to group with. Release the mouse pointer to create the group:

 *As you drag the palette, you'll most likely see the docking rectangle mentioned in the previous section. However, as you bring the mouse pointer alongside the title tab of the palette you want to group with, the rectangle will change slightly. The change is subtle, but you can see it if you're looking for it.*

Collapse and Close Palettes

If you want to keep a palette in the work area but don't need it right at the moment, you can hide its contents by clicking the minimize button in the upper-right corner. This collapses the palette, leaving only the title tab and More menu visible:

To redisplay the full palette, click the maximize button (which replaced the minimize button).

If you are done using a palette, you can close it to get it out of your way. To close the palette, click the close button in the upper-right corner of the palette. What happens at this point depends on the setting of the Close Palette to Palette Well item in the More menu, as explained here:

Close Palette to Palette Well is enabled (check mark)   The palette is removed from the work area and appears in the palette well.

Close Palette to Palette Well is disabled (no check mark)   The palette is closed and no longer visible, either in the work area or the palette well.

To access the menu options just mentioned, click the More button in the upper-right corner of the palette.

Turn Palettes On and Off with the Window Menu

At this point you might be wondering how you're going to turn a palette on once it's no longer visible. Of course, Photoshop Elements provides you with a solution—the Window menu:

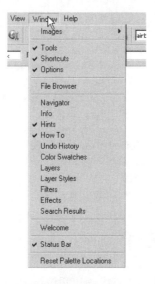

The center section of this menu provides a list of all the palettes. Those palettes with a check mark are visible in the work area, and those without a check mark are not visible in the work area (they may be docked in the palette well). To view a palette in the work area, select an unchecked palette in the Window menu to turn on the check mark. To close (hide) a palette, select a checked palette in the Window menu to clear the check mark.

 *If you select an unchecked palette that is docked in the palette well, the palette displays its contents, and remains in the palette well.*

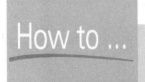 **Maximize Your Work Area**

Since the work area is where you do all your editing, you will want to maximize this area to give yourself more room to work. Here are some steps you can take to make the most of your work area:

Close any open palettes   By default, Photoshop Elements displays some palettes in the work area, rather than in the palette well. To retrieve the work area taken up by these palettes, you can move them to the palette well by clicking the close button. Make sure that Close Palette to Palette Well is selected in the More button of the palette.

Dock palettes together   Docking palettes causes the docked palettes to overlap, sharing space in the work area. See "Dock and Undock Palettes" earlier in this chapter for details on how to group palettes.

Set your desktop resolution to the highest value you can   You may be able to increase the resolution of your Windows desktop. This makes everything appear smaller on your monitor, but enables you to display more items in Photoshop Elements (as well as any other application). If your graphics card and monitor support it, you can increase the resolution to 1024 × 768 (good for a 15-inch monitor), 1280 × 1024 (good for a 17-inch monitor), or even higher (for 19-inch and larger monitors). To change the resolution of your desktop, right-click the desktop and choose Properties from the context menu. Choose Settings from the Display Properties dialog box, and choose the resolution you want from the Screen Area section of the dialog box.

Upgrade your hardware   If you are serious about digital photography, you may wish to consider upgrading your monitor and graphics card, especially if you can't use the resolution you'd like. 17-inch monitors can be purchased for about $300, and larger monitors (19-inch and 20-inch) can be purchased for around $500 (sometimes even less). An upgraded graphics card not only can provide increased resolution, but better performance as well. The graphics card is often the bottleneck when rendering digital images. After adding more memory, replacing your graphics card is the wisest investment you can make.

Depending on your graphics card, increasing the display resolution may limit the number of colors available in your palette. The higher resolution requires more graphics memory, so if the graphics card doesn't have enough memory to display a high resolution with a full palette of colors, it will offer only a reduced number of colors as an option when you try to increase the resolution.

Use the Palette Menus

Each of the palettes has a palette menu to provide commands appropriate to that palette. For example, the Layer Style palette enables you to pick how you want to view the Layer Styles—either as thumbnails or as a list. Palettes such as the Swatches palette provide options for managing the contents of the palette, such as loading a set of swatches, saving a set of swatches, and creating new swatches:

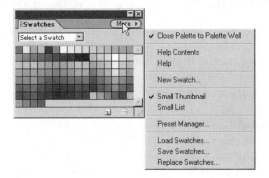

Finally, palettes such as the Layers palette (covered in Chapter 9) provide a long list of menu items suitable for working with layers.

Where the palette menu is located and what it looks like depends on where the palette is located. If the palette is located in the work area, you access the palette menu by clicking the More button, as shown in the previous illustration. However, if the palette is in the palette well, you can access the palette menu by clicking the triangle at the right side of the title tab:

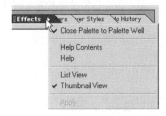

Correct Mistakes You've Made

It may take you many steps to correct an image, and it is easy to make a mistake along the way. Fortunately, Photoshop Elements has a number of mechanisms to allow you to undo your work with the Edit menu and the Undo History palette.

Correct the Last Action

If you just want to undo the last action you took, you can choose Edit | Undo. You can also select Edit | Step Backward or choose Step Backward from the Undo History palette menu. You can continue undoing single changes in the reverse order you made them by selecting Step Backward as many times as you want.

Use the Undo History Palette to Make Corrections

The Undo History palette (shown in Figure 1-5) displays a list of actions you have taken with an image. Each line in the palette represents a *history state*. By default, you can keep track of the last 20 changes you made to an image; after you exceed 20, the oldest change rolls off of the Undo History palette and is no longer available. However, you can configure the number of history states to keep track of using Preferences (choose Edit | Preferences | General) as discussed in Chapter 2.

To view an image at a previous state (before certain changes were applied), click the state in the Undo History palette. Photoshop Elements moves the history state slider to that state, indicating that it is selected. At this point, Photoshop Elements displays the image as it looked then, but no actual changes will have been made to the image. However, if you make any changes while you are viewing the image in a previous state, all subsequent states you had made are discarded and you begin editing the image from the selected state. You can also return the image to a previous state by selecting it (click the state), then either choosing Delete from the context menu or clicking and dragging the state to the trashcan.

You must be careful to first select the state, then delete it or drag it to the trashcan. If you click and drag the state to the trashcan without first making it the selected state, you are simply deleting the state from the Undo History palette. No changes are made to the image, but since the state is no longer available in the palette, you cannot revert to that state.

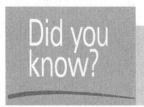

You can recover memory by purging the Undo History palette once you no longer need the previous history states. To do so, choose Edit | Purge | History or choose Clear History from the palette menu.

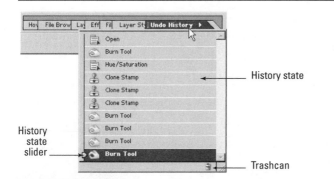

History state

History
state
slider

Trashcan

FIGURE 1-5   Return to a previous state—or delete changes you have made—using
the Undo History palette.

Chapter 2

Configure Photoshop Elements

How to...

■ Manage palette contents

■ Set Photoshop Elements preferences

You can configure Photoshop Elements by not only loading different contents (called *presets*) into a palette, but also by modifying those contents and saving them as a new file. Photoshop Elements includes a tool called Preset Manager to make the job of managing the palette contents easier.

Photoshop Elements also supports a large number of preferences you can set. While some of these are somewhat esoteric and beyond the scope of this book, other preferences are very important to getting the most from the software and making it work efficiently with your computer.

Manage Presets with the Preset Manager

The Preset Manager enables you to manage collections of brushes, swatches, gradients, and patterns. Each item (brush, swatch, and so on) is called a *preset*. Although I'll use swatches in the examples in this chapter, all the collections of presets work the same.

To view the Preset Manager, choose Edit | Preset Manager. You can also open the Preset Manager by choosing Preset Manager from the Swatches palette menu:

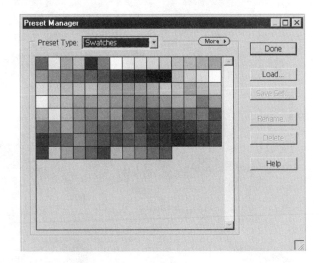

You can resize the Preset Manager window just like any other window: Click and drag a border or corner.

The next step is to pick the type of presets you want to work with by choosing it from the Preset Type drop-down list. Once you have chosen the preset type, you can perform the tasks described in the next few sections with the Preset Manager. When you are done making changes, click the Done button to close the Preset Manager window.

Load a Library of Presets

Loading a library of presets adds the contents of that library to the presets visible in the Preset Manager. This action makes additional presets available for you to use with the appropriate tool.

To load a library, click the Load button, then select the library of presets you want from the Load dialog box.

Replace a Library of Presets

Replacing a library of presets replaces the existing set(s) with a new set.

To replace the current set with a new library, click the More button and choose Replace (followed by the type of preset you are working with) from the menu. Select the library of presets you want from the Load dialog box.

To replace the current set with one of those provided with Photoshop Elements, choose the library from the list at the bottom of the More menu:

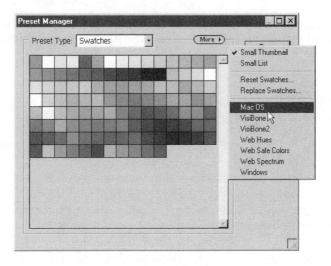

When you use a tool or palette that uses a set of presets, only those presets that have been loaded are available. For example, if you choose the Pattern Stamp tool in the toolbox, only the default set of pattern presets are available unless you have previously used the Preset Manager to load more presets.

Modify the Presets

You can make the following changes to the presets in a group:

Rearrange the presets   To rearrange the presets, click a preset and drag it to a new position in the group.

Rename a preset   To rename a preset, either double-click the preset or click the preset and then click the Rename button. In the resulting Name dialog box, type in the new name:

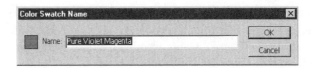

Delete a preset   To remove a preset from the group, click the preset and click the Delete button.

Return the presets to their default condition   To return the presets to the way they were when you installed Photoshop Elements, click the More button and choose Reset from the list.

 **Save a Custom Preset Library**

One of the limitations of the Preset Manager is that the Save Set button saves only the selected swatches, even if you rename or rearrange swatches (after which the swatches are no longer selected). So what do you do if you want to rearrange the presets, rename a few of them, and then save the whole thing as a new library? As it turns out, the answer is easy, if a bit tedious. Perform the customization steps, then select *all* the presets, and click the Save Set button. To select all the presets, you must click the first preset (selecting it), then hold down the SHIFT key and click each of the other swatches.

Save a Subset of Presets

You can save a subset of the presets in their own library. To do so, follow these steps:

1. Click the first preset you want in the group.

2. Hold down the SHIFT key and continue clicking presets until you have selected all of those you want to save.

3. Click the Save Set button in the Preset Manager window. This opens the Save dialog box.

4. Type the filename for your new library into the File Name field, and click Save.

Change the Appearance of the Presets

Photoshop Elements has the capability to display the presets in four different formats. To choose one of the formats, click the More button and select the format you want from the list:

Text Only   A list that displays only the names of each preset. This is not available for Swatches.

Small Thumbnail   A small thumbnail representation of each preset. This is the default, and represents a good tradeoff between presenting information to the user and using space in the Preset Manager dialog box.

Large Thumbnail   A larger version of the thumbnail. This is a good choice, especially for patterns, but it does take more room. Therefore, you have to enlarge the dialog box or scroll around to see all the thumbnails. This choice is not available for Swatches.

Small List   A list that contains a very small thumbnail as well as the name of the preset:

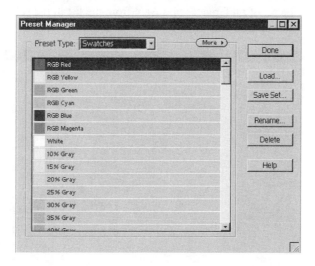

Large List A list that contains larger thumbnails as well as the name of the preset.

Stroke Thumbnail This option is available only for brushes. It displays what the brush stroke would look like in the image:

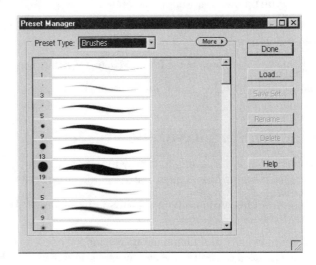

Set Your Own Preferences

Photoshop Elements features a multitude of preference settings so you can customize the program to work the way you want. To access these settings, choose Edit | Preferences. You can then pick the set of preferences you want from the list in the submenu. Whichever choice you make, Photoshop Elements opens the Preferences dialog box:

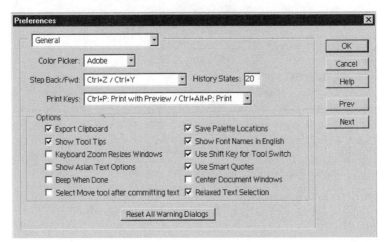

To switch to a different set of preferences, choose the preferences you want to set from the drop-down list at the top of the Preferences dialog box.

Set General Preferences

The General Preferences dialog box contains many options; only some are covered here because they are most relevant to digital photography. These options are:

Color Picker   The color picker is a tool for (can you guess?) picking the color you want to use. There are two color pickers available in the drop-down list: the Adobe color picker and the standard Windows color picker. Which one you use is your choice. Personally, I prefer the Adobe color picker, and it is the one we will use in examples throughout this book.

History States   The History States field specifies the number of history states—that is, the levels of Undo—available to you. More History States enables you to step back further to correct mistakes, but also requires more memory.

Show Tool Tips   Tool tips are those handy little flags that pop up when you hover your mouse over a tool or button. If you tire of having these little helpers appear, clear the Show Tool Tips check box.

Save Palette Locations   If you want your palettes to appear exactly where you left them the next time you open Photoshop Elements, check the Save Palette Locations check box. If, instead, you'd prefer to have the palettes appear in their default locations the next time you open Photoshop Elements, clear this check box.

Use Shift Key for Tool Switch   The toolbox contains some tool buttons that can be used to select several different tools. For example, the Marquee button in the upper-left corner of the toolbox can be used to select either the Rectangular Marquee or the Oval Marquee. The Use Shift Key for Tool Switch check box controls how you switch between these multiple tools using the keyboard. When the check box is checked, you must press SHIFT and the keystroke (M in the case of the Marquee tools) to switch between them. When the check box is cleared, you need only to press the keystroke; the SHIFT key is *not* required.

Reset All Warning Dialogs   Sometimes when you execute an action in Photoshop Elements, a dialog box will appear warning you of the consequences of your actions. As you become familiar with the program, you may find these warning dialogs annoying. Fortunately, each warning includes a check box that enables you to disable the dialog box so that it doesn't appear in the future. However, if you have been away from Photoshop Elements for a while, or a new person has started to use it, you may wish to re-enable these warnings. To do so, simply click the Reset All Warning Dialogs button.

Set Saving Files Preferences

The options in the Saving Files Preferences dialog box enable you to set some choices related to saving files:

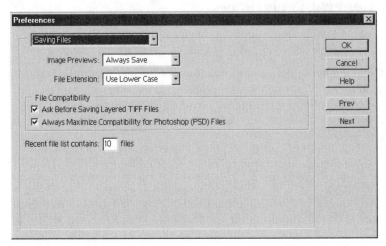

Here are some relevant options you may wish to set:

Image Previews Make a selection from the drop-down list to choose whether to always save a preview of the file with the file itself, never to save a preview, or to ask each time you save a file. However, this option has an effect only on Photoshop Elements (PSD) files. It makes the files larger, and other than providing a quicker preview in the Load or Open dialog box, and enabling the File Browser palette (see Chapter 3) to display the preview thumbnail while it builds a larger preview of a new PSD file, it doesn't seem to serve much of a useful purpose.

Recent File List Contains Type a number into this field to control how many files are displayed in the menu list that appears when you select File | Open Recent.

Set Display and Cursors Preferences

The Display & Cursors Preferences dialog box enables you to control how the cursors look when you are working with tools, as well as how previews are rendered (see illustration on opposite page):

Use Pixel Doubling Checking this check box doubles the size of pixels in dialog boxes that show previews of the effect of a tool or a command. The resolution is reduced, but the preview renders much faster. This command has no effect on the actual image; it just affects how the preview is presented.

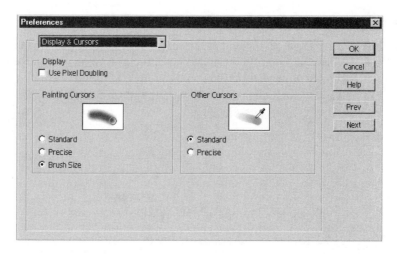

Painting Cursors   This option controls how the cursor is displayed when you use painting tools (such as brush, sponge, sharpen, blur, and others). Choose Standard to display the cursor as an icon of the tool you are using, choose Precise to display the cursor as a cross-hair, and choose Brush Size to display the cursor as a shape (usually a circle or oval) that represents the area that will be affected when you use the tool.

Other Cursors   This option controls how the cursor is displayed when you use other tools (such as the eyedropper). The options are identical to those detailed in the Painting Cursors description.

Set Transparency Preferences

The Transparency Preferences dialog box enables you to control how the background of an image appears when it is transparent.

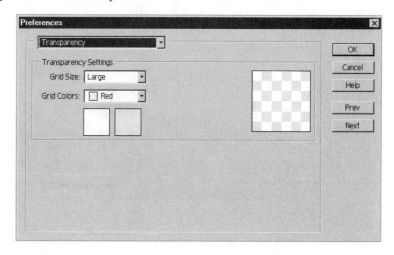

The two options you can set are:

Grid Size   You can set the grid of rectangles that represent a transparent area to None, Small, Medium, or Large. Photoshop Elements displays a preview of the grid in a square on the right side of the dialog box.

Grid Colors   You can choose the color of the colored rectangles from this drop-down list:

Options include three shades of gray (Light, Medium, or Dark) or several other colors mixed with white. If you select the Custom option, you can choose the color you want to use from the Color Picker (see Chapter 4).

Set Units and Rulers Preferences

Photoshop Elements provides rulers to help you align your work. To turn rulers on and off, choose View | Rulers. Here is an image with rulers turned on:

You can set the unit of measure for the ruler and the precision of the grid (size of the grid elements) in the Units & Rulers Preferences dialog box:

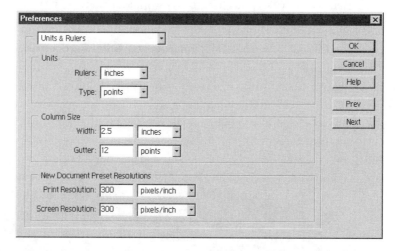

Set the unit of measure from the Rulers drop-down list (inches, pixels, cm, mm, points, picas, and percent). Set the unit of measure for type (see Chapter 16) from the Type drop-down list (points, pixels, and mm).

You can also use this dialog box to set the resolution of newly created documents. Choose the Print Resolution (in pixels/inch or cm/inch) and the Screen Resolution from the appropriate drop-down lists.

You can relocate the zero point on the ruler. To do so, click the hollow dot that appears at the intersection of the two lines in the upper-left corner of the ruler.

Drag this dot down or right and release it where you want the new 0,0 point to be. To reset the zero point to its default, double-click the dot.

Set the Grid

Photoshop Elements provides grids to help you work accurately. To turn the grid on and off, choose View | Grid. Here is an image with the grid turned on.

The items you can set in the Grid Preferences dialog box are:

Color   Click the Color drop-down list to pick the grid color. If you choose the Custom selection from the list, the Color Picker appears so you can pick the color you want (see Chapter 4).

Style   The grid can be one of three styles: lines, dashed lines, or dots. Pick the one you want from the Style drop-down list.

Gridline Spacing   You can specify the distance between the major gridlines by typing a value into the Gridline Every field and picking a unit of measure from the adjacent drop-down list. In addition, you can specify how many subdivisions are drawn between each of the major gridlines by typing a value into the Subdivisions field.

Set Up Scratch Disks

When you don't have enough memory in your computer to perform an operation, Photoshop Elements uses a section of your hard drive for temporary storage. This section is called a *scratch disk*. By default, Photoshop Elements uses the same hard drive that the operating system is installed on. However, Photoshop Elements enables you to choose a different primary scratch disk, and assign up to four scratch disks that will be used in order as each fills up.

To configure your scratch disks, open the Plug-Ins & Scratch Disks Preferences dialog box:

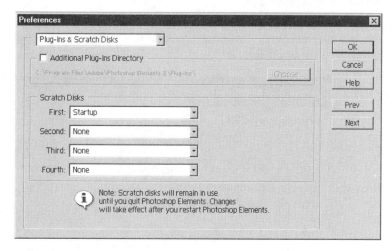

From each drop-down list, choose the drive you want to designate as the scratch disk.

 *The scratch disk designations actually take place after you exit Photoshop Elements and rerun it.*

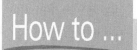 **Optimize Your Scratch Disk**

The scratch disk should be the fastest hard drive connected to your system—don't use a network drive or a removable disk as a scratch drive. You should also defragment your scratch drive regularly to make it as fast as possible, using a commercial defragmenting utility like Norton SpeedDisk. Ideally, the scratch disk should be a different disk from the disk on which your image file is stored, but unless you have two physical hard drives in your computer, this isn't possible. Finally, no matter how fast your hard drive is, memory is *much* faster. If you see your hard drive light up a lot when you are performing complex operations, you'll probably want to increase the amount of memory in your computer. You can also tell whether Photoshop Elements is accessing the hard drive for storage by viewing the Efficiency Percentage in the status bar, as described in Chapter 1. If the Efficiency Percentage is less than 100%, it's time to add memory!

Set Up the Memory Cache

Many of the tasks you perform with Photoshop Elements are quite memory intensive. You can
configure how much memory Photoshop Elements will take for itself by using the Memory &
Image Cache Preferences dialog box:

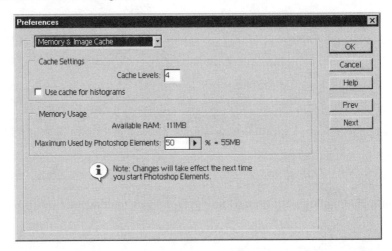

The Memory Usage section of the dialog box tells you how much memory is available. You
can then select the percentage of available memory you want to use by either typing a number
in the Maximum Used by Photoshop Elements field, or by clicking the arrowhead and using
the slider to set the percentage.

Chapter 3

Get Your Images Into Photoshop Elements

How to...

- Create a new image
- View and open a file
- Obtain a file from a scanner or camera
- Navigate around an image in the work area
- Use the ruler and grid
- Save a file

Photoshop Elements is a program for working with images, so the first thing you will need to know is how to get images into the program. You can create an image "from scratch," open an image file, or import a file from an external source, like a digital camera. Of course, when you are done working on an image, you'll need to save the result.

Once the file is open in the work area, Photoshop Elements provides tools for zooming in and out, and moving the image around. You can also get an idea of the alignment and size of an image by using the ruler and grid tools.

Create a New Image

Photoshop Elements provides two ways to create a new image: You can either create an empty image, or create an image from the contents of the clipboard.

Create a New, Empty Image

To create a brand-new empty image in Photoshop Elements, select File | New or choose the New button in the Welcome screen. Either way, Photoshop Elements displays the New dialog box:

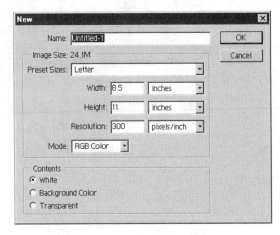

Fill out each of the fields in the dialog box as described in the following sections, and click OK to create the new image.

As you change the size, resolution, and mode of an image, Photoshop Elements updates the estimated image size.

3

Specify an Image Name

Type the name of the image into the Name field. This name is used to identify the image by displaying the name in the upper-left corner of the image title bar, as shown in Figure 3-1. It is also used as the default filename when you save the image (although you can change the filename at that point if you want).

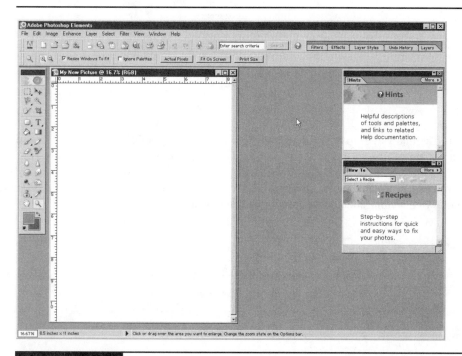

FIGURE 3-1   The new image file, showing the name and background color.

Choose an Image Size

You have two ways to select the initial size of an image. The first way is to choose a size from the Preset Sizes drop-down list:

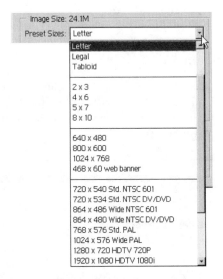

The second way is to type values into the Width and Height fields. If you first choose a size from the Preset Sizes list, and then you modify the choice by typing a value into either the Width or Height fields, the Preset Sizes list displays the word "Custom."

You can also select the unit of measure for the width and height by selecting it from the drop-down list alongside the numeric width and height values.

You can measure the image height and width in *picas* or *points*. There are roughly 6 picas (or 72 points) to an inch.

Set the Resolution

Set the resolution of the image by typing a value into the Resolution field. The default value of 72 pixels per inch (or 28.346 pixels per centimeter) results in an image on your monitor that is roughly the same size (has the same dimensions) as the height and width you set when you created the image. If you set a higher resolution (for example, 300 pixels per inch), the image will appear to be larger on the screen (at full magnification) than your specified dimensions because your monitor can't display a resolution that high. However, as we'll see later in this chapter, you can scroll around the image if it is too big, or you can reduce the magnification so you can see the entire image.

If your intention is to later print the image, you'll want to use a resolution of at least 250 pixels per inch, as lower resolutions don't print with enough detail. This is the same reason you'd want to set your scanner to a high resolution (300 pixels per inch is common) if you want to be able to print the results.

Set the Color Mode

Choose the color mode from the Mode drop-down list. The choices are:

RGB Color   Used for photos and most other color images.

Grayscale   Used for continuous grayscale images such as black and white photos.

Bitmap   This mode draws only in pure black or white. If you draw or paint with a light foreground color (such as light blue), Photoshop Elements uses white; if you draw or paint with a dark foreground color (such as dark blue), Photoshop Elements uses black.

Choose the Background Color of the New Image

Pick one of the options in the Contents section of the New dialog box to set the background color of the image to white, the currently selected background color, or to leave the background transparent.

Create an Image from the Clipboard

If you copy either an entire image or a portion of an image to the clipboard, you can create a new image from the contents of the clipboard. The image can come from anywhere. For example, it might be an image you downloaded or are viewing in another graphics application. You can even create a new image from an image you have open in Photoshop Elements. To create a new image this way, follow these steps:

1. Open the image you want to use as the source of your new image.

2. Choose one of the selection tools in the upper-left corner of the toolbox. For more information on using these tools, see Chapter 8. Alternatively, you can select the entire image by choosing Select | All.

3. Copy the selected portion of the image to the clipboard by selecting Edit | Copy.

4. Create the new image from the clipboard contents by choosing File | New From Clipboard:

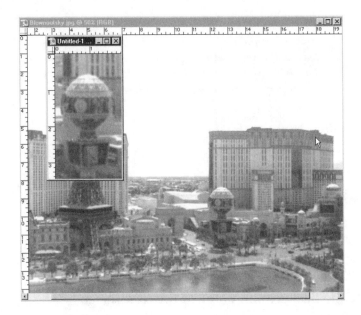

 *When you first create an image, the contents of the image are selected. Thus, you can use the Move tool (upper-right corner of the toolbox) to move the image around on the canvas, or click and drag one of the sizing handles to change the image size (see Chapter 11 for more information about these techniques).*

Open a File from a Disk Drive

You can open a file for editing from any drive attached to your system or network: your internal hard drive, external hard drive, floppy disk, Zip, CD-ROM, DVD, or even one of the new MP3 players or memory card readers that come with drivers to make them appear like drives.

To open a file in Photoshop Elements, select File | Open to view the Open dialog box:

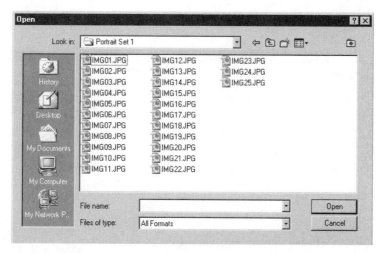

By default, the Open dialog box shows you all files that Photoshop Elements is capable of opening. If you want to see files only of a certain type, select the file type from the Files of Type drop-down list at the bottom of the Open dialog box. Navigate to the file location and either double-click the file or click the file and then click Open.

You can convert a file to another file type by choosing File | Open As. This action opens the Open As dialog box. Click the file you want to open, then select the type of file you want to open the image as (from the Open As drop-down list).

You can quickly reopen a file you've used recently by selecting File | Open Recent and choosing the file you want from the menu list that appears.

Open a File Using the File Browser

Photoshop Elements includes a powerful tool—the File Browser palette—for previewing and opening images on any drive attached to your system. As shown in Figure 3-2, the File Browser palette provides mechanisms for navigating your file structure, a display of the images as thumbnails, and a considerable amount of information about each image. To open a file, simply double-click the image thumbnail.

It is easier to keep the File Browser palette open if you drag the palette out of the palette well (as shown in Figure 3-2). Once you have opened the file you want, you can quickly return the palette to the palette well by selecting Dock to Palette Well from the palette menu.

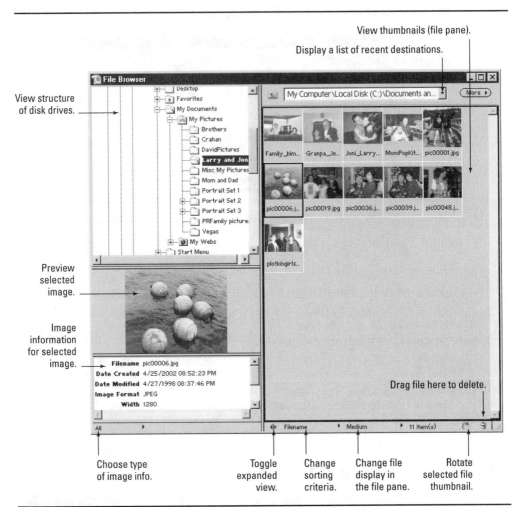

View thumbnails (file pane).

Display a list of recent destinations.

View structure of disk drives.

Preview selected image.

Image information for selected image.

Drag file here to delete.

Choose type of image info.

Toggle expanded view.

Change sorting criteria.

Change file display in the file pane.

Rotate selected file thumbnail.

FIGURE 3-2   View your thumbnails and pick an image to open in Photoshop Elements using the File Browser.

View Your Drives and Files

The upper-left pane of the File Browser displays the structure of the drives on your computer. You can navigate this "tree" much like you do in Windows Explorer. To see the contents of a folder in the upper-right section of the File Browser, click that folder. To expand the contents of the folder or drive and display any subfolders, click the plus (+) sign next to the folder or drive name. To collapse (hide) the list of subfolders, click the minus (–) sign next to the folder or drive name.

The pane on the right side of the File Browser displays the contents of the current folder. If those contents are graphic images, the display includes a thumbnail of each image. Subfolders of the current folder are displayed as icons. From this pane, you can open a file or "drill-down" into the contents of a subfolder by double-clicking it or by clicking the folder icon and choosing Open from the palette menu. You can also select an image by clicking it to display a preview of the image in the middle-left pane and the image information in the lower-left pane.

You can control how Photoshop Elements displays images in the pane on the right by using the palette menu. Your display options are:

Small Thumbnail   A tiny thumbnail image followed by the filename. This option is not very useful because the thumbnail is so small.

Medium Thumbnail   A larger thumbnail with the filename below the thumbnail. The thumbnails are still quite small. This is the version that is shown in Figure 3-2.

Large Thumbnail   The largest version of the thumbnails.

Details   This view displays a thumbnail along with all the image information, including the filename, image type (JPEG, GIF, and so on), date the file was created and modified, file size, image dimensions, and the color space.

You can also change the display option by clicking the current display option in the middle of the status bar at the bottom of the file pane. This list presents the options as "Small," "Medium," "Large," and "Details."

NOTE   *This section describes the expanded view of the File Browser. You can turn off the expanded view by unchecking the Expanded View entry in the palette menu, or clicking the Expanded View toggle in the status bar at the lower-left corner of the file pane. In this unexpanded view, you can see only the thumbnails in the file pane; the file tree and file information are not visible.*

Sort the Files

You can sort the contents of the file pane by filename, width, height, file size, resolution, file type, date created, and date modified. To customize the sorting criteria, choose from the list you get when you click the current sorting criteria that appears in the status bar near the lower-left corner of the file pane. The normal sort order is ascending, but you can switch to descending sort order by clearing the check mark on the Ascending Order option in the list.

Choose the Type of Visible Image Information

The data in the image information pane (lower-left pane of the File Browser) consists of two types of information. The first is related to the physical image file, and includes (as noted earlier) such information as file size, when the file was created, and the file format (JPEG, TIFF, and so on). The other type of information is Exchangeable Image File (EXIF) data. EXIF data is present only if you took a picture with a digital camera in JPEG format (or created the image from scratch with compatible software, such as Photoshop Elements). The camera writes this information into the file header and the data is preserved with the digital image file. The data includes the exposure, date the image was taken, the ISO setting, and other image-related information (depending on the camera). You can choose whether to view all the information or just EXIF information by choosing *All* or *EXIF* from the list you get when you click the button at the far-left end of the File Browser status bar.

The EXIF data is preserved even if you edit the image and save it, provided you use a JPEG format. However, if you convert the image to some other format (such as TIFF), the EXIF data is lost.

Rotate File Thumbnails

It can be handy to rotate an image while viewing the thumbnail. It is especially useful if the image is presented sideways, which can happen if you rotated a 35mm camera on its side when you took the picture (for example). To rotate an image thumbnail, select the image in the file pane and choose the rotation option you want (Rotate 180, Rotate 90 CW, or Rotate 90 CCW) from the palette menu. You can also click the rotation button in the status bar at the lower-right corner of the file pane. Clicking this button rotates the thumbnail clockwise; holding ALT while clicking this button rotates the thumbnail counter-clockwise.

Rotating the thumbnail does not rotate the image; it simply changes the way the thumbnail is displayed in the file pane. Once you load an image into Photoshop Elements, you can rotate it by following the instructions in Chapter 4.

Rename and Delete Files

You can rename a file in the file pane by selecting it and choosing Rename from either the context menu or the palette menu. Photoshop Elements makes the filename editable and you can change it. Complete the rename operation by pressing ENTER.

To delete a file in the file pane, select the file and either drag it to the trashcan or choose DELETE from the context menu or the palette menu.

You can rename a whole batch of files at one time. To do so, follow these steps:

1. Make sure that none of the files you want to rename are open. Click the first file in the list to select it.

2. Select the rest of the files by holding down the CTRL key and clicking the additional files. If you change your mind about including a file, click it again (with the CTRL key still pressed).

You can select a set of contiguous files by clicking the first file, holding down the SHIFT key, and clicking the last file. Photoshop Elements selects all files in between the two you chose.

3

3. Choose Batch Rename from either the context menu or the palette menu. This opens the Batch Rename dialog box:

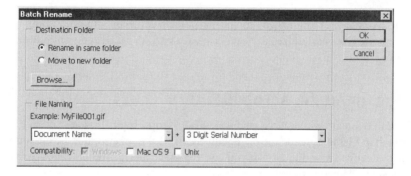

4. Choose the destination folder for the renamed files by clicking the radio buttons in the Destination Folder section of the dialog box. If you choose Rename In Same Folder, the files are renamed in place. If you choose Move To New Folder, the files are copied to the destination folder and then renamed. To choose the destination folder, click the Browse button and choose the folder from the Browse For Folder dialog box:

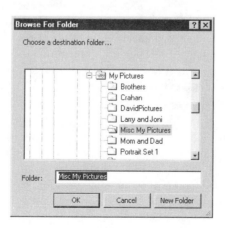

5. Choose how you want Photoshop Elements to construct the new filenames by using the two drop-down lists. You can use serial numbers, serial letters, dates, the original document name, and other options. As you make selections from the lists, the dialog box displays a sample of what the filename will look like. For example, if you choose to use a 3-digit serial number followed by the date (in mmddyy format), the filename might look like 001042402.

6. Click OK to perform the renames.

Open Acrobat, Photo CD, or PostScript Files

Some types of files require you to specify parameters when you open them. The most common of these file types are Adobe Acrobat (PDF), Kodak Photo CD, and encapsulated PostScript (EPS) images.

Open an Adobe Acrobat File

You can open an Adobe Acrobat file in Photoshop Elements, but only one page at a time. Photoshop Elements reads the page and *rasterizes* the image—that is, turns it into a graphic that you can work with, just like you can any other image. To open an Adobe Acrobat file in Photoshop Elements, follow these steps:

1. Choose File | Open and select the PDF file you want to open in the Open dialog box.

2. Use the PDF Page Selector dialog box to choose the page you want to open:

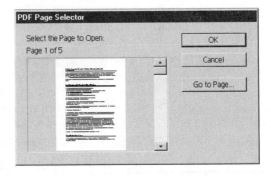

3. Click OK and use the Rasterize Generic PDF Format dialog box to set the parameters for opening the document:

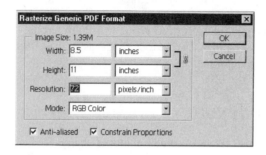

4. Click OK to open the document.

The Width, Height, Resolution, and Mode fields in the Rasterize Generic PDF Format dialog box have the same meaning as discussed earlier in this chapter. Unless you want a severely distorted image, you'll want to leave the Constrain Proportions check box checked. This forces the width and height to maintain the same proportions as in the PDF file.

If the PDF file page you want to open contains mostly text (and most of them do), turn off the Anti-aliased check box. If you allow Photoshop Elements to anti-alias the text, it becomes unreadable. Anti-aliasing adds intermediate colors to smooth sharp edges, which is exactly what you don't want for text.

Open a Kodak Photo CD File

Photo CD is something you can get at most film developers—your photographs are placed on a CD in a variety of different sizes and resolutions. To open a Photo CD file, choose File | Open and select the file. In the resulting dialog box, fill in the following parameters:

Pixel Size   Specify the pixel dimensions of the image. The actual size of the image on the screen depends on both the pixel size and the selected resolution.

Profile   Specify the device profile for color management.

Resolution   Choose the resolution of the opened image.

Color Space   Specify the color profile to use with the opened image.

Orientation   Choose either landscape or portrait for the orientation of the opened image.

Open a Postscript Image

Postscript is a language (originally interpreted by printers) that describes an image in terms of a set of instructions for recreating the image. You can open a postscript image in Photoshop Elements by selecting File | Open, choosing the file (it has the extension *.eps*), and specifying the Width, Height, Resolution, and Mode fields, as well as whether to constrain the dimensions and anti-alias the resulting image.

Import a PDF Image

Adobe Acrobat (PDF) files can contain multiple images. You can open one or more of these images directly in Photoshop Elements, modify it, and save it. To import a PDF image, follow these steps:

1. Choose File | Import and select PDF Image from the menu list. This opens the Select PDF For Image Import dialog box.

2. Choose the PDF file from which you want to import the image and click Open. This opens the PDF Image Import dialog box.

3. Using the scroll bar on the right side of the dialog box, locate the image you want to use, and click OK.

4. Photoshop Elements opens the selected image in the work area.

You can also open all the images in the PDF document by clicking Import All. However, depending on how much memory you have in your computer, if there are a lot of images in the document, you may get an error message.

Obtain an Image from Your Scanner or Camera

Once you install the drivers that come with your scanner or digital camera, you can bring an image directly into Photoshop Elements. To do so, choose File | Import or choose Acquire from the Welcome screen. Your scanner or digital camera will appear as an option in the Import menu. Choose the device you want from the menu and it will launch the software that comes with your scanner. What happens next depends on your scanner or camera software. With my HP scanner, the scanning software launched and I could apply all the controls I normally use to select a portion of the picture to scan, set the resolution, adjust the color, and so on. However, I now have a new button available in the Scanner software—Save to Photoshop. When I click this button, my scanner scans the picture and then closes down, leaving the picture in Photoshop Elements for me to work with.

Some devices (many digital cameras) appear as a hard drive when connected to your computer. These devices do not appear in the Import menu. Instead, you can open an image directly using File | Open and picking the "hard drive" that corresponds to your camera (or other device).

3

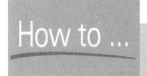

Control Which Program Opens Which File Type

As you are probably aware, you can double-click many different types of files and automatically open an application that can handle that file type. For example, if you double-click a file that ends in ".doc," it will open in Microsoft Word (provided you have Microsoft Word installed on your computer). Essentially, the "doc" file type (identified by the ".doc" ending to the filename) is associated with Microsoft Word. However, graphics files can be opened by many different programs. For example, a JPEG graphic file (which ends in .JPEG or .JPG) can be opened in Photoshop Elements, Internet Explorer, PhotoDeluxe, Paint Shop Pro, or just about any other graphic program you have.

Photoshop Elements makes it easy to associate a file type with it, so that when you double-click a file in Windows Explorer, Photoshop Elements opens automatically and loads the program. To do so, choose Edit | File Association to open the File Association Manager dialog box:

File Association Manager	
Select the file types you would like Adobe Photoshop Elements to open.	OK
	Cancel
☑ Photoshop PSD (*.PSD, *.PDD)	Help
☑ JPEG (*.JPG, *.JPE)	
☑ JPEG 2000 (*.JPX, *.JP2)	
☐ Bitmap (*.BMP, *.RLE)	
☐ Photoshop EPS (*.EPS)	Default
☑ TIFF (*.TIF)	
☑ CompuServe GIF (*.GIF)	Select All
☑ Photoshop PDF (*.PDF, *.PDP)	
☐ PICT File (*.PCT, *.PCT)	Deselect All
☐ RAW (*.RAW)	

To associate one of the file types in the dialog box with Photoshop Elements, simply check the check box for that file type. Since all of these files can be opened by Photoshop Elements, there is no danger you'll end up associating a file type that can't be opened by the program. However, you may want to be careful because some of the file types are actually handled better by other programs. For example, a Photoshop PDF file can be opened only one page at a time, so you're much better off leaving that file type associated with an application like Adobe Acrobat that can open the entire document.

Figure Out Where You Are with the Navigator Palette

If you open a large picture, Photoshop Elements provides the Navigator palette (see Figure 3-3) to help you view the portions of the picture you want to see, as well as scroll quickly to a different section of the picture.

The Navigator palette is most useful if you drag it out of the palette well so it will stay open.

This rectangle indicates the portion of the image visible in the window.

Type a zoom level here.

Adjust this slider to change the zoom (magnification) level.

FIGURE 3-3   Change magnification and scroll around a picture with the Navigator palette.

To quickly scroll around an image you are viewing, move the mouse inside the rectangle in the Navigator palette. Once the mouse cursor turns into a hand, click and drag the rectangle. As you do so, the portion of the image shown in the window changes to match.

You can also quickly change the magnification level by either typing a zoom level into the field at the lower left corner of the palette, or by using the slider along the bottom border. The buttons to either side of the slider also control the zoom level, zooming down (the left button) or zooming up (the right button) to preset levels.

If you don't like the color of the rectangle in the Navigator palette (it is light red by default), choose Palette Options from the palette menu, and pick a different color from the resulting dialog box:

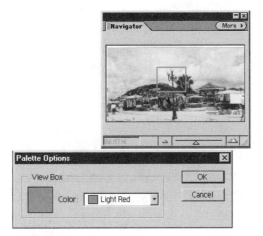

Zoom In and Out

As you work on your images in Photoshop Elements, you'll find that you need to change the magnification (zoom) level. Sometimes you'll need a low magnification (zoom out) so you can see a lot of the image; at other times you'll need to zoom in (high magnification) to work on individual pixels and do other detailed work. We've already seen that we can use the Navigator palette to control zoom, but Photoshop Elements provides another way: the Zoom tool in the toolbox.

Use the Zoom Tool

To use the Zoom tool (it looks like a magnifying glass), select it from the toolbox. Move the tool over the image and either click the image to increase magnification or ALT-click to decrease magnification.

 *The magnifying glass displays a small plus sign (+) in the middle, which changes to a minus sign (–) if you press the ALT key.*

You can also zoom in on a specific section of the image. To do so, click and drag a rectangle in the image with the Zoom tool. When you release the mouse button, Photoshop Elements zooms to fit the rectangle in the window.

Use the View Menu

The View menu has a number of ways to control the zoom level of the image. These items enable you to:

Zoom In   Zooms *in* one standard level. For example, if you are viewing an image at 100%, choosing this option will zoom in to a 200% magnification.

Zoom Out   Zooms *out* one standard level. For example, if you are viewing an image at 100%, choosing this option will zoom out to a 50% magnification.

Fit On Screen   Increases the magnification until either the height or the width of the image fills the work area:

Actual Pixels   Displays the image at 100% magnification.

Print Size   Displays the image at the size it will print. For example, if you create an image using the letter size template, this option will display the image at 8.5 inches by 11 inches. Note that this will be different from 100% magnification if the resolution is not 72 dpi (the resolution of the screen). For example, if the resolution of your image is 144 dpi, Photoshop Elements will shrink the image to 50% to display it at the print size.

The View menu has an option to enable you to open additional views of your image. To do so, select the window containing the image for which you want an additional view, and choose View | New View. The new window opens, and any changes you make to the image are displayed in both windows.

Drag Your Photo Around with the Hand Tool

If the image you are working with is larger than the viewing window, you can pan the image using the Hand tool. Simply choose the Hand tool from the toolbox, then click and drag the image. As you drag, the image moves, displaying the hidden portions of the image in the window.

As you can probably imagine, the Zoom tool and the Hand tool work well together—using them in tandem, you can change zoom levels, move the image, change zoom levels again, and so on. Photoshop Elements makes it easy to use these two tools together.

Switch from the Zoom tool to the Hand tool   If you are using the Zoom tool, hold down the SPACEBAR to switch temporarily to the hand tool. When you release the SPACEBAR, the mouse turns back into the Hand tool.

Switch from the Hand tool to the Zoom tool   If you are using the Hand tool, press the CTRL key to switch temporarily to the Zoom In tool to increase magnification. Press the ALT key to switch temporarily to the Zoom Out tool to decrease magnification. While either tool is visible, click the image to increase or decrease the zoom level.

Reorient the Image

Believe it or not, sometimes you need to rotate an image—or even flip it over completely! Here is an example: If you use a 35 mm camera to take a picture of a tall object in portrait mode (the normal orientation of the camera is landscape mode), you would need to rotate the camera. However, when you have the pictures scanned and put on a CD after you have the pictures processed, the portrait-mode pictures will come out in landscape mode—lying on their sides! Thus the need to rotate the image. An example of when you might need to flip an image over completely is if you scan a picture upside down. This is pretty easy to do with a flat-plate scanner. Rather than starting over and rescanning the photograph, simply use Photoshop Elements to flip it over.

Rotating or flipping images is all done by choosing options from the Image | Rotate menu.

90° Left　Rotates the image a quarter turn counter-clockwise.

90° Right　Rotates the image a quarter turn clock-wise.

180°　Rotates the image a half turn.

Flip Horizontal　Flips the image left to right. That is, imagine a vertical line from the top to the bottom of the image. This rotates the image around the vertical line so the former left edge becomes the right edge.

Flip Vertical　Flips the image top to bottom. That is, imagine a horizontal line from the left edge to the right edge of the image. This rotates the image around the horizontal line so the former top becomes the bottom.

Custom　You can use the Custom dialog box to specify any degree of rotation you want:

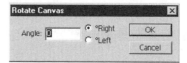

Type in the angle of rotation and then pick either the Left (counter-clockwise) or Right (clockwise) radio button. Click OK to rotate the image. The canvas expands automatically to contain the new (larger) shape of the image:

 *The new areas that are added to the image will use the background color, so be sure to set the background color to the one you want before performing the rotation.*

3

Set Up a Contact Sheet to See the Contents of a Folder

Keeping track of your photos can be quite a job. Rather than hunting through the contents of your disk drive using the file browser, you can choose to create a *contact sheet*:

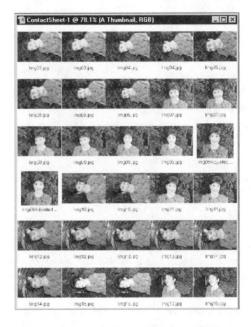

As you can see, a contact sheet is an image that Photoshop Elements creates by laying out the images available in a folder as thumbnails. You can then save the contact sheet as a Photoshop Elements image, or print it out to use for reference.

 A *contact sheet* gets its name from an old photographer's trick. Since it was difficult to tell what was on a film negative, photographers would take the strips of negatives and lay them on a sheet of photo paper in a darkroom. They would expose the combination of photo paper and negatives to light (and develop the result), making tiny prints of each negative on the paper. This contact sheet would then serve as a reference to tell what was on the negatives.

To create a contact sheet, follow these steps:

1. Choose File | Print Layouts | Contact Sheet. This opens the Contact Sheet dialog box:

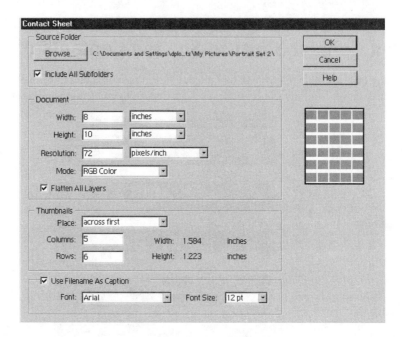

2. Choose where the photos will come from by clicking the Browse button and selecting a folder. Check the Include All Subfolders check box if you want all the pictures in the subfolders of the selected folder to be included.

 *If you choose more photos than will fit on a single-page contact sheet, Photoshop Elements automatically creates additional pages. Also, if a folder contains non-graphic files, Photoshop Elements will warn you that it couldn't open those files, nor could it create thumbnails from those files.*

3. Set the overall document width, height, and resolution by typing values in the appropriate fields and picking units of measure from the drop-down lists.

4. Choose the color mode (RGB Color or Grayscale) from the Mode drop-down list.

5. Choose whether to flatten all the layers in the various images by checking or clearing the Flatten All Layers check box. The purpose of layers is to add considerable editing power to an image. These images are really too small for you to meaningfully edit, so it is best to leave the check box checked (it is checked by default). Layers are further explained in Chapter 9.

6. Specify the layout and size of the thumbnails. For a layout, pick whether you want the thumbnails laid out across and then down, or down and then across. To set the size of the thumbnails, specify the number of rows and columns (integers only!) and Photoshop Elements will automatically calculate the size of the thumbnails.

7. Choose whether you want Photoshop Elements to place the filename as a caption to each thumbnail by checking or clearing the Use Filename as Caption check box. If you do use the filename as a caption, choose the font and type size you want to use for the caption text.

8. Click OK to create the Contact Sheet.

Save a File in Any Format

Photoshop Elements can save files in a large number of formats, including:

Photoshop's native format   The Photoshop Elements' native file format uses the .psd extension. It is ideal for works in progress, as it doesn't compress the file (the way JPEGs do) with resulting loss of information. It also preserves all the special Photoshop Elements features, such as multiple layers. and color spaces. This format is also excellent for sending files to professional printers, many of whom require files in Photoshop format.

JPEG   JPEGs (indicated by a file extension of .jpg or .jpeg) are the file type of choice for storing photographs for the Web. They can be opened and displayed by any browser. JPEGs are compressed as they are saved, so some information can be lost. However, by setting the compression parameters during the save (as described later in this chapter), you can balance the resulting file size with the quality of the image. Higher compression ratios degrade the image more, but can reduce the size of the file considerably. High-quality JPEGs take up less room than other good photo file types, such as TIFF files. However, because JPEGs lose information each time you save them, it is best to work on images in some other file format (such as TIFF or Photoshop format), then convert the finished product to a JPEG when you're done. You should keep a copy of the TIFF or Photoshop file in case you need to apply further changes.

CompuServe GIF   A GIF file (indicated by a file extension of .gif) is a good choice for clipart and other images that don't require more than the 256 colors possible with a GIF file. You can store photos in GIF format, but the smooth color gradations may be lost due to the limited number of colors available. GIF files are compressed, but unlike JPEGs, they do not lose information when compressed.

TIFF   TIFF files (indicated by a file extension of .tif) are also a good choice for storing photographs. These files can be really huge, but unlike JPEGs, information is not lost when you save a TIFF file. Browsers cannot read TIFFs (except with special plug-ins), but many graphic programs and office applications *can* use TIFFs, but not Photoshop files. In addition, the TIFF format has the capability to preserve layers when saving a file. Thus, if you need to preserve the photo quality and use photographs in other applications (or trade them with someone who doesn't own Photoshop), TIFFs are a good choice.

EPS Encapsulated PostScript (EPS) format is good for exchanging images with desktop publishing and illustration programs. It is also the most effective type of file to send to a PostScript-enabled printer.

There are many more file types that Photoshop Elements can handle, but these are the main ones for working with digital images such as photographs and clipart.

Save a File in Photoshop Elements Format

Saving a file in Photoshop Elements' native format is pretty simple: Just choose File | Save As to open the Save As dialog box, and choose Photoshop (*.PSD, or *.PDD) from the Format drop-down list. Specify the filename, choose whether to save the ICC color profile along with the image, and click the Save button.

Save a File as a JPEG

Saving a file as a JPEG provides you a number of choices for formatting and compression. The first step is to choose File | Save As to open the Save As dialog box. Choose the JPEG (*.JPG, *.JPEG, or *.JPE) option from the Format drop-down list, specify the filename, choose whether to save the ICC color profile, and click Save. This opens the JPEG Options dialog box:

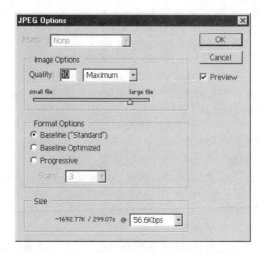

From this dialog box, you can specify the amount of compression to apply to the file in one of three ways: Type a number between 1 and 10 into the Quality field, select an option (Low, Medium, High, or Maximum) from the Quality drop-down list, or drag the small file/large file slider. Each of these operations does basically the same thing—adjusts the amount of compression and the resulting file size. As noted earlier, these two quantities are related. A small amount of compression preserves image quality, but results in a large file, while a large amount of compression results in a small file, but the image can be noticeably of poorer quality.

> **NOTE** *The file size can change quite a bit depending on the amount of compression you choose. In the example file I was using, the file size changed from 82KB at the lowest quality to 1130KB (1.1 megabytes!) at the highest quality.*

As you make adjustments to the quality/file size, Photoshop Elements provides an estimate of the size of the resulting file and how long it will take to download in the Size section near the bottom of the JPEG Options dialog box. You can choose the assumed download speed from the drop-down list in the Size section. In addition, if you check the Preview check box, the image changes to show (approximately) the amount of degradation you can expect.

> **TIP** *To view and judge the effect of compression, you should zoom the image to 100%, and view an area with subtle gradations of color. At higher compression levels, the subtleties are lost and the areas become patchy.*

> **NOTE** *It's pretty hard to provide good guidelines as to what choices to make for compression. Images that don't contain subtle color variations or lots of detail can stand quite a bit of compression without too much damage. You can also apply a fair amount of compression (medium or 5) to low-resolution images designed for the Web. But for archival images that you may wish to print out or work on later, it is best to use very little compression and pay the price of the larger file. After all, large hard drives have gotten very inexpensive, and burning your own CDs to hold the images is very cheap.*

The JPEG Options dialog box also provides some formatting options. They are:

Baseline   The standard format for JPEG. This format has been around a long time, and all browsers can read it, as can all image cataloging programs.

Baseline Optimized   This format provides a more sophisticated algorithm for compression, and is thus able to compress a file with less loss of quality. However, not all browsers and image cataloging programs can read this format.

Progressive   This format displays the image in a series of scans. Each scan displays a progressively higher quality. This is especially useful for photos published on the Web—the viewer can get an idea of what the photo looks like without waiting for the entire photo to load. If the viewer discovers he or she doesn't care about the photo, the viewer can move on to something else. If you choose this format, you can specify the number of scans to use from the Scans drop-down list (3 or 4 is a good number to choose). Virtually all modern browsers can read this format, but older ones (versions 3 and earlier) may not be able to. Still, it is considered good web etiquette to publish large photos using this format.

Save a File as a GIF

When you choose to save a file as a GIF, Photoshop Elements opens the Indexed Color dialog box:

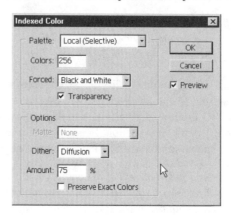

Since GIF files support only up to 256 (or fewer) colors, you have to make some choices about how you want Photoshop Elements to reduce the number of colors from what was originally in the photo. The options in the Indexed Color dialog box are as follows:

Palette   Pick the palette of colors you want to use from the palette drop-down list. The three Local palettes use different algorithms to estimate the best colors to use. For example, the Local (Perceptual) palette gives preference to colors that the eye is most sensitive to, while the Local (Adaptive) palette samples the colors from the spectrum appearing most frequently in the image. The Web palette is a preset combination of 216 colors that are guaranteed to be available and displayed properly by all web browsers. You can also choose the System palettes for Windows or the Mac, although these (in general) don't do as good a job as the Local palettes. Finally, you can choose a Custom palette, which displays the Color Table dialog box:

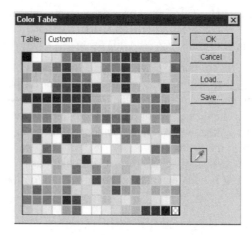

From this dialog box, you can click a color to open the Color Picker, choose a color to replace the selected color (as described in Chapter 5), and click OK to return to the Color Table dialog box. Once you have the palette adjusted the way you want, click the Save button to save the palette. You can also load a palette you saved earlier.

If the image you are trying to save has fewer than 256 colors, there is another palette option: Exact. This option saves the image by using the exact colors present in the image.

3

Colors   Type the number of colors you want to use (up to a maximum of 256) into the Colors field. The fewer colors you use, the smaller the file becomes (especially with photographs), but the quality of the image degrades as well.

Forced   The Forced drop-down list enables you to force the palette to contain certain colors. Options include Black and White (includes both pure black and pure white); primaries (includes all primary colors of red, green, blue, cyan, magenta, yellow, black, and white); Web (includes all 216 colors from the Web palette); and Custom. If you choose Custom, Photoshop Elements opens the Forced Colors dialog box:

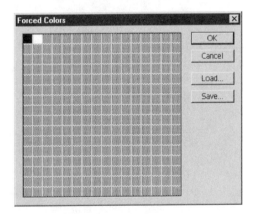

To create a list of forced colors, which you can Save and Load, click on each rectangle to open the Color Picker. Choose a color from the Color Picker and click OK to return to the Forced Colors dialog box to choose the next forced color.

Dither   Dithering is a technique by which Photoshop Elements attempts to simulate colors that exist in the original image but are not available in the chosen palette. You can choose the algorithm to use for dithering from the Dither drop-down list. Options include None, Diffusion, Pattern, or Noise. Diffusion uses an error diffusion method that does a pretty good job of simulating colors without introducing a noticeable structured pattern the way the Pattern option does. The Noise option introduces additional random elements, doing an even better job of dithering along edges than Diffusion, but at a cost of a slightly larger file.

Amount If you choose the Diffusion dithering algorithm, you can adjust the error diffusion calculation by entering a number in the Amount field. This number does not have a large effect on dithering, and I have found purely through experience that between 75% and 100% seems to work well, minimizing patchiness in large areas containing subtle gradations of color.

When using the Diffusion algorithm, Photoshop Elements will sometimes dither colors that are actually in the palette. To prevent this, check the Preserve Exact Colors check box.

Save a File as a TIFF

If you choose to save a file as a TIFF, Photoshop Elements opens the TIFF Options dialog box:

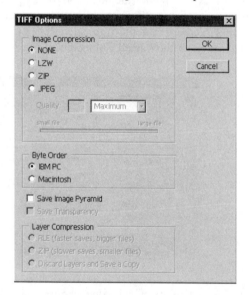

From the TIFF Options dialog box, you can set the following options:

Image Compression Normally, TIFF files are not compressed, which can make them very large. However, you can, if you wish, apply compression to a TIFF file when you save it. The compression types are

LZW This is the most common compression scheme used with TIFF files, as most TIFF editors can still open a TIFF file that has been compressed using LZW. This is a *lossless* compression scheme, meaning that (unlike JPEG compression) no data is lost when the image is compressed this way.

ZIP   Zip is a common file-compression scheme. It is quite efficient and also lossless, but is uncommon, so many TIFF editors cannot read files that have been "zipped." If your editor won't read a zipped TIFF file, you'll have to "unzip" it first using a utility like Winzip (go to http://www.winzip.com for an evaluation copy of this useful utility).

JPEG   You can apply JPEG compression to a TIFF. The same tradeoffs between compression and image quality apply when you use JPEG compression for a TIFF file. Additionally, like Zip, many TIFF editors cannot read files that have been compressed using JPEG. And, unlike Zip, there aren't any utilities that can decompress a TIFF file that has been compressed using JPEG compression.

Byte Order   Although TIFF is supposed to be a standard, there are two different byte orders that can be used when creating a TIFF file—IBM PC and Macintosh byte orders. Choose the one you want to use from the radio buttons in the Byte Order section of the dialog box. IBM PC order is the safest, as most Macintosh TIFF editors (including Photoshop Elements running on a Macintosh) can read a TIFF in IBM PC byte order.

Save Image Pyramid   You can create a TIFF file that contains multiple-resolution versions of the image. The highest resolution is the image resolution itself, but lower-resolution versions are stored in the file as well. Unfortunately, because Photoshop Elements opens and displays only the highest resolution version, there is really no reason to select this option.

Layer Compression   As described in Chapter 9, Photoshop Elements can use layers of information to build up an image or make adjustments "on top" of the original. If your image contains layers, you can choose how these layers will be handled when saving to a TIFF file. The three options include RLE, Zip, or simply discarding the layers and saving the image as a copy. RLE is very fast but creates bigger files than Zip. However, RLE is also more widely recognized by TIFF editors. As mentioned earlier, most TIFF editors cannot handle TIFF files (or TIFF file layers) that have been compressed with Zip.

Save a File as EPS

If you choose to save a file as Encapsulated PostScript (EPS), Photoshop Elements displays the EPS Options dialog box:

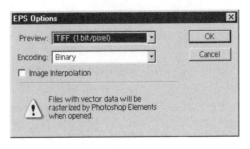

The options you can choose are:

Preview　To be able to see the contents in an EPS file as a thumbnail, a preview of the file is needed. This preview version is stored with the file and used by graphic editor software to display the thumbnail. You have two options for the preview: 1 bit/pixel and 8 bits/pixel. The 8 bits/pixel generates a much higher-quality preview, but the file is a little larger than the 1 bit/pixel.

Encoding　You can specify the encoding method used to generate the EPS file. ASCII encoding creates a larger file than Binary encoding and is slower to work with. You can also use JPEG encoding (in low, medium, high, or maximum quality), but as with everything else JPEG, image quality suffers. Also, PostScript Level 1 printers cannot read and print a JPEG-encoded file.

Image Interpolation　If your image is low resolution, check the Image Interpolation check box in order to apply anti-aliasing to the image for better print quality.

Part II

Make Simple Adjustments to Your Images

Chapter 4

Make General Fixes to an Entire Image

How to...

- Crop pictures to reduce their size
- Change the canvas and picture size
- Adjust brightness, contrast, and color
- Preview multiple corrections with color variations
- Fix deep shadows with fill flash
- Fix focus problems
- Rotate and straighten images
- Apply special effects

Now that we've gotten some of the "housekeeping" out of the way, it's time to dive in and start using Photoshop Elements to fix problem photographs. These fixes are applied to the photograph as a whole, and later in this book, you'll see how to apply fixes to specific areas of a photo. As is typical of Photoshop Elements, there are several ways to get a lot of these fixes done. Photoshop Elements offers automated tools that do a pretty good job of making corrections, but you'll also want to learn how to fine-tune the corrections in case the photo presents too much of a challenge for the automated tools.

Crop Your Picture to Remove Unneeded Portions

Pictures often include large areas that take away from the overall effect. For example, your main subject may be off-center, or there may be a lot of "busy" background. An example of such a photograph is shown in Figure 4-1. Editing a picture to remove unwanted areas is called "cropping." The result may well be a more attractive composition.

Crop with the Crop Tool

To crop with the Crop tool, select it from the toolbar. Click and drag a rectangle in the photograph to define the area you want to crop. By default, the outside of the rectangle (which will be removed when you actually perform the crop) is masked to display the effect of the crop, as shown in Figure 4-2.

To adjust the crop mask, you can do the following:

Move the crop mask   Click inside the rectangle and drag it to move the crop mask.

Change the size   Click one of the sizing handles and drag to increase or decrease the size of the crop mask.

Rotate the mask   Move the mouse pointer around the outside of the crop mask (it turns into a bent, double-headed arrow) and drag to rotate the crop mask.

When you are ready to execute the crop, choose Image | Crop or choose any other tool from the toolbox.

You can adjust the properties of the crop mask by using the options in the options bar. To turn off the mask altogether, clear the Shield check box. To change the color of the mask, click the Color square, then pick the color you want from the Color Picker (described later in this chapter). Finally, to change the opacity of the mask, either type a value into the Opacity field or click the arrow and use the slider to change the opacity. Opacity of 100% hides (masks) the cropped portions of the picture completely.

4

> **TIP**
>
> *A good value to use for opacity is 75%, as shown in Figure 4-2. This percentage darkens the cropped area without hiding it completely, so you can see the portions that will be removed and make small adjustments to improve the picture composition.*

Crop with the Crop Command

An alternate way to crop a picture is to designate the crop area with one of the selection tools (see Chapter 8 for more details). The easiest selection tool to use is the Rectangular Marquee. Simply select the tool from the upper-left corner of the toolbox, then click and drag to define a rectangle in your image. Select Image | Crop to crop the image to the selected rectangle.

> **NOTE**
>
> *You can actually use any selection tool, including the Oval Marquee or one of the Lassos. However, if you choose a non-rectangular area, Photoshop Elements will crop to the smallest rectangle that includes the selected area.*

FIGURE 4-1   In this photo, the background takes away from the impact of the photo.

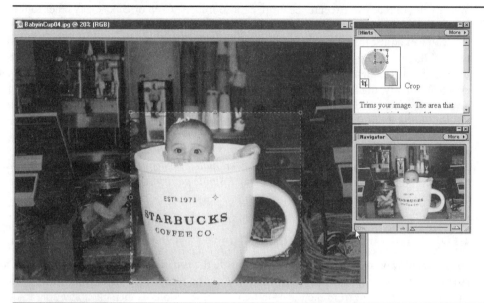

FIGURE 4-2
Using the Crop tool to edit unwanted areas of the photo.

Change the Canvas Size

Each image you open sits on a canvas, the area in which you can work. You don't normally see the canvas because it is usually the same size as the image. However, you may wish to change the size of the canvas. For example, if you want to add a frame border effect around the outside of the image, you'll want to make the canvas larger to make room for the border.

To change the canvas size, choose Image | Resize | Canvas Size. This displays the Canvas Size dialog box:

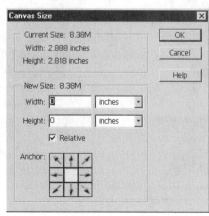

Simply type in new numbers in the Width and Height fields. If you make the canvas smaller, Photoshop Elements will warn you that clipping will occur—that is, portions of the picture outside the reduced canvas size will be lost.

Checking the Relative check box enables you to specify the new dimensions relative to the existing dimensions. If you type positive numbers into the Height and Width fields, the resulting canvas will be that much larger than the original. If you type negative numbers into these fields, the resulting canvas will be smaller, and clipping will occur.

Normally, the image sits in the middle of the canvas. Thus, if you make the canvas larger, there will be a blank space all the way around the outside of the image (as shown in the illustration below on the left).

You can choose the anchor point from the grid in the Canvas Size dialog box. Click a square in the grid to set where the image will be anchored after the resize operation. For example, if you click in the upper-left corner and make the canvas larger, the existing image will be located in the upper-left corner of the resulting canvas (as shown below on the right).

4

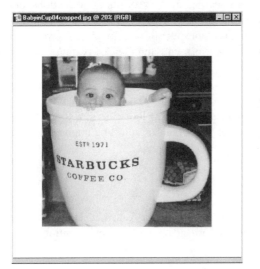 

Let Photoshop Elements Correct Your Pictures

One the slickest features of Photoshop Elements is its ability to make many corrections automatically—analyzing the errors in your pictures and correcting them with little or no input from you. As you get more practiced with Photoshop Elements, you'll probably find yourself using these automatic tools less and less, but they are very handy when you are just getting started and aren't quite sure how to fix your pictures.

Using an automatic tool is very easy. Simply select the tool you want to use from the Enhance menu. The tools available to you are:

Auto Levels   Adjusts brightness *and* contrast.

Auto Contrast   Adjusts the contrast of the image.

Auto Color Correction   Adjusts the hue (color) of the image. This tool is handy if the image has an overall color cast—that is, the colors aren't truly represented. For example, areas that should be white can come out with a greenish tint. This can often happen when you shoot a picture under fluorescent lights with film that is designed for sunlight.

Make Quick Fixes to Your Photos

The automatic tools described in the previous section are fine for minor corrections, but there is no opportunity for you to have any say in the process. Thus, you'll outgrow the automatic tools very quickly. The Quick Fix dialog box provides lots of help in adjusting your images, as well as presenting you with instant feedback. To work with the Quick Fix dialog box (shown in Figure 4-3), choose Enhance | Quick Fix.

The Quick Fix dialog box is divided into four categories: Brightness, Color Correction, Focus, and Rotate. Some of the adjustment categories, especially brightness, contrast, and color correction, have not been covered in this book. In the following sections, I'll discuss how to use the Quick Fix dialog box, and later in this chapter, I'll cover the finer points of adjusting brightness, contrast, and color.

Adjust the Brightness

From the Brightness category, you can select Auto Contrast or Auto Levels, which have the same effect as making those selections from the Enhance menu. The other options in the Brightness category are:

Brightness/Contrast   Use the Brightness and Contrast sliders to adjust these quantities:

Fill Flash   Use the Lighter and Saturation sliders to correct photographs that are too dark or that have dark shadows (see the illustration on the following page). The Lighter slider adjusts the amount of lighting in the photo, while the Saturation slider makes the colors more or less vivid.

1. Select Adjustment Catagory	2. Select Adjustment	3. Apply Fill Flash
⊙ Brightness	○ Auto Contrast	Lighter: [9]
○ Color Correction	○ Auto Levels	
○ Focus	○ Brightness/Contrast	Saturation: [0]
○ Rotate	⊙ Fill Flash	
	○ Adjust Backlighting	

Adjust Backlight   Use the Darker slider to correct photographs where the foreground looks good but the background is too bright or is washed out.

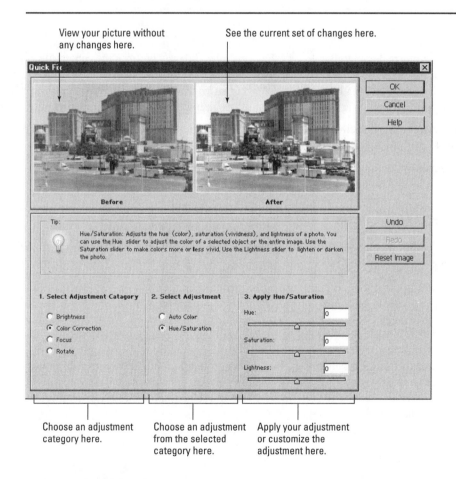

View your picture without any changes here.

See the current set of changes here.

Choose an adjustment category here.

Choose an adjustment from the selected category here.

Apply your adjustment or customize the adjustment here.

FIGURE 4-3   Make your changes and view the results instantly with the Quick Fix dialog box.

4

Correct the Color

The Color Correction category makes two adjustments available: Auto Color (which works just like the menu selection) and Hue/Saturation:

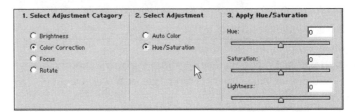

Use the sliders to make the following corrections:

Hue   Adjusts the overall color. As you move the slider away from the center, the color cast of the picture changes. You can use this slider to adjust a picture that was taken with film that is not designed for the type of light that was available when the picture was taken, or to correct overly warm tones that may occur in low light or late afternoon photographs.

Saturation   Adjusts the vividness of the color from no color (slider all the way to the left) to very intense color (slider all the way to the right).

Lightness   Lightens (move right) or darkens (move left) the photo.

Enhance the Focus

The focus adjustment category has two adjustments available: Auto Focus and Blur. Auto Focus applies a sharpening filter to high-contrast edges in the photo, sharpening the apparent focus.

The focus adjustments are difficult to master—too much, and the edges look jagged. You are probably better off using the Unsharp Mask to get more control over the sharpening effect (discussed later in this chapter).

The Blur focus adjustment has exactly the opposite effect of Auto Focus. This adjustment blurs edges and sharp details, and works well in portraits for that reason. As you will see in Chapter 8, you can use Blur in combination with the selection tools to bring out a foreground subject in a photograph.

Use the Rotate Quick Fix

The last Quick Fix category is the Rotate category. The adjustments available (see the illustration on the following page) enable you to rotate or flip your photograph.

1. Select Adjustment Catagory	2. Select Adjustment	3. Apply Rotation
○ Brightness	⦿ Rotate 90° CW	
○ Color Correction	○ Rotate 90° CCW	Apply
○ Focus	○ Rotate 180°	
⦿ Rotate	○ Flip Horizontal	
	○ Flip Vertical	

Simply click the rotation or flip direction you want and then click Apply.

Preview Multiple Variations

One of the more difficult but effective ways to adjust a photograph is to make a series of small changes, and then preview what they look like before committing to the changes. The Color Variations dialog box enables you to make color, saturation, and brightness changes in small steps, and also shows you the effect of applying various changes via a series of thumbnails, as shown in Figure 4-4. To use the Color Variations dialog box, choose Enhance | Adjust Color | Color Variations.

The large "before" picture in the upper-left corner of the dialog box displays your original photo. The image immediately to its right ("after") shows you the cumulative effect of your changes. The radio buttons at the left side of the dialog box determine whether your changes apply to midtones (middle shades of color), the shadows (dark areas), or highlights (very bright areas). The series of thumbnails across the bottom of the dialog box displays previews of various changes, such as increasing the amount of blue in the photo or lightening the photo. These previews change as you pick different radio buttons. To apply a change (such as increasing red), simply click the thumbnail and watch the "after" image change. You can click a thumbnail multiple times to apply the effect multiple times. If you go too far, simply click the opposite thumbnail (decrease red, in this example) to back out of the change. The amount of each change is controlled by the Amount slider in the lower-left corner. Moving this slider to the left decreases the amount of each change; moving it to the right increases the amount.

The Saturation radio button works a little differently from the other radio buttons. When you select this button, you are limited to two options: add more saturation (more intense color) or less saturation:

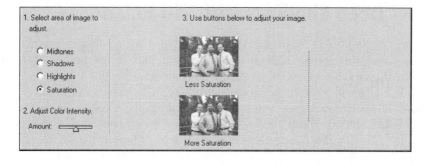

Original photo   View the changes you've made here.

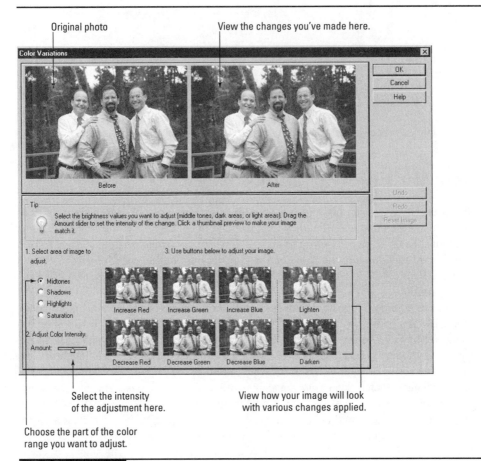

Select the intensity
of the adjustment here.

View how your image will look
with various changes applied.

Choose the part of the color
range you want to adjust.

FIGURE 4-4   Make color adjustments and see how they'll look with the Color
Variations dialog box.

Correct Deep Shadows with Fill Flash

Using "fill flash" is an old photographer's trick. When you photograph a subject against a bright
background, the exposure meter in the camera is "fooled" by the background, and exposes for
it, leaving the subject too dark, as shown in Figure 4-5.

To brighten the subject, the photographer turns on the camera's flash and forces it to fire. The
flash "fills in" the dark area, hence, the name "fill flash." Of course, up until now, there was no
way to correct the problem after the fact. But Photoshop Elements fixes that with its fill flash
facility. This nifty tool selectively lightens dark areas of the photograph, as shown in Figure 4-6.

FIGURE 4-5   When the background is bright, the face of the subject is under-exposed and left in deep shade.

To use fill flash, choose Enhance | Adjust Lighting | Fill Flash to open the Adjust Fill Flash dialog box:

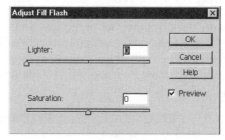

To lighten the dark areas of the image, drag the Lighter slider to the right or type a value into the field. As you lighten the image, the colors may begin to appear "washed out." You can correct this by adjusting the saturation with the slider. A slight increase in saturation (between 10 and 20) is usually enough to fix the problem.

NOTE   *As with many other dialog boxes, you can preview the changes you apply in the actual image by checking the Preview check box. However, if the change is complex or you have a slower computer, there may be a delay before the change is reflected in the image.*

FIGURE 4-6   After using fill flash, the ruined photo was rescued!

Bring Out the Background with Backlighting

Some photographers use backlighting (such as a bright sky) to emphasize the main subject in the image. However, backlighting may result in an overexposed photo, which can mean a loss of detail (the main subject is too dark or underexposed), as shown in Figure 4-7.

To correct this problem, choose Enhance | Adjust Lighting | Adjust Backlighting to display the Adjust Backlighting dialog box:

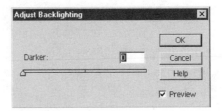

Drag the Darker slider to adjust the tonal range of the picture, darkening the backlighting and lightening the darker area, as shown in Figure 4-8. You may find that the lightened foreground loses contrast, so you'll need to apply additional contrast, as described later in this chapter.

FIGURE 4-7   The foreground is a little dark, and the interesting cloud pattern in the sky is partially lost because the sky is so bright.

FIGURE 4-8   The sky looks better—and so does the foreground—after we adjusted the backlighting.

Sharpen a Photo to Correct Focus Problems

You can make a photo look sharply focused by increasing the contrast in several different ways. To sharpen the entire photo (good for when the whole picture is a little out of focus), choose Filter | Sharpen | Sharpen. To increase the effect, you can choose Filter | Sharpen | Sharpen More. These commands do not allow you to exercise any control, and they sharpen the entire photograph rather indiscriminately.

A somewhat more effective tool is Sharpen Edges (Filter | Sharpen | Sharpen Edges). This detects the edges of objects, and sharpens only those edges.

The most powerful sharpening tool in the arsenal carries the odd name of Unsharp Mask. It locates pixels that are different from surrounding pixels by the amount (threshold) you specify in the dialog box, thus locating edges according to your instructions. You can also specify the distance (radius) that Photoshop Elements uses to compare pixels to the original pixel, again controlling what is assumed to be an edge. The mask then increases the contrast of those pixels by the amount you specify.

To use Unsharp Mask, choose Filter | Sharpen | Unsharp Mask to display the Unsharp Mask dialog box:

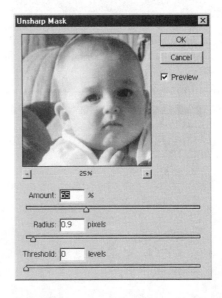

You can control the preview image in the dialog box by clicking the two small buttons below the image. The plus button (+) increases the magnification level, while the minus button (–) decreases the magnification. You can also click and drag the preview image to display a different portion of the main image.

To view the preview image without the sharpening effects being visible, position the mouse pointer over the preview image, then click and hold the mouse button. When you release the mouse button, the sharpening effects become visible again.

Use the following steps to adjust the effect of Unsharp Mask:

1. Drag the Amount slider or type a number into the Amount percent field. This value determines how much to increase the contrast of the detected pixels. Amounts between 150% and 200% usually work best.

2. Drag the Radius slider or enter a value into the Radius pixels field. This determines the number of pixels surrounding the edge pixels that are sharpened. I recommend a radius of between 1 and 2 pixels. Lesser amounts sharpen only the edge pixel itself, while a larger number sharpens a wider band of pixels. Taken to the extreme, this has the same effect as just sharpening the entire image.

3. Drag the Threshold slider or type a value into the Threshold levels field. This determines how different the sharpened pixels must be from the surrounding area before they are considered edge pixels. A value of between 2 and 20 works well. Lower values detect every color change as an edge; very high values fail to find edges at all.

4. Click OK to apply the effect to the image.

Make Color Corrections for Yourself

As you become more experienced with Photoshop Elements, you'll find yourself wanting to exercise a very fine degree of control over color, brightness, and contrast adjustments. This is primarily because "exactly right" for you is very much a matter of personal preference, and the automatic adjustments—or the stepped adjustments available from Color Variations—may not allow you to apply corrections the way you want.

Fortunately, Photoshop Elements sports a number of controls that enable you to fiddle with color corrections to your heart's content. These controls include Hue/Saturation, Color Cast, Brightness/Contrast, a histogram of the image's color distribution, and the Levels dialog box.

Understand the Color Wheel

A color wheel (see Figure 4-9) will help you understand how to make adjustments to colors in an image. You can use a color wheel to keep track of how changes to one color affect another color.

As you can see from the figure, each color has an "opposite" or complementary color and is indicated on the color wheel by the lines connecting different colors. For example, the complementary color of green is magenta (they are at opposite ends of the same line).

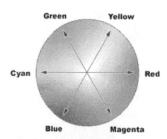

FIGURE 4-9   A color wheel shows the relationship between related colors.

The rules for color interaction are pretty simple:

You can increase the amount of one color by decreasing the amount of its opposite color.   For example, if you increase the amount of yellow, you automatically decrease the amount of blue (yellow's opposite on the color wheel).

You can increase the amount of a color by increasing the amount of both its adjacent colors.   For example, to increase the amount of cyan, you can increase the amount of blue and green (cyan's adjacent colors on the color wheel). You can also increase the amount of a color by *decreasing* the amount of both adjacent colors of its opposite color. Thus, to increase the amount of cyan, you can decrease the amount of yellow and magenta.

To decrease the amount of a color, you can decrease the amount of both its adjacent colors.   You can also decrease the amount of a color by *increasing* the amount of both adjacent colors of its opposite color. Thus, to decrease the amount of cyan, you can increase the amount of both yellow and magenta.

The color wheel also displays the saturation (purity of the color). Moving toward the center of the color wheel decreases the saturation, while moving toward the perimeter increases the saturation.

Resampling is the process of re-analyzing the contents of an image when making color corrections. Resampling, however carefully done, can introduce subtle errors to the image. This is most apparent when saving JPEG files, but it occurs at other times too. The effects of resampling are most apparent around the edges in an image, which is why your last step should be to sharpen your image.

Plan Your Color Corrections

To get the best results from a color correction, you should make the corrections in a certain order. The correct order enables you to focus on what is important, as well as to more easily see the results of making the corrections to the image.

The first step is to make corrections in the extreme areas of the image—the deep shadows and the extreme highlights. For the deep shadow areas, you'll want to lighten and bring out whatever details are available. You may also need to increase the color saturation and slightly increase the contrast. The contrast adjustment is tricky, since it tends to darken areas you just took great pains to lighten!

Making adjustments in the extreme highlights enables you to take the "edge" off specular (pure white) areas. These tend to get introduced either from reflection (from your flash or snow and water reflections) or high-intensity light sources (car headlights, and so forth.). There isn't much you can do except tone down the trouble spots so they aren't as distracting, since these areas have lost all detail. With other bright areas (sky, bright water reflections, overexposed faces), you can decrease the brightness and increase the color saturation and contrast.

After you have modified the extremes of the image, focus your attention on the midranges. Adjusting the extremes will have modified the midranges somewhat, but additional adjustments may be necessary to get them just right. You should focus on correcting the brightness and contrast because the next step is to adjust the overall color balance of the image, which is most visible in the midranges. This step removes color casts (where white shows up as another color, such as light green) and over- and under-saturated colors.

The last step in making a correction is to sharpen the image using the Unsharp Mask or one of the other sharpening filters. By correcting the extremes, overall color balance, and overall contrast *first*, you will find edge sharpening to be more effective, and avoids introducing false color and moiré patterns around the edges. This step also helps to correct softness in the focus introduced by previous steps (due to *resampling* of the image).

Analyze Color Distribution with the Histogram

A histogram illustrates how pixels in an image are distributed from dark to light, otherwise known as the "tonal range." The histogram can tell you whether an image has enough detail in the shadows (at the left end of the graph), the midtones (the middle section of the graph), and the highlights (at the right end of the graph). To view the histogram for an image, choose Image | Histogram:

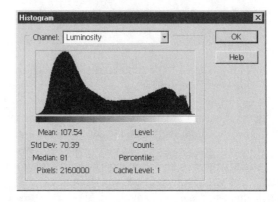

The horizontal axis of the histogram shows the levels from dark (0) at the far left to light (255) at the far right. The height of each line in the histogram represents the number of pixels at each level. Thus, a well-exposed photo will have most of the pixels in the middle of the window, tailing off at the dark and light ends (what we used to call a "bell-shaped curve" when we were in school).

The quantities on the left below the histogram provide information about the entire image. These quantities are:

Mean The average intensity level.

Std Dev (Standard Deviation) A measure of how widely the intensity values vary.

Median The middle intensity level. This means that half the pixels fall within intensity levels above the median, and half fall within intensity levels below the median.

Pixels Total number of pixels in the image.

You can choose whether to view a histogram for the overall luminosity (choose Luminosity from the Channel drop-down list) or a histogram for any of the three color channels (red, green, or blue). Select one from the Channel drop-down list.

You can obtain information about a particular level in the histogram by moving the mouse pointer over that level. The three quantities on the right side of the area below the histogram (Level, Count, and Percentile) display the values for the chosen level. Here is what they mean:

Level The intensity level of the area under the pointer. As discussed earlier, this varies from 0 (dark) to 255 (light).

Count The total number of pixels that has this intensity level.

Percentile   The percentage of all the pixels in the image at or below the selected intensity level.

You can also click and drag to select a portion of the histogram. As long as you hold down the mouse button, these quantities display information about the selected portion, including the range of levels (in the Level field) and the percentage of pixels in the selected area (in the Percentile field).

Correct a Color Cast

4

A color cast is a situation in which the entire tonal range of the photograph has too much of one color. "Warm" photographs tend to have a reddish cast, and "cold" photographs tend to have a bluish cast. Color casts usually occur because the film was not "balanced" for the type of light you were using. For example, a daylight-balanced film (most films) will show a greenish color cast when shooting under fluorescent or mercury vapor lights. For digital cameras, a color cast can occur if the automatic white balance is fooled by the lighting conditions. You will usually notice a color cast in photos that have large areas that should be white, but instead have faint (and sometimes not so faint) overtones of the cast color. Figure 4-10 shows an image with a strong color cast. In this case, the color cast occurred because I shot the picture through a tinted window.

To correct color cast, choose Enhance | Adjust Color | Color Cast to open the Color Cast Correction dialog box:

Follow the instructions in the dialog box to click an area of the photo that *should be* white, gray, or black. Photoshop Elements does the rest, correcting the color cast. If you change your mind, simply click the Reset button to put things back the way they were. As you can see from Figure 4-11, Photoshop Elements does a good job of removing even a strong color cast.

The difference between Figures 4-10 and 4-11 is difficult to see because it depends on a color difference and these figures are printed in black and white. However, I have included these images in the color insert section, where you can really see the change that results when you remove the color cast.

FIGURE 4-10   The strong bluish cast of this photo detracts from the quality.

FIGURE 4-11   Click where the picture should be white, black, or gray, and Photoshop Elements adjusts the picture to set the colors properly.

Adjust the Hue and Saturation

Photoshop Elements provides Hue/Saturation tools to adjust the color (hue), purity of color (saturation), and lightness of the image. To open the Hue/Saturation tool, select Enhance | Adjust Color | Hue/Saturation, as shown in Figure 4-12.

Adjust the Master Channel

If you choose Master from the Edit drop-down list, your changes affect all the colors in the image equally. Here is what you can do:

Adjust the Hue   Use the Hue slider or type a value into the Hue field to shift all the colors in the image. The values in the Hue field reflect a move around the perimeter of the color wheel (from –180 degrees to +180 degrees). As you change the hue, the bottom color bar shifts to show how the new color in the image aligns with the original colors (shown in the upper color bar). In my example photo, an adjustment of +30 degrees changes everything that used to be yellow to lime green.

Adjust the Saturation   Use the Saturation slider or type a value into the Saturation field to increase (positive values) or decrease (negative values) the intensity of the color.

Adjust the Lightness   Use the Lightness slider or type a value into the Lightness field to increase (positive values) or decrease (negative values) the brightness of the image. A value of +100 turns the image completely white, while a value of –100 turns the image completely black.

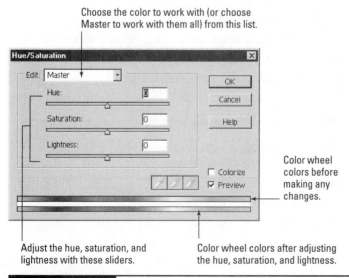

Choose the color to work with (or choose Master to work with them all) from this list.

Color wheel colors before making any changes.

Adjust the hue, saturation, and lightness with these sliders.

Color wheel colors after adjusting the hue, saturation, and lightness.

FIGURE 4-12   Adjust the colors and brightness of an image—for both the overall color and for each individual channel—with the Hue/Saturation tool.

Adjust the Individual Color Channels

The Hue/Saturation tool works quite differently when you select one of the individual channels from the Edit drop-down list. In fact, it even *looks* different, as shown in Figure 4-13.

Once you choose a color from the Edit menu, any changes you make to the sliders or fields affect only that color. For example, if you choose yellow from the Edit menu, adjusting the Hue slider or field changes the color of only the yellow areas of the image. Similarly, adjusting the saturation increases or decreases only the amount of yellow, and adjusting the lightness changes the brightness of only the yellow.

When you choose a color in the Edit drop-down list, the Eyedropper tools become available for you to use. These tools enable you to choose a color from the image and modify it, overriding the selection you made in the Edit drop-down list. For example, if you choose yellow in the Edit drop-down list, then click a blue area in your image with the eyedropper, any adjusting you do to the hue, saturation, and lightness will affect only the blues tones. The Edit drop-down list will then change to "blues." You can expand the range of colors affected by the Hue/Saturation tool by choosing the middle Eyedropper tool (the one with the plus sign) and clicking a color in the image. Similarly, you can decrease the range of colors affected by the Hue/Saturation tool by selecting the right-hand eyedropper (the one with the minus sign) and clicking a color in the image.

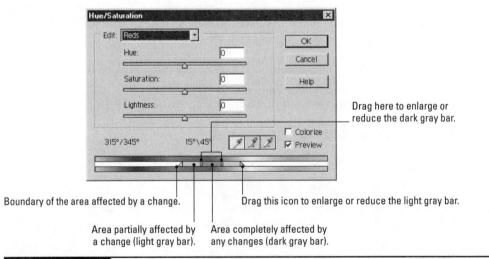

Drag here to enlarge or reduce the dark gray bar.

Boundary of the area affected by a change.

Drag this icon to enlarge or reduce the light gray bar.

Area partially affected by a change (light gray bar).

Area completely affected by any changes (dark gray bar).

FIGURE 4-13 When you pick a color channel, the Hue/Saturation dialog box changes to show color information.

As you experimented with the Edit drop-down list; the eyedroppers; and the Hue, Saturation, and Lightness sliders, you may have noticed changes to the new set of icons that appeared between the color bars after you chose a color from the Edit drop-down list. These bars and icons represent valuable information. Here is what they mean:

Adjustment Slider   The dark gray bar in the center of the icons represents the color range that is affected by the changes you make to the Hue, Saturation, and Lightness sliders. For example, if the Adjustment slider spans blue and magenta, changing the hue will affect both blue and magenta, but no other colors in the image. You can expand or reduce the size of the Adjustment slider by dragging the small rectangle icon at either end of the dark gray bar.

Fall-off Color Range   The light gray bar at either end of the Adjustment slider represents the color range that will be only partially affected by the changes you make to the Hue, Saturation, and Lightness sliders. The color changes you make progressively "fall off" in effect as you move away from the edge of the Adjustment slider. They will cease to have any effect at the triangle icon that represents the edge of the Fall-off Color Range. You can drag the triangle icon to expand the Fall-off Color Range, making the change less abrupt.

By default, the range of the color that is affected (the dark gray Adjustment slider) is 30 degrees wide (30 degrees around the circumference of the color wheel) with a 30-degree fall-off area on each side.

You have already seen how you can change the affected color you choose by using the Edit drop-down list or the Eyedropper tools. You can also drag the Adjustment slider right or left between the color bars. If you drag the Adjustment slider to a color that is different from the one selected in the Edit drop-down list, Photoshop Elements will provide a new name in the Edit drop-down list (such as "Red2") to indicate that you're not really editing the color you chose originally.

Watch the bottom color bar as you make changes to individual colors. You'll see the affected color change, with the most intense change in the affected color range (dark gray bar). The color change will become progressively less intense in the Fall-off Color Range (light gray bar).

Convert to Black and White

It's very easy to convert a color image to black and white for artistic effect. To do so, simply choose Enhance | Adjust Color | Remove Color. You aren't limited to just plain black and white, however. Instead, you can tint the result to give the effect of a sepia-tone photograph, like the photos of old. You can achieve this effect either with a color photo or with a black and white photo.

To tint a photograph, choose Enhance | Adjust Color | Hue/Saturation to open the Hue/Saturation dialog box, and check the Colorize check box:

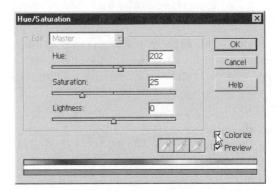

This version of the Hue/Saturation dialog box displays variations of a single color in the lower color bar. To adjust the toning of the photograph, adjust the three sliders as follows:

Hue   Adjusting the hue changes how the original colors (in the top color bar) map to the single colorizing color (in the bottom color bar). The only variation in the bottom color bar is the intensity of the single color.

Saturation   Adjusting the saturation changes the amount (saturation) of the single color, affecting how the colorized photo looks.

Lightness   Adjusting lightness changes the brightness of the single color.

Adjust the Brightness and Contrast

One of the most common problems with photographs is over or underexposure. Take, for example, the photo shown in Figure 4-14. It is washed out, with much detail apparently lost. But with Photoshop Elements' Brightness and Contrast controls, you can fix this problem, as well as fix problems with photos that are too dark.

To access the Brightness and Contrast control, choose Enhance | Adjust Brightness/Contrast | Brightness/Contrast to display the Brightness/Contrast dialog box:

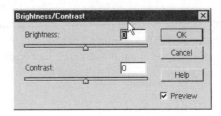

FIGURE 4-14   You can fix a photo that is overexposed like this one.

Simply drag the Brightness slider up or down, or type a number into the Brightness field to correct exposure problems. Dragging the slider left or typing a negative number darkens the photo; dragging the slider right or typing a positive number brightens the photo.

Making corrections to brightness often leads to contrast problems. Usually, lightening a photo decreases contrast, while darkening a photo increases contrast. Thus, it is quite convenient that the Contrast slider is available in the Brightness/Contrast dialog box. Drag the slider right (or type a positive number into the Contrast field) to increase the contrast; drag the slider left (or type a negative number into the field) to decrease contrast. As you can see from Figure 4-15, it is pretty easy to correct even severe exposure problems with the Brightness/Contrast dialog box.

Correct Your Photos with the Levels Controls

The Levels dialog box (see Figure 4-16) enables you to adjust the brightness and contrast for an image. However, unlike the Brightness/Contrast dialog box described earlier, the Levels dialog box enables you to adjust the brightness and contrast not only for an image as a whole, but also for each of the primary colors (red, green, or blue) individually. To get started with the Levels dialog box, choose Enhance | Adjust Brightness/Contrast | Levels.

FIGURE 4-15   Reducing the brightness and decreasing the contrast makes this photo much better.

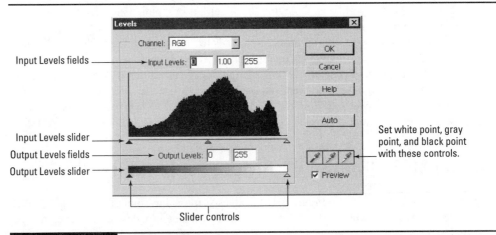

FIGURE 4-16   Change the brightness of an image with Input Levels and the Output Levels in the Levels dialog box.

The histogram in the center of the dialog box shows the distribution of color for the image. If you select Master from the Channel drop-down list (as shown in the previous figure), the histogram displays the overall brightness of the image. If you select one of the primary colors, the histogram displays the distribution of the brightness of that color. For example, with the Blue channel selected, the histogram shifts to show that the color blue is more concentrated than the overall brightness at the ends of the ranges:

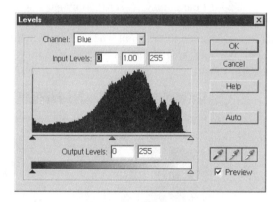

Adjust the Tonal Range with the Input Levels

One way to adjust the tonal range is by using either the Input Levels fields or the slider. Remember that the entire range stretches from a value of 0 at the low end to 255 at the high end. Here is what adjusting the Input Levels does:

Adjust the Maximum Input level   The Maximum Input level (white point) is controlled by the value in the right-most Input Level field or the white Input Level slider control. Setting the value of this field (or dragging the control to set the value) to a number less than 255 resets all pixels in the image that had a value greater than the new Maximum Input Level equal to pure white (255). It also remaps the remaining pixels so that the color balance is unaffected. The overall effect is to increase the tonal range (contrast) at the high end of the image. The image appears to lighten because pixels are being mapped to higher values.

Adjust the Minimum Input level   The Minimum Input level (black point) is controlled by the value in the left-most Input Level field or the black Input Level slider control. Setting the value of this field (or dragging the control to set the value) to a number greater than 0 resets all pixels in the image that had a value less than the new Minimum Input Level equal to pure black (0). It also remaps the remaining pixels so that the color balance is unaffected. The overall effect is to increase the tonal range (contrast) at the low end of the image. The image appears to darken because pixels are being mapped to lower values.

Adjust the midtones   The midtones are controlled by the center Input Levels field or the gray Input Level slider control. To darken the midtones, decrease the value in the field by typing a number or dragging the gray slider to the right. To lighten the midtones, increase the value in the field or drag the gray slider to the left. Note that these corrections do not change either the white point or the black point.

The normal way to adjust the Input Levels for an image is to drag the maximum level *down* to the point where a significant number of bright pixels appear in the histogram. Likewise, you would drag the minimum level *up* to the point where a significant number of dark pixels appear in the histogram. For example, here is the histogram of an image that contains virtually no pixels in the very bright range:

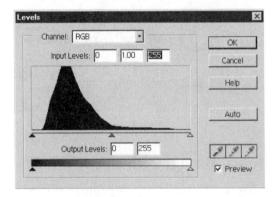

By dragging the white Input slider down to the point where the histogram shows bright pixels occurring, the brightest pixels that *do* exist are mapped to white; the rest of the pixels are remapped proportionally, increasing the tonal range. You can do the same at the black end of the range as well.

To you accept the changes you just made, click OK, then reopen the Levels dialog box. You'll find that the tonal range has been adjusted so that pixels now stretch across the entire range:

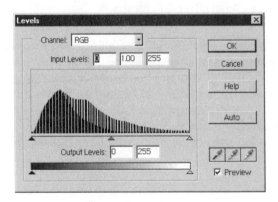

If you want Photoshop Elements to automatically set the maximum Input point and the Minimum Input point, click the Auto button.

It is easy to overdo the adjustments to the Input levels. For example, if you drag the white Level slider down past the point where a lot of bright pixels appear in the histogram, you'll lose all details in those bright areas because all the bright pixels above the value of the slider are mapped to pure white. You can also lose details in the shadows by dragging the black Level slider up past the point where a significant number of pixels appear at the dark end of the histogram.

Adjust the Tonal Range with Output Levels

Unlike the Input levels discussed previously (which increase tonal range as you adjust the maximum down or the minimum up), Output levels have the opposite effect. That is, as you decrease the maximum Output level or increase the Minimum Output level, the tonal range decreases, thereby decreasing the contrast of the image. The Output fields and sliders work as follows:

Decrease the Maximum Output level   When you decrease the value of the maximum Output field (either by typing in a number less than 255 or dragging the white Output slider left), the value of the white pixels are remapped to the new maximum Output level. Pixels with lower values are remapped down proportionally. This compresses the tonal range of the bright areas, dulling the brightest areas (they become a shade of gray rather than white) and reducing the contrast. For example, if you set the maximum Output level to 225, all bright white (255) pixels are reset to 225, and all pixels that had a value less than 255 are remapped to have values less than 225. Since there are no longer any pixels with a value of 255, there are no longer any bright white areas in the image.

Increase the Minimum Output level   When you increase the value of the Minimum Output level (either by typing in a number greater than 0 or by dragging the black Output slider right), the value of the black pixels are remapped to the new minimum level. Pixels with higher values are remapped up proportionally. This compresses the tonal range in the dark areas and reduces the contrast.

Set the Target Colors with the Eyedroppers

The lower-right corner of the Levels dialog box contains eyedropper buttons. You can set the target colors for the black point, gray point, and white point using these three eyedroppers. To do so, simply choose each Eyedropper tool in turn, and then click the image to choose the matching color. For example, click the Set Black Point tool (left-most eyedropper) and then click the darkest area in the image.

TIP

Before you use the three Eyedropper tools, make sure to set the eyedropper sample size to 3 × 3 so that the point you click will be a representative sample of the area. To set the eyedropper sample size to 3 × 3, choose the Eyedropper tool from the toolbox, and choose 3 × 3 Average from the Sample Size drop-down list.

There are a few things you should realize if you decide to pick the black, gray, and white points using the Eyedropper tools. First, when picking the white point, do *not* pick specular white. Specular white is an area that has no detail, such as a spot of glare. You should pick a white that shows some detail. Next, when picking the gray point, be careful to pick a point that is actually gray (or should be). When you choose the gray point, Photoshop Elements adjusts the color balance to make that point gray. For example, if you pick a medium blue for the gray point, the color balance of the image will shift toward yellows, transforming the selected shade of blue to gray.

NOTE

Finding the white, gray, and black points in the image can be tricky. A good way to proceed, before choosing the Levels dialog box, is to display the Info palette. Then choose the Levels dialog box and move any of the Eyedropper tools over the image. As you do, the Info palette displays the RGB values. Locate the point in the image where the three values are at their maximum (but not a specular point), where they are at their lowest values, and where they are about even and close to 128. Use these points to set the white, black, and gray points.

Rotate and Straighten Images

One of the more common ways to get images into Photoshop Elements is to scan a photograph. If the scan comes out slightly crooked, you could end up with a skewed image:

Set the Black, White, and Gray Points Using the Color Picker

The Adobe Color Picker is a versatile tool that will be covered in more detail in Chapter 5. You can use the Color Picker to set the black, white, and gray points. To do so, double-click one of the Eyedropper tools in the Levels dialog box to open the Color Picker. For example, you can double-click the Set Black Point tool (left-most eyedropper) to open the Color Picker, which is preset to Black (R,G, and B all set to 0):

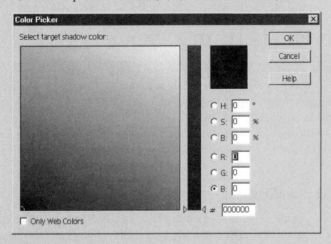

Choose a color in the Color Picker either by clicking the color or filling in values in the HSL or RGB fields. Click OK to close the Color Picker. Then move the mouse pointer over the points you selected for black, white, or gray (depending on which tool you chose) and click.

Choosing the right color this way can be tricky, so here are some guidelines for choosing each of the three color points:

Pick the black point   A good choice for the black point is to set R, G, and B to 10, or Brightness (B in the HSB section) to 4. However, if the image has little detail in the shadows (high key), you may wish to set the Brightness (B) to a higher value to preserve those details. Experiment with values between 4 and 20.

Pick the white point   A good choice for the white point is to set R, G, and B to 244, or to set Brightness (B in the HSB section) to 96. However, if the image has details concentrated in the shadows (low key), you may want to preserve the highlight detail by setting the Brightness (B) to a lower value. Experiment with values between 80 and 96.

Pick the gray point   A good choice for the gray point is where R, G, and B are all assigned the same values—128 is a good number. This is the same as assigning Brightness (B in the HSB section) to 50.

You have two ways to correct this—Straighten and Straighten and Crop.

Straighten   To simply straighten an image, choose Image | Rotate | Straighten. This option detects the edges of the photo and rotates the photo to straighten them (as well as everything else in the photo). The resulting image has a transparent area around the border as a result of the straightening operation.

Straighten and Crop   To straighten the image and crop off the unnecessary edges, choose Image | Rotate | Straighten and Crop. As with Straighten (see the previous bullet), this operation straightens the image, but it also crops off the resulting extra space around the edges. On occasion, corners of the photo may be cropped off, so it is best to enlarge the canvas slightly before doing a Straighten and Crop.

Apply Special Effects to a Photo

Photoshop Elements can apply a huge number of special effects to a photo. Many of the effects are either not really appropriate for the digital photographer, need to be applied to only a selected area of the photo (see Chapter 8), or should be applied to layers (see Chapter 9). However, you can achieve some interesting (and even surreal) effects on an entire photo using the effects discussed in the next few sections. If you don't overdo it, you can make your images slightly out of the ordinary.

Posterize a Photo

Posterizing an image reduces the number of colors, and creates large blocks of a single color from adjacent areas of similar colors. To posterize a photo, choose Image | Adjustments | Posterize to open the Posterize dialog box:

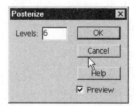

In the Posterize dialog box, choose the number of levels of each color you want to use. Remember that each color has 255 levels initially, so any number below 255 will result in some posterization, but it may not be very noticeable until you reduce the number of levels to 10 or below.

For example, take a look at the photos in Figures 4-17 and 4-18. In Figure 4-17, you can see the initial photo, and in Figure 4-18, you can see the result when the photo is posterized using four levels of each color.

FIGURE 4-17   The unposterized photo…

FIGURE 4-18   … that has been posterized using four levels of each color.

Apply a Gradient Map

You can apply a gradient map to an image by choosing Images | Adjustments | Gradient Map to open the Gradient Map dialog box:

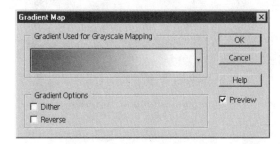

Click the down arrow to display the set of available gradients. Choose the gradient you want to use, or load an alternate set of gradients from the menu that appears when you click the arrow button. Then choose the gradient.

FIGURE 4-19   Map a color image to pure black and white with the Threshold function.

 *Most of the available gradients make such drastic changes to the image that you won't want to use them, but a few (such as the black/white gradient and some of the gradients in the pastels set) do provide an attractive result.*

Convert to High-Contrast with Threshold

The Threshold option renders an image in just two colors—black and white. As shown in Figure 4-19, this function maps all colors above the threshold to pure white, and all colors below the threshold to pure black.

To set the threshold, either type a value into the Threshold Level field or drag the slider below the histogram.

4

Chapter 5

Choose and Customize Paint and Brush Tools

How to...

- Pick a paint tool
- Set the options for a paint tool
- Set up the brush dynamics
- Choose a color to use
- Use brush parameters
- Create and edit brushes
- Build custom brushes

Photoshop Elements provides a number of tools in the toolbox for applying changes to images. You can customize how these tools work, including the opacity (how well the tools cover what you're painting over), color, Blending Mode (how the tools combine with what you're painting over), and many other options, some of which vary depending on which tool you use. You can also create custom versions of some tools, such as the brush tools.

Don't be fooled by the references to "brushes" and "brush tools." Many of the options you'll learn about in this chapter can be applied to useful tools such as smudge, blur, and sharpen. In fact, you'll probably use these other tools more than the paintbrush tools when working with digital photographs.

Pick a Paint Tool to Do Touch-Ups

The main paint-type tools available in the toolbox include the Brush, Pencil, Sponge, Smudge, Blur, and Sharpen tools. Each of these tools has a different effect when you use it on an image, but many of the options (as described later in this chapter) are similar for each.

Each of the tools can be constrained to marking in a straight line horizontally or vertically by holding down the SHIFT key while dragging the mouse pointer. You can also "draw" a straight line with any of these tools by clicking the starting point, holding down the SHIFT key, and clicking the end point. For example, you can apply a smudge along a straight line by first choosing the Smudge tool and then following the instructions to "draw" a straight line.

Table 5-1 describes each tool and in what ways they are most useful. In Chapter 6 you will see how each of these tools can be used to modify images.

Icon	Tool Name	Description
	Brush	Creates soft strokes of the chosen color, size, and brush type. For photographs, the Paintbrush tool is of limited use. However, you can use it touch up or (if you're artistic) add detail to limited areas at high magnification.

TABLE 5-1   Each Paint-Type Tool Is Useful for Modifying Your Image in a Different Way.

Icon	Tool Name	Description
	Pencil	Creates hard-edged lines of the chosen color, size, and brush type. The Pencil tool works virtually identically to the Paintbrush tool except that the default setting is a narrower line (1 pixel) and a type-1 brush type (a solid, hard-edged line). You can, however, change all the settings. Also, unlike the Brush tool, you can't define custom brushes for the Pencil.
	Sponge	Adds and removes color saturation from the effected area.
	Smudge	Picks up color where you begin the stroke and pushes the color in the direction you drag. This tool is of limited use with digital photos, although landscapes (especially with water reflections) can benefit from the judicious application of this tool.
	Blur	Softens hard edges to reduce details. It is useful to take the "edge" off background edges that draw the eye away from the main subject of the photo. In general, however, blurring the entire background as a whole is more effective, as detailed in Chapter 8.
	Sharpen	Focuses soft edges to sharpen details. This tool is useful for sharpening the area around an important detail. In general, however, applying sharpening to all edges—or to all edges in a selected area of the image—is a more efficient way to sharpen an image (see Chapter 8 for details).

TABLE 5-1   Each Paint-Type Tool Is Useful for Modifying Your Image in a Different Way (*continued*).

Set the Options for Your Paint Tool

You can control exactly how a brush tool behaves by setting various options for the tool. The options that are available depend on the tool you are using. In addition, available values for an option (such as for the Blending Mode) also depend on the tool. For example, a brush allows you to pick from no less than 24 different Blending Modes, while the Smudge tool allows only seven Blending Modes.

The easiest way to set options for a tool is to choose the options from the options bar. The options bar changes to show only the allowed options for each tool you choose. For example, here is the version of the options bar that appears when you choose a brush tool:

The options available for the paintbrush-type tools include opacity, Blending Mode, brush size, and strength. As I describe each option, I'll also discuss which brush tools have which options available, and any special options available for each tool.

Set the Brush Size and Style

You can set the brush size and style for all the brush tools, as well as for many of the other tools in the toolbox, including the Red Eye brush tool (which, despite its name, is not really a brush tool), Dodge and Burn (discussed in Chapter 7), and the Clone Stamp (also discussed in Chapter 7).

There are two controls in the options bar that you can use to set the brush size and style. The first is the Brush Size/Style drop-down list near the left end of the options bar. When you click the down arrow, Photoshop Elements displays a list of brush size/style combinations in the Brush palette:

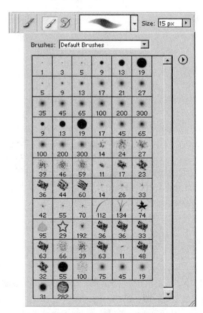

You can choose how you want to view the brushes by clicking the palette menu button (the small button in the upper-right corner of the Brush palette). Choices include various sizes of thumbnails and lists, as discussed in Chapter 1. Depending on how you have chosen to view the brushes, you can see a brush size (for thumbnails) or a brush size and name (for lists) for each available brush. Each brush is represented in the palette by an image that shows the style of the brush. The options bar shows the selected brush. For example, the options bar in the previous illustration shows a hard, round, 15-pixel brush. When you choose a brush from the palette, Photoshop Elements sets the size of the selected brush in the Size field (immediately to the right of the Brush Size/Style drop-down list).

You can override the selected size by typing a number into the Size field or using the Size slider. The style of the brush stays the same, but Photoshop Elements resets the size to match your choice.

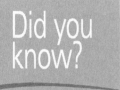

You can choose to load another set of brushes by opening the Brush Size/Style drop-down list (which displays the Brush palette). Click the Brushes drop-down list near the top of the palette and choose the set of brushes to load.

5

Set the Opacity

You can set the opacity for the gradient, as well as the Brush and Pencil, Paint Bucket, Clone Stamp, and Pattern Stamp tools. The opacity varies from 0% to 100%, and determines how much of the existing image "shows through" the change you apply. At 0%, the change is invisible (the background is unchanged), and at 100% the change completely hides the background. At values *between* 0% and 100% the background partially shows. For example, here is an image where a wide brush stroke has been applied with an opacity of 40%:

Notice how the background shows through the brush stroke. Thus, a low opacity can be used to tint an area with a new color, while a high (100%) opacity can be used to completely cover the details of an area by applying the brush.

Set the Blending Mode

One of the more complex effects to master is varying the Blending Mode—that is, how the *base* color and the *blend* color mix together to form the *result* color. To understand how the Blending Mode works, you need to understand what these three colors mean:

Base color   The original color of the image.

Blend color   The color being applied by the brush or editing tool.

Result color   The color resulting from mixing the base color and the blend color.

You can set the Blending Mode for all the brush tools as well as the Gradient, Paint Bucket, Clone Stamp, and Pattern Stamp tools. However, the Sharpen, Blur, and Smudge tools use only a small subset of the modes: Normal, Darken, Lighten, Hue, Saturation, Color, and Luminosity. In addition, the Sponge tool uses two modes that are described later in this chapter.
The Blending Modes are:

Normal   Turns each pixel into the result color, which is identical to the blend color. That is, regardless of the base color, the pixel ends up being the blend color.

Dissolve   Sets the result color randomly to either the base color or the blend color, depending on the value of the opacity.

Behind   Edits or paints only on the transparent part of a layer (see Chapter 9 for more information on layers). This mode works only in layers with Lock Transparency deselected.

Clear   Paints or edits each pixel and makes it transparent. You'll only see a difference from Normal mode if you are painting on a layer with Lock Transparency deselected.

Darken   Selects either the base color or the blend color as the result color, whichever is darker. Pixels lighter than the blend color are replaced with the blend color; pixels darker than the blend color are not modified.

Multiply   Multiplies the base color by the blend color for each color channel. The result is always a darker color unless the blend color is white, in which case there is no change to the image. Multiplying any color with a black blend color always results in a black result color. Except for black or white, successive strokes result in progressively darker colors.

Color Burn   Takes the color information in each channel and darkens the base color to reflect the blend color. The darker the blend color, the more the base color is darkened. If the blend color is white, there is no change.

Linear Burn   Darkens the base color to reflect the blend color, like the Color Burn. The darker the blend color, the more the base color is darkened. However, the overall effect of the Linear Burn is to darken colors more than the Color Burn, especially when the blend color is light. When the blend color is dark, the overall effect is similar to Color Burn, but highlighted areas are darkened more than with Color Burn.

Lighten   Selects either the base color or the blend color as the result color, whichever is lighter. Pixels darker than the blend color are replaced with the blend color; pixels lighter than the blend color are not modified.

Screen   Multiplies the base color by the inverse of the blend color for each color channel. The result is always a lighter color unless the blend color is black, in which case there is no change to the image. Screening any color with a white blend color always results in a white result color. Except for black or white, successive strokes result in progressively lighter colors.

Color Dodge   Takes the color information in each channel and lightens the base color to reflect the blend color. The lighter the blend color, the more the base color is lightened. If the blend color is black, there is no change.

Linear Dodge   Takes the color information in each channel and brightens the base color to reflect the blend color. If the blend color is black, there is no change.

Overlay   Overlays the blend color on the base color, preserving the highlights and shadows of the base color. Thus, if you paint a medium purple over a checkerboard pattern of white and dark brown, the white becomes light purple, and the dark brown becomes dark purple. In essence, the Overlay mode has either the effect of Multiply (if the blend color is dark) or Screen (if the blend color is light).

Soft Light   Darkens or lightens the base color, depending on the blend color. If the blend color is light (less than 50% gray), the image is lightened. If the blend color is dark (greater than 50% gray), the image is darkened. The result color is achieved by mixing the base color with the blend color, so that the base color picks up the tint of the blend color. Using pure black or pure white for the blend color darkens or lightens the image considerably, but does not produce a result color of pure black or pure white. The effect is similar to shining a diffused spotlight on the image.

Hard Light   Darkens or lightens the base color, depending on the blend color. If the blend color is light (less than 50% gray), the image is lightened, as if it were screened. If the blend color is dark (greater than 50% gray), the image is darkened, as if it were multiplied. Thus, Hard Light is a more intense effect than Soft Light, and using pure black or pure white *does* result in a result color of pure black or pure white. The effect is similar to shining a harsh spotlight on the image.

Vivid Light   Darkens or lightens the image, depending on the blend color, like the Soft Light and Hard Light effect. Vivid Light is more intense than Soft Light, but not as intense as Hard Light. The effect is similar to shining a bright, non-directional light on the image.

Linear Light   Darkens or lightens the image, depending on the blend color, like the Soft Light and Hard Light effect. However, Linear Light tints the base color with the blend color and removes most of the contrast, so the difference between dark and light areas of the base color are much less pronounced than with the other Light tools.

Pin Light   Works similarly to Linear Light in that it tints the base color with the blend color. However, it maintains more of the contrast between light and dark areas than Linear Light.

Difference   Derives the result color by subtracting either the base color from the blend color or the blend color from the base color, depending on which is lighter (has the greater brightness value). If the blend color is white, the result color is the inverse of the base color. There is no change if the blend color is black.

Exclusion   Produces a result similar to Difference, but with a lower contrast.

Hue   Creates the result color by taking the luminance and saturation of the base color and the hue of the blend color. If the base color is white, there is no change. If the blend color is black (0 hue), the result is the grayscale version of the picture. This is useful for converting selected portions of an image to grayscale.

Saturation   Creates the result color by taking the luminance and hue of the base color and the saturation of the blend color. If blend color is black, the result is the grayscale version of the image. If the base color is white or the blend color is gray (0 saturation), there is no change.

Color   Creates the result color by taking the luminance of the base color and the hue and saturation of the blend color. If the base color is white, there is no change. If the blend color is black or white, the result is a grayscale version of the image. This option is useful for colorizing grayscale images because it preserves the grayscale of the original image.

Luminosity   Creates the result color by taking the hue and saturation of the base color and the luminance of the blend color. A blend color of black or white completely replaces the base color.

Configure the Sponge Tool

The Sponge tool either increases or decreases the saturation of the base color. To switch modes, choose either Desaturate or Saturate from the Mode drop-down list. The amount of saturation or desaturation applied is controlled by the Flow control. To set the Flow control, type in a number between 1 and 100 (percent), or use the Flow slider.

NOTE   *The Sponge tool has no effect on pure white or pure black areas of the image.*

Set up Special Tool Options

Many of the brush tools have their own special options available, such as the Auto Erase check box for the Pencil tool. The Brush tool options are:

Auto Erase (Pencil)   If this check box is selected, the pencil draws in the background color if the point where you start drawing in the image is the foreground color. This option is of limited use because the image color and the foreground color need to match exactly before Auto Erase will work.

Strength (Blur, Sharpen, and Smudge)   The Strength field (and its slider) control how much blur or sharpen is applied for each stroke. You can vary this between 1% and 100%.

Use All Layers (Blur, Sharpen, and Smudge)   If this check box is selected, the effect will be applied to all layers of the image (see Chapter 9 for more details on layers). This check box is also available for the Clone Stamp tool.

Finger Painting (Smudge)   If this check box is cleared, the Smudge tool starts smudging with the image color present at the starting point. It pushes that color ahead of the Smudge tool, mixing it with the other image colors in the path of the tool, creating the smudge effect. However, if you check the Finger Painting check box, the Smudge tool begins smudging with the foreground color. Within a very short distance, the foreground color has mixed thoroughly with the image colors and is no longer visible. For example, Figure 5-1 shows two smudges—the top one was done with the Finger Painting check box cleared; the bottom one was done with the Finger Painting check box checked.

Set the Brush Dynamics

You can specify a variety of quantities that control how the Brush tool works. These options include Spacing, Fade, Color Jitter, Hardness, Scatter, and Brush Shape. To set the brush dynamics, click the More Options button to display the control panel:

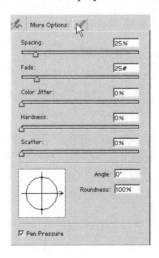

Smudge done with Finger Painting on.

Smudge done with Finger Painting off.

FIGURE 5-1   The two smudges show the effect of using the Finger Painting check box with the Smudge tool.

NOTE   *As you make adjustments to the brush dynamics, the image of the selected brush in the options bar changes to show the effect of your choices.*

The spacing control varies from 1% to 1000%, where 100% represents the size of the current brush. Setting the spacing determines the distance between the brush marks in a stroke. If you set this quantity to a very low number (like 1%), the brush strokes completely overlap.

Setting this quantity to a high number (such as 200%) makes the brush skip. For example, at 200%, two brush marks in the stroke are skipped for each one that is painted:

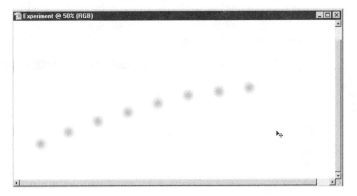

The Fade control varies from 0 to 9999, and controls how quickly the paint flow diminishes. Setting a low value for Fade means that the flows diminishes to zero quickly, whereas a high value means that the paint flows longer before starting to fade. Setting Fade to zero suppresses fading altogether—the paint never decreases in intensity as you stroke. Here is an example of two different values for Fade, where each stroke went from left to right. The one on the top is a low number; the one on the bottom is a much larger number:

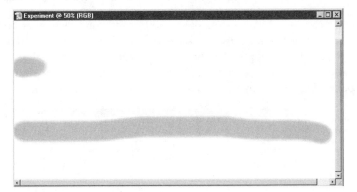

The Color Jitter control varies from 0% to 100%, and controls whether (and how often) Photoshop Elements switches between the foreground and background colors while applying paint. If you set the value of this control to 0%, Photoshop Elements paints only with the foreground color. As you increase the Color Jitter value, Photoshop Elements inserts brush strokes in the background color more frequently, until, at 100%, it uses the foreground color for half of the strokes, and the background color for the other half.

The Hardness control varies from 0% to 100% and controls the size of the hard center of the brush stroke. At a setting of 100% (the right part of the following illustration), the hard center of the stroke takes up the entire brush size, and the edges of the brush stroke are well defined. As you reduce the value in the hardness control, the edges become feathered and the size of the hard center is reduced, as seen in the left portion of the image:

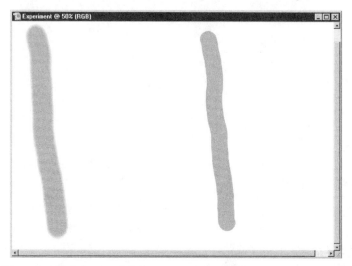

The Scatter control varies from 0% to 100%, and controls how much paint is scattered away from the center of the brush stroke as you paint. At 0% scatter, no paint is scattered; that is, Photoshop Elements applies paint only where you stroke the brush (as seen on the left side of the illustration that follows). With a high value in the Scatter control, Photoshop Elements sprays paint pretty wildly in a wide radius (as shown on the right side of the illustration):

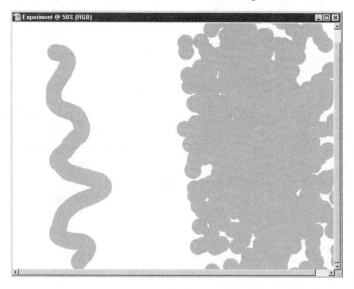

The Angle and Roundness controls at the bottom of the Brush Dynamics drop-down list controls the shape of the brush stroke. You can change the roundness either by typing in a value between 0% (flat) and 100% (round), or dragging one of the two black dots:

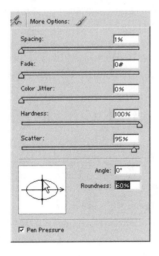

NOTE *All values between 1% and 99% are various oval shapes.*

You can tilt the oval you created by modifying the value of the Angle field. To modify the angle, type in a value or drag the arrowhead. Values from 0 degrees to 180 degrees rotate the arrow counter-clockwise, while values from 0 degrees to –180 degrees rotate the arrow clockwise.

Did you know?

An airbrush is an artist's tool that sprays a fine pattern of paint. You can turn on an airbrush effect for the Brush, Burn, and Dodge tools in Photoshop Elements. You can turn the airbrush on in one of two ways:

- Choose your brush and then click the Airbrush button in the options bar. This button is immediately to the right of Opacity control (Brush tool) or Exposure control (Burn and Dodge tools).

- Choose a brush that already contains airbrush effects built in. The name of the brush indicates that it uses an airbrush (for example, "Airbrush Hard Round 9").

Pick a Color to Use with Your Brush Tools

Near the bottom of the toolbox are a pair of rectangles, as shown in Figure 5-2. The top rectangle displays the foreground color, and the bottom rectangle displays the selected background color. These colors are used with the Brush, Pencil, Paint Bucket, Eraser, Red Eye Brush, and Gradient tools.

There are a number of ways to choose either a foreground or background color, including using the Color Picker, Swatch Palette, and Eyedropper tools.

Exercise Color Control with the Adobe Color Picker

The Color Picker is a powerful tool for working with colors. To access it, click either the Foreground Color square (to pick the foreground color) or the Background Color square (to pick the background color). Photoshop Elements displays the Color Picker dialog box as shown in Figure 5-3.

The square near the upper-right corner displays the current color. The top three fields (H, S, and B) display the current *H*ue, *S*aturation, and *B*rightness values for the color. The bottom three fields (R, G, and B) display the current *R*ed, *G*reen, and *B*lue values for the color. The last field at the bottom (with the # symbol alongside) is the hexadecimal (base 16) value of the color.

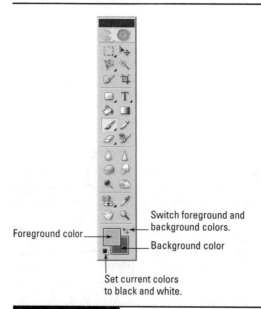

Foreground color

Switch foreground and background colors.

Background color

Set current colors to black and white.

FIGURE 5-2   Set the foreground and background colors by using the rectangles in the toolbox.

Current color displayed here.

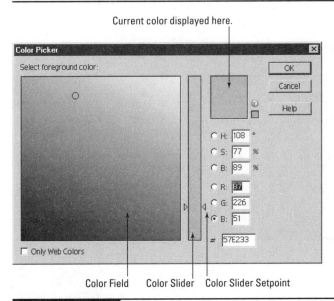

Color Field   Color Slider   Color Slider Setpoint

FIGURE 5-3   Use the Adobe Color Picker to set a foreground or background color.

If you know the HSB, RGB, or Hex values for the color you want, you can type the values into the appropriate fields.

You can visually pick a color using the Color slider and the Color field. To do so, select one of the fields (H, S, B, or R, G, B) by clicking the radio button alongside the letter. The Color slider changes to display the range of color levels available for the selected color component, while the Color field displays the range of colors for the remaining two components—one on the horizontal axis, the other on the vertical axis. For example, if you choose Hue (click the radio button next to H), the Color slider shows the range of hues (colors), while the Color field displays the Saturation (S) along the horizontal axis and the Brightness (B) along the vertical axis. If you choose Green (G) instead, the Color slider shows the range of greens, while the Color field displays the range of Blues along the horizontal axis and the range of Reds along the vertical axis.

Choose a value from both the Color slider and the Color field. With the Color slider, you can either click somewhere in the slider, or drag the Color Slider Setpoint arrows. When you make your choices for the new color, the Current Color rectangle changes to show two colors.

The top of the rectangle displays the newly selected color, while the bottom of the rectangle displays the original color:

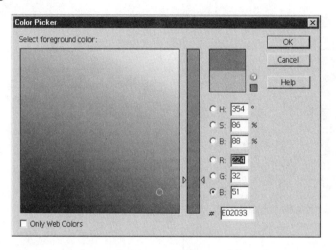

   *If you want to limit your choices to the 216 "web-safe" colors (guaranteed to be available to any web browser), check the Only Web Colors check box.*

Pick a Color with the Eyedropper

The Eyedropper tool in the toolbox also enables you to pick a foreground or background color. Choose the Eyedropper tool and move it over the image. When the eyedropper is over the new foreground color, simply click to set that color as the new foreground color. To set the background color, ALT-click a color in the image.

It can be tricky picking exactly the right color with the eyedropper. The Sample Size option in the options bar provides three choices for selecting the color. They are:

Point Sample   Picks the color of the single pixel under the tip of the tool. At low magnifications, it can be hard to pick exactly the right pixel.

3-by-3 Average   Picks the color determined by averaging the colors of a sampling of 3 by 3 pixels under the tip of the eyedropper.

5-by-5 Average   Picks the color determined by averaging the colors of a sampling of 5 by 5 pixels under the tip of the Eyedropper.

Choose a Color from the Swatch Palette

One of the easiest ways to choose a color is to use a palette designed specifically for that purpose—the Swatch palette, as shown in Figure 5-4.

As you move the mouse pointer over the color swatches in the Swatch palette, it turns into the Eyedropper tool. To pick the foreground color, click the color. To pick the background color, hold down the CTRL key and click the color.

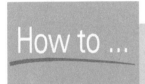

Manage Colors in the Swatch Palette

5

With a simple set of commands, you can add colors to or remove colors from the Swatch palette. You can also load and save a set of color swatches.

To add a swatch of the foreground color to the Swatch palette, move the mouse pointer over an empty area of the palette (it turns into the Paint Bucket tool), and click. The Color Swatch Name dialog box appears, and you can enter the name of the new swatch:

Alternatively, you can choose New Swatch from the palette menu or click the New Swatch icon along the bottom of the palette.

To remove a swatch, click and drag the swatch to the small trashcan icon in the lower-right corner. Or, you can hold down the ALT key and click the swatch you want to be rid of.

The palette menu enables you to save your modified set of swatches. Simply choose Save Swatches, and choose a name for the swatch file in the Save dialog box.

There are two ways to load a set of swatches into Photoshop Elements. If you choose Load Swatches from the palette menu, you can pick a set of swatches from the Load dialog box. These swatches are *added* to those already available, giving you access to more colors in the Swatch palette.

If you choose Replace Swatches from the palette menu, you can (as with Load) pick a set of swatches from the Replace dialog box. This time the set of swatches you pick replaces all those in the Swatch palette. If you pick a set of swatches from the drop-down list just below the palette title, it has the same effect as using Replace Swatches. If you need to return to the default set of swatches, choose Default from this drop-down list.

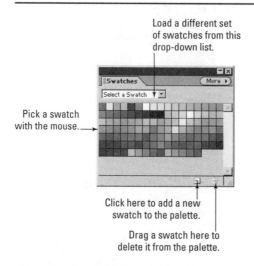

Load a different set
of swatches from this
drop-down list.

Pick a swatch
with the mouse.

Click here to add a new
swatch to the palette.

Drag a swatch here to
delete it from the palette.

FIGURE 5-4   Easily pick a color from the Swatch palette.

Create and Edit Brushes

Photoshop Elements displays a list of available brushes when you click the Brushes drop-down list in the options bar to display the Brush palette. To choose a brush to use, simply click the brush you want.

The Brush List palette is available for many tools in the toolbox. These include the Brush, Pencil, Red Eye Brush, Blur, Sharpen, Sponge, Smudge, Dodge, Burn, Clone Stamp, Pattern Stamp, and Selection Brush tools. Some of these tools have been covered already; the others will be covered later in this book.

You can create, edit, and save your own brushes for future use. Once you do, you can save a set of brushes so you can load your set of custom brushes in the future.

Build a Brush

To create a custom brush, follow these steps:

1. Choose the Brush tool from the toolbox. This makes all the brush options available.

2. Choose a brush from the drop-down list in the options bar to serve as a starting point. For example, you could choose "Soft Round 21 pixels" from the Default Brushes list.

3. If you wish, change the size of the brush using the Size field. For example, you could change the size to 35 pixels.

4. Use the options in the More Options list to further customize your brush (this was discussed earlier in this chapter). For example, you could set the Color Jitter to 50%, Fade to 1500%, and Hardness to 50%.

5. Display the list of brushes (click the Brushes drop-down list), and right-click any brush in the list. Choose New Brush from the context menu. Alternatively, you can choose New Brush from the palette menu. Either way, the Brush Name dialog box appears:

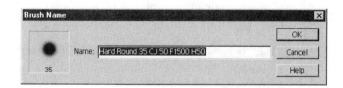

6. Fill in the name of the brush and click OK. The newly defined brush is added to the list of brushes.

   *You can use an already customized brush as the starting point to build a new brush.*

You can delete a brush by right-clicking the brush and choosing Delete Brush from the context menu. You can also select the brush and choose Delete Brush from the palette menu.

You can rename a brush by choosing Rename Brush from either the context menu or the palette menu. Photoshop Elements redisplays the Brush Name dialog box so you can change the name.

Save and Load Sets of Brushes

You can perform the following functions using the palette menu:

Reset Brushes   Returns to the default set of brushes. You can also choose Default Brushes from the Brushes drop-down list at the top of the Brush List palette.

Load Brushes   Displays a list of files that contain brush sets. Choosing one of these files adds those brushes to what is already available in the brush list.

Save Brushes   Enables you to name and save the current set of brushes as a file so you can reload them later.

Replace Brushes   Displays a list of files that contain brush sets. Choosing one of these files replaces the currently available brush set with the brushes in the file.

Create a Custom Brush Shape

If you have a portion of an image that you want to turn into a brush, Photoshop Elements makes it easy. To do so, you must select the portion of the image you want to turn into a brush. Although the selection tools aren't described until Chapter 8, you can try this out by choosing the Rectangular Marquee selection tool in the upper-left corner of the toolbox.

 *If the Elliptical Marquee tool is showing in the upper-left corner, either use it or click and hold down the left mouse button to display the list of Marquee tools. Then choose the Rectangular Marquee.*

Click and drag the Marquee (or other selection tool) to select the portion of the image to turn into a brush. Select Edit | Define Brush to open the Brush Name dialog box to name the brush:

The brush is not only created, but added to the list of available brushes. Once you select it, you can customize its size as well as its brush dynamics—just like any other brush.

 *Even though the portion of the image you originally chose was probably rendered in many colors, brushes can only be one color. Thus, Photoshop Elements converts the image to a single color. Light areas are transparent, and darker areas have the foreground color (which you can, of course, choose for yourself).*

Chapter 6

Touch Up Your Photo with Brushes and Shapes

How to…

- Paint and draw with the toolbox tools
- Add blur to hide features
- Sharpen areas of the photo
- Saturate and desaturate with the Sponge tool
- Smudge an image to soften details
- Remove red eye

Now that I've introduced the major portions of Photoshop Elements, and you understand how to choose and use the brush tools in the toolbox, you'll gain some experience using these tools while touching up real photos.

Paint an Area of a Photo with the Brush Tool

Given that most of the focus of this book is on digital photographs, you might be wondering under what circumstances you would want to use the Brush tool. As it turns out, the Brush tool and the other brush-type tools are so versatile that you can really clean up a picture without making major modifications. For example, take a look at Figure 6-1.

The background is very "busy," and mostly mottled with shades of green. To brighten up the more muted greens in the background, follow these steps:

1. Click the Foreground Color tool at the bottom of the toolbox to display the Color Picker.
2. Choose a shade of green that meets your needs. I chose a shade that had the following characteristics: R = 50, G = 164, B = 42.
3. Choose the Brush tool from the toolbox.
4. Select a brush from the Brushes drop-down list in the options bar. A good starting point for this kind of work might be the Soft Round 45 pixels brush.
5. Adjust the size of the brush to about 50 pixels using the Size control in the options bar.
6. Set the blending mode to Soft Light (you may want to try others, such as Hue in the lighter areas).
7. Begin painting in the darker areas of the background by clicking and dragging the Paint Brush (displayed as a round circle).
8. When you are done, choose File | Save As and provide a new filename to save your changes.

Notice in Figure 6-2 that the deep greens in the background are now much more noticeable (the stronger contrast in the black-and-white reproduction indicates the change). This illustrates the usefulness of the various blending modes in touching up a digital photo.

FIGURE 6-1   The busy background needs to be recolored in this photo.

FIGURE 6-2   I adjusted the colors to give the picture a more "spring-like" feel.

Draw with the Pencil

The Pencil tool draws fine lines (unless you choose a wide brush), but more importantly, it makes it easy to draw straight lines. Done carefully, adding lines can provide the illusion of additional detail, especially in old, faded photographs where the information along object edges has been lost.

Take, for example, the image shown in Figure 6-3. The cathedral in the background is actually the most important part of this badly faded photo.

To add lines of detail, follow these steps:

1. Select the Eyedropper tool from the toolbox, and click in a medium gray area of the cathedral near the edge to set the foreground color.

2. Choose the Pencil tool from the toolbox. Choose the Hard Round 3 pixels brush from the Brushes drop-down list in the options bar.

3. Move the Pencil tool to the point in the image where you want to start a line, and click.

4. Move the Pencil tool to the point in the image where you want to finish the line, and click. Photoshop Elements draws a gray line from the starting point to the ending point.

FIGURE 6-3   This photo could benefit by the addition of some lines to provide additional definition.

5. Continue until the object is well defined:

6

The Pencil tool is also useful if you need to label items in a photo. As we'll see in Chapter 16, you can add text to an image, and then connect that text to the item it describes.

Add Blur to Hide Features of a Photo

Many photos (like the one in Figure 6-4) have a subject that should capture your attention. Unfortunately, as also illustrated in Figure 6-4, the background may have one or more very distracting items that draw attention away from the subject. Although it is possible (as we'll see later in the book) to remove a distracting object—or change the background altogether—it is often sufficient to blur the sharp outlines of a background object so that it is not as distracting.

To blur an object, follow these steps:

1. Choose the Blur tool from the toolbox.

2. Choose a brush style from the Brushes drop-down list. I have found that a soft-edged brush works well (my favorite is Soft Round 45 pixels) because it "feathers" the edges of the blur effect.

3. Use the Size control to set the size of the brush to match the kind of work you are doing. The size of the brush should be large enough to encompass the hard edges you are going to blur, but not so large that the blur effect spills over into the surrounding area. In the example image, I found that a 30-pixel brush worked fine.

4. Use the Strength control to set the amount of blurring. Lower values may require multiple passes over an area to achieve the desired effect, whereas higher values may apply too much blurring at once. I have found that about 50% strength is a pretty good value.

5. Set the blending mode using the Mode control.

6. Position the Blur tool over the beginning of the area you want to blur, hold down the left mouse button, and move the mouse over the area you want to blur. Repeat this motion in long strokes until you get the desired amount of blurring:

Sharpen Areas to Bring Them Into Focus

Another problem with some photos is that the main subject may be slightly out of focus. This is often caused by the auto-focus feature on a camera being fooled by the background or another object in the picture. Whatever the reason, you can selectively "sharpen" an area of a picture using the Sharpen tool. For example, take a close look at Figure 6-5. The two main subjects in this photo are slightly out of focus, probably because they are not centered in the image, and so the camera was fooled by the background.

TIP   *Before finishing with this picture, you'll probably want to crop the unimportant parts of the picture.*

FIGURE 6-4   The subject in the foreground and an object in the background compete for attention in this photo.

FIGURE 6-5   A man and his dog—both out of focus!

To sharpen an object, follow these steps:

1. Choose the Sharpen tool from the toolbox.

2. Choose a brush style from the Brushes drop-down list. I have found that a hard-edged brush works well (my favorite is Hard Round 19 pixels) because it tightly controls the effected area.

3. Use the Size control to set the size of the brush to match the kind of work you are doing. The size of the brush should be large enough to encompass the edges (and any other areas) you are going to sharpen, but not so large that the sharpen effect spills over into the surrounding area. In the example image, I found that the 19-pixel brush size I picked earlier worked fine.

4. Use the Strength control to set the amount of sharpening in each pass. Lower values may require multiple passes over an area to achieve the desired effect, whereas higher values may apply too much sharpening at once. As with blur, I have found that about 50% strength is a pretty good value.

5. Set the blending mode using the Mode control.

6. Position the Sharpen tool over the beginning of the area you want to sharpen, hold down the left mouse button, and move the mouse over the area you want to sharpen. Repeat this motion in long strokes until you get the desired amount of sharpening:

 *The Sharpen tool (as well as all the other sharpening effects) actually works by adjusting the pixel color to increase the contrast. If you try to sharpen too much, you'll start to see aberrations in the picture, especially along sharp edges.*

Saturate and Desaturate with the Sponge Tool

The Sponge tool either increases or decreases color saturation. This can be handy if one area of a photo needs a little more or a little less color. This effect is easy to overdo, though, so be careful. One good reason to apply this effect is when brightly colored clothing detracts from other interesting aspects of a picture—such as the face of the person wearing the clothes! This is evident in Figure 6-6, where the person's shirt is pretty overwhelming.

To saturate or desaturate the color in an object, follow these steps:

1. Choose the Sponge tool from the toolbox.

2. Choose a brush style from the Brushes drop-down list. I have found that a hard-edged brush works well (my favorite is Hard Round 65 pixels) because it extends over a fairly wide area, and you are usually working with a decent-sized area when applying the Sponge tool.

6

FIGURE 6-6   A fashion (or at least a photographic) faux pas: Brightly colored clothing captures all the attention.

3. Use the Size control to set the size of the brush to match the kind of work you are doing. The size of the brush should be large enough that you don't have to make many passes over the area (which makes it difficult to blend the adjacent areas), but small enough to be able to get "into the corners." I have found that I usually need to change the size of the brush, using a 50-pixel or larger brush to begin with, then shrinking the size to about 25 pixels for the touchups.

4. Use the Flow control to set the amount of change for each pass. I have found that about 60% flow is a pretty good value.

5. Set the Mode to either Saturate or Desaturate.

6. Position the Sponge tool over the beginning of the area, hold down the left mouse button, and move the mouse over the area. Repeat this motion in long strokes until you get the desired amount of saturation or desaturation (desaturation in this example). You can see the change in the woman's dress here:

Smudge a Photo to Soften Details

The Smudge tool does just what you might think—it smudges an area of the photo. It's as if you put your finger onto a slightly wet watercolor image and slid your finger through the picture. Although the tool isn't of much use when working with digital photos, I have found one use for it—to soften the effect of glare on glass or metal. For example, Figure 6-7 shows light reflecting from a shiny surface in a very distracting way.

pic00047.jpg @ 66.7% (RGB)

FIGURE 6-7   The glare from a metallic or glass surface plays havoc with this photo.

Here are the steps I took to fix this condition:

1. Choose the Smudge tool from the toolbox.

2. Magnify the image so you can work on the problem area. In this case, I used a magnification of 200%.

3. Choose a brush size from the Brushes drop-down list. I found that a soft-edged brush works well because it feathers the effect of the smudge. In this case, I used a Soft Round 5 pixels brush on my dad's glasses, and a Soft Round 15 pixels brush on the TV screen behind my parents.

4. Use the Strength control to set the amount of the effect applied with each pass and also the distance that the smudge is effective. Too much Smudge can really ruin an image, so I tend to set the Strength to a low number like 25%. But in the case of the TV screen, the area was so large that I had to set the Strength to 90% to drag the dark areas into the glare areas.

5. Use the Mode control to set the blending mode. Either Normal (smudges everything) or Darken (smudges darker into lighter) works best in eliminating glare.

6. Position the Smudge tool in the dark area around the edges of the glare and drag into the glare area. Here is the result:

Selecting the glare area (see Chapter 8 for information on selecting an area) with the Magnetic Lasso tool, and then reducing the brightness also helps quite a bit.

Remove Red Eye

Many photos of people and animals (especially dogs and cats) display "red eye," as shown in Figure 6-8. Red eye occurs when you use a flash on your camera, and the flash is situated too close to the camera lens. The light from the flash bounces off the back of the eye, causing the center of the eye (which would normally be brown or blue) to glow red. This effect is more common with people who have blue eyes, but it occurs with any eye color.

Photoshop Elements has a special tool to remove red eye, called, oddly enough, the Red Eye Brush. This tool makes it relatively easy to remove red eye. Here is what you do:

1. Zoom in on the portion of the image containing the red eye so you can work on the correction with precision.

2. Choose the Red Eye Brush tool from the toolbox.

FIGURE 6-8   No, it's not "devil dog." This is an example of red eye, but you can fix it!

3. Select a brush size that is large enough to include the entire red eye portion of a single eye. You can judge whether the brush is sized correctly by comparing the size of the brush in the image to the red eye section. As you'll see in a moment, an exact fit is not necessary:

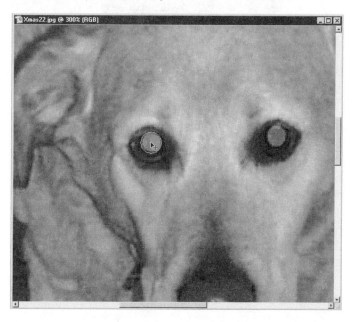

4. There are two color rectangles in the options bar. The right-hand rectangle specifies the color that Photoshop Elements will use to replace the red eye. You can either click the Default Colors button in the options bar to obtain the default replacement color, or click the right-hand rectangle and choose the replacement color from the Color Picker.

5. The Sampling drop-down list determines *how* Photoshop Elements decides which color to replace with the color you selected in step 4. I recommend choosing First Click.

The First Click option uses the color where you click as the color to replace. This is the normal option because you can simply maneuver the Red Eye Brush over the red eye and click to make the replacement. The Current Color option uses the foreground color as the color to be replaced (I have never used this option).

6. Use the Tolerance control to determine how different the color must be before the Red Eye Brush will leave it unchanged. A good value to use is 30% because the red eye is typically surrounded by areas (either skin/fur or the white of the eye) that are widely different in color. Choosing a reasonable value like 30% will guarantee that all of the various shades of red will be uniformly replaced.

7. Move the Red Eye Brush over the red eye effect and click. If you miss a section, simply include that section with the Red Eye Brush and click again. All done!

Chapter 7

Clean Up Areas with Darkroom-Like Tools

How to…

- Lighten areas with the Dodge tool
- Darken areas with the Burn tool
- Repair old photographs and remove "scan noise"
- Erase parts of an image
- Clone parts of an image to hide defects

Once you have corrected the overall image by cropping and adjusting the color, brightness, and contrast, the next step is to make corrections to specific portions of the image, leaving the balance of the image unchanged. Photoshop Elements provides tools that enable you to darken and lighten specific areas of an image, simulating the Dodge and Burn tools. In addition, you can remove portions of a photograph altogether using a variety of erasers. Finally, if you need to remove an object from the image, or hide a defect, you can clone another part of the image, or even a section of a different photo.

Lighten an Area with the Dodge Tool

If an area of a photograph is underexposed—and therefore prints too dark—a photographer can try to fix the problem in the darkroom. Because the underexposed area of the negative is too light, too much light from the enlarger reaches the photo paper. The photographer would need to block some of the excessive light from the enlarger (the cause of the problem) by attaching a piece of opaque material (usually cardboard) to a stick, and holding it over the photo paper during the printing process. Then, the photographer moves this "tool" around to feather the effect on the photo paper. This is called "dodging" (and is why the Dodge tool looks like a lollipop in the toolbox).

Photoshop Elements provides the Dodge tool to simulate this effect. In Photoshop Elements, you have a much higher degree of control over how much light to hold back than a photographer does working with an enlarger. In addition, you can control the size of the dodging tool by setting the brush size, and even set whether the Dodge tool affects deep shadows, the midtones, or highlights.

Since the effect of the Dodge tool is to hold back light (lightening an area), it is normally most useful in shadows and, to a lesser extent, in the midtones.

The Dodge tool can be used to lighten some distracting deep shadows, as shown in Figure 7-1.

FIGURE 7-1   Removing deep shadows will make this picture much more pleasing.

To lighten the image, follow these steps:

1. Choose the Dodge tool from the toolbox.

2. Choose the brush type and size from the Brush drop-down list and the Size control. The size and shape of the brush should approximate the area you want to lighten because if you apply the Dodge tool multiple times with an overlapping area, the lightening effect will become noticeable in the overlaps. Instead, you should size your brush (multiple times if necessary) to lighten the area with a minimum of overlaps.

3. Choose the range that the dodge should affect. For example, if you choose Shadows, using the Dodge tool on a very light area won't produce a change.

4. Choose the amount of dodge to apply from the Exposure control.

NOTE   *Lower settings for exposure apply less lightening, but a setting of 100% does not lighten the area all the way to white. Instead, a setting of 100% applies a moderate amount of lightening. A reasonable value is 50%, to avoid having to apply the effect too many times, which can lead to inadvertent overlap.*

5. Position the Brush tool over the area that needs lightening, and click to apply the Dodge tool. You can also hold down the mouse button and move the Brush tool over the area with quick motions, although care must be taken to not overdo this.

6. Continue applying the tool, moving it, and (if necessary) resizing it to cover the entire area. See Figure 7-2 for an example of how much better dodging can make an image.

"Burn in" an Area with the Burn Tool

Another photographer's trick is to "burn in" an area that is overexposed. When the overexposed area of the negative is too dark, not enough light passes through the negative so the print is too light in that area. The photographer "applies" a trick similar to dodging in order to fix this problem. First, the photographer exposes the photo paper for the properly exposed portion of the negative. Next, the photographer re-exposes the paper, holding back light from everywhere except the area that needs to be "burned in." Although some photographers cut holes in cardboard to achieve this effect, many just used their hands to block the light, allowing the extra light to pass through the area between the thumb and forefinger. And that, boys and girls, is why the Burn tool looks like a cupped hand!

Photoshop Elements provides the Burn tool to simulate this effect. As with the Dodge tool, you need to choose the brush size and shape, the range (shadows, midtones, highlights), and the exposure (amount of the effect applied on each pass).

FIGURE 7-2   Correcting the underexposed areas of the image make it look much better.

TIP *Unlike the Dodge tool, the Burn tool works best when you hold down the mouse button and sweep the brush across the affected area.*

A really excellent use for the Burn tool is apparent in Figure 7-3. The bald areas of the men's heads are overexposed compared to the rest of the photo. Since I come from a family of prematurely bald men (including yours truly, there on the left), I find that most family pictures require the judicious use of the Burn tool!

However, this condition is easy to fix, and doesn't even require Rogaine. To do so, I chose the Burn tool, set the brush size to 65 pixels, set the range to midtones, and the exposure to 50%. A quick pass over each bald spot resulted in Figure 7-4—a much better picture!

Repair Old Photos with the Dust & Scratches Filter

You may have some old photographs lying around that are not in very good shape. You've already seen how you can correct some fading and discoloration, and you'll see later in this chapter how you can make detailed repairs to these photos. You can use Photoshop Elements to fix some types of damage automatically. This is especially true of ingrained dust spots and small speckles of missing photo emulsion, which show up as tiny white spots. If you scan a photo to get it into an electronic format, you may also find that large dark areas display tiny white dots, as shown in Figure 7-5.

7

FIGURE 7-3   That shiny area where there should be hair can ruin a picture.

FIGURE 7-4   Now we are not being blinded by that reflection from the bald spots.

FIGURE 7-5   These tiny white dots and lines are noise introduced during the scanning process.

Although some of these spots may be caused by dust, much of it is "noise" introduced during the scanning process. The noise is most noticeable in large, dark areas. Fortunately, it is also easiest to fix when located there.

Photoshop Elements provides the Dust & Scratches filter to automatically correct some of these defects. To use the Dust & Scratches filter, choose Filter | Noise | Dust & Scratches. This opens the Dust & Scratches dialog box:

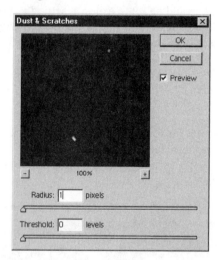

The square area in the center of the dialog box displays a small portion of the image and shows you the effect that the current settings will have. You can increase or decrease the magnification of this preview area by clicking the plus (+) or minus (–) buttons. To specify the portion of the image displayed in the preview area, you can:

Scroll the preview area   Move the mouse over the preview area, where it turns into a hand. Click and drag in the preview area. This scrolls the portion of the image previewed.

Pick the image area   Move the mouse over the image, where it turns into a small square. Click the area of the image you want to preview.

The Dust & Scratches filter applies changes to the image to hide dust, noise, and scratches. It does this by locating a noise spot and applying the color adjacent to the noise so that the noise is no longer visible.

To pick the amount of correction you want to apply, you must set the Threshold and Radius controls. These controls do the following:

Radius   The Radius control determines how far away from a particular pixel Photoshop Elements will search to find pixels of a different color.

Threshold   The Threshold control determines how different the color of a pixel has to be before the Dust & Scratches filter eliminates that pixel.

Here are some guidelines for applying the Radius and Threshold controls. In general, the difference in color between a noise spot and its surrounding color is very distinct. As stated earlier, the most common symptom is a white noise spot on a black or very dark area. Therefore, it is best to set the Threshold control to as high a value as possible. If you set it low, minor differences in color—such as in the edges—may be identified as noise and softened when you apply the filter. I have found that a Threshold value of about 40 works well in most circumstances.

The Radius control should be set to as low a setting as possible that still eliminates the noise. Setting the Radius to a high value makes the image blurry because edges are misidentified as noise. Since noise tends to be quite small, a Radius of about 3 works well in most circumstances.

 *Very high-contrast areas—such as highlights in the eyes—are blurred or eliminated by the filter. To avoid this, you may wish to select the problem areas (detailed in Chapter 8) prior to applying the filter to mask the filter effects from eyes.*

By experimenting with the Radius and Threshold controls, it is possible to eliminate much of the noise without too much detrimental effect on the rest of the image. Figure 7-6 shows the same image as Figure 7-5, but with most of the noise removed. Note, however, how much softer the highlights are in the baby's eyes.

FIGURE 7-6   Removing noise and dust really "cleans up" an image.

Paint with the Background Color Using the Eraser

Chapter 6 explored how to work with various tools that use the foreground color. However, there is another color available—the background color. As discussed earlier, you can set the background color by clicking the Background Color square at the bottom of the toolbox and choosing the color from the Color Picker. To use the Background Color tool, choose the Eraser tool from the toolbox.

There are actually three eraser tools available via the Eraser button in the toolbox. This section explains how to use the tool known simply as the Eraser tool. We will discuss how to use the other two eraser tools (Background Eraser and Magic Eraser) in the next two sections.

As mentioned earlier, the Eraser tool "paints" in the background color. To use it, select the tool and pick one of the three available modes:

Brush   Applies color just like the Brush tool. You can adjust the brush style, size, and opacity.

Pencil   Applies color just like the Pencil tool. You can adjust the brush style, size, and opacity.

Block   Applies color using a fixed-size square.

There is one circumstance where the Eraser tool does not use the background color. When you are erasing on a layer (see Chapter 9), and the layer transparency is not locked (that is, you are allowed to erase items to transparency on that layer), the Eraser tool will erase to transparency.

Remove Extraneous Backgrounds with the Background Eraser

The Background Eraser enables you to tightly control your erasures. This tool consists of two parts: the boundary of the tool and the hotspot (as shown in Figure 7-7). The brush erases everything that falls inside the boundary that is the same color as the color under the hotspot.
To use the Background Eraser, follow these steps:

1. Select the Background Eraser tool from the toolbox.

2. Choose the size of the Eraser "brush" from the Size option in the options bar. Everything within the edges of the tool is subject to erasure.

7

3. Choose the limits from the Limits drop-down list. "Contiguous" erases only areas of the selected color that are adjacent to the hotspot. "Discontiguous" erases all areas of the selected color within the tool edge.

4. Choose the Tolerance setting. The tolerance controls how similar a color must be to the hotspot color in order to be erased. A higher Tolerance setting erases a broader range of colors.

5. Choose an area in the image, and click. Photoshop Elements detects the color under the hotspot, and erases all areas within the tool boundary that are of the same color. You can also click and drag, erasing a swath.

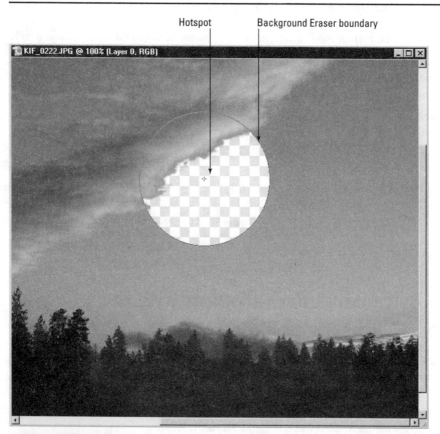

FIGURE 7-7   Click an area with the Background Eraser to erase everything of a given color within the tool boundary.

Erase Blocks of Color

You can use the Magic Eraser to erase large blocks of a similar color. For example, you can remove much of the background from a studio portrait (see Figure 7-8), perhaps to allow another background to show through.

With a single click of the Magic Eraser, the image in Figure 7-8 can be transformed into the image shown in Figure 7-9, where the entire background was erased.

To use the Magic Eraser, select it from the toolbox, and follow these steps:

1. Choose the Tolerance setting in the options bar. The tolerance controls how similar a color must be to the color present at the point where you click in the image in order to be erased. A higher value of tolerance erases a broader range of colors.

2. Check or clear the Anti-aliased check box. If you select anti-aliasing, the edges of the remaining portions of the image are less sharp and don't appear abrupt against any new background.

3. Check or clear the Contiguous check box. If you check this check box, only areas of the selected color that are adjacent to the point at which you click in the image are erased. If you clear the check box, all areas of the selected color in the image are erased.

4. Choose the Opacity setting of the erased area.

5. Select a point in the image that is rendered in the color you want to erase, and click.

6. Continue using the Magic Eraser to erase all the sections you want.

DnM 2001 NCI Sun-300dpi-apd.jpg @ 25% (RGB)

FIGURE 7-8   It is easy to erase large blocks of color using the Magic Eraser.

DnM 2001 NCI Sun-300dpi-apd.jpg @ 33.3% (Layer 0, RGB)

FIGURE 7-9   The background is all gone now, ready to be replaced with something more interesting.

Make Fine Repairs with the Clone Stamp

One of the most useful tools included with Photoshop Elements is the Clone Stamp. Essentially, this tool enables you to clone a portion of an image—or a portion of another image—to hide a blemish, repair a damaged area of a photo, or eliminate an object or a person from an image altogether.

To use the Clone Stamp, select the tool from the toolbox and follow these steps:

1. Move the Clone Stamp to the area that you want to clone. Hold down the ALT key and click to set the clone start point.

2. Move the mouse pointer to the area you want to paint over.

3. Click and drag the Clone Stamp to paint over the target area. As you move the Clone Stamp (with the left mouse button held down), Photoshop Elements displays a small moving indicator to show you the area you are currently cloning, as shown in Figure 7-10.

Clone source indicator
(area you are cloning)

Clone stamp
(area you are painting over)

FIGURE 7-10 The clone source indicator and the Clone Stamp are both visible while you are cloning an area of an image.

NOTE

The clone source indicator (the area you are cloning) moves in concert with the movement of the Clone Stamp. That is, if you move the Clone Stamp to the right, the clone source indicator moves to the right as well. Thus, you can clone a whole section of an image by holding down the left mouse button and moving the Clone Stamp so that the indicator travels over the entire section you want to clone. You'll see an example of that later in this section.

You can configure the following parameters in the options bar:

Brush type and size   You can select the type and size of brush from the drop-down list and Size field. Larger brushes clone larger areas, but give you less detailed control.

Mode   You can choose the Blending Mode from the Mode drop-down list. These modes were described in Chapter 5, and they have the same meaning here. To be honest, the only mode I've ever used with the Clone Stamp is Normal, which simply paints over an area with the cloned area.

Opacity   As described earlier, the Opacity setting controls how much of the existing background shows through the cloned area. Again, for most repairs, you don't want *any* of the background to show through, so set the Opacity to 100%. However, it can be fun to add a "ghost" to your image by cloning a person at a low opacity so that the background does show through.

Alignment   When the Alignment check box is cleared, each stroke of the Clone Stamp clones from the same starting point (source). That is, if you use the Clone Stamp, then move the tool across the image and use the Clone Stamp again, the cloned area starts from the same source for both strokes. However, if the Alignment check box is checked, the clone source moves each time you start a new stroke. For example, if you set the clone source and execute a stroke, then move the Clone Stamp two inches to the right and execute another stroke, the clone source starts two inches to the right of your originally specified clone source.

Fix Scan Noise with the Clone Stamp

One of the most common uses for the Clone Stamp is to clean up scan noise that you couldn't correct with the Dust & Scratches filter. Figure 7-11 shows an image that was scanned, leaving white dots (noise) and lines (scratch) in most of the dark areas of the image.

To fix this photo, I followed these steps:

1. Used the Magnify tool to increase the magnification of the image to clearly display the noise and dust imperfections.

2. Chose the Clone Stamp from the toolbox.

3. Picked a spot to work on, and set the size of the brush to approximately the same size as the noise spot. I also made sure the Mode was set to "Normal," the Opacity to 100%, and that the Aligned check box was checked.

4. Held down the ALT key, and chose an adjacent area to use as the clone source.

5. Positioned the Clone Stamp over the noise spot and clicked. I then clicked again if the spot was not completely hidden, or clicked and dragged to hide an irregularly shaped spot.

FIGURE 7-11   Clean up scan noise with the Clone Stamp.

Remove an Object with the Clone Stamp

The Clone Stamp can do far more than just clean up some dust and noise. The photo on the left side of Figure 7-12 was taken on my parents' fiftieth wedding anniversary. A few seconds later, I took the photo on the right of Figure 7-12. However, just as I was snapping the shot, my brother jumped into the picture. Unfortunately, I like my parents' expressions better in the right-hand picture, and the Clone Stamp enables me to remove my errant brother from the right-hand photo.

The trick is that the two photos were taken just seconds apart, and have identical backgrounds. Essentially, I can clone a portion of the background in the left photo to paint over my brother in the right photo.

TIP   *Sometimes, two pictures can have different brightness and color even when they were taken at the same time because of sloppy commercial printing. Thus, you may have to make some corrections to one of the photos to make both as identical as possible before cloning a portion of one image to another.*

To remove my brother from the right-hand photo, I followed these steps:

1. Enlarged both photos so they would both fit on the screen and would display the problem area (my brother in the right photo) or the background clone source (the left photo).

2. Chose the Clone Stamp tool and set the brush size. A fairly large brush size (about 50 pixels) works well for the large areas; a much smaller brush (about 10 to 20 pixels) is necessary to work along the edges of my parents for detail work.

3. Checked the Alignment check box in the options bar to make sure the movement of the clone source mirrored the movement of the Clone Stamp.

4. Moved the Clone Stamp over the left-hand image, held down the ALT key, and clicked to pick the clone source. It is extremely important that the clone source be a point that is recognizable in order to properly execute the next step. In this case, I chose one of the stumps sticking out of the tree visible over my brother's shoulder in the right photo.

5. Moved the Clone Stamp over the left-hand image, and clicked on exactly the same feature of the tree I had picked as the clone source in the right-hand image.

6. Began stroking with the Clone Stamp while holding down the left mouse button, replacing my brother with the background from the other photo:

FIGURE 7-12   Using the left photo, I can correct the right photo to remove my brother from the picture.

7. Continued working, moving carefully around the edges of my parents, until my brother was all gone, as shown here:

Repair an Old Photo with the Clone Stamp

Recently my mother-in-law found an ancient photo of my wife's aunts and uncles in a drawer. It was badly deteriorated, as you can see from Figure 7-13. There are creases, missing flecks of emulsion (the photo coating that contains the image information), and portions are faded. Still, there is enough information to attempt a repair.

The main job is to fill in the missing pieces using the Clone Stamp. I had to exercise care to choose areas that were the same color as the missing flecks. Fortunately, since the photo is not in color, it was easy to find another area of the photo that matched. I had to reproduce a missing section of the wooden wall alongside my wife's grandfather (standing in the background), and recreate a missing portion of his face using the Brush tool. Finally, I adjusted the brightness and contrast of selected portions of the image, especially the dirt areas around the car and girl's dresses. You can see the result in Figure 7-14.

Paint a Pattern with the Pattern Stamp

Photoshop Elements includes a large number of patterns, and you can "paint" with these patterns. For example, you can replace a boring concrete sidewalk with a pattern of red rocks, as shown in Figure 7-15. To add patterns to an image, use the Pattern Stamp tool (it shares a button with the Clone Stamp in the toolbox).

Old Car n Kids-600dpi.JPG @ 33.3% (RGB)

FIGURE 7-13   Even a photo in bad shape—as this one is—is repairable.

FIGURE 7-14   After about six hours of working on the photo, it is in much better shape.

7

FIGURE 7-15   Replace a flat surface with a pattern using the Pattern Stamp tool.

The Pattern Stamp tool works much like the Brush tool. Thus, you can specify the brush type and size, Blending Mode (from the Mode drop-down list), opacity, and alignment. In the case of a pattern, checking the Alignment check box aligns the pattern from one paint area to the next. That is, you can stop painting and resume painting, and the pattern remains aligned—as you paint over the existing edge of the pattern, the newly painted area is in perfect alignment with the previously painted area. Clearing the Alignment check box causes the pattern to realign each time you resume painting. Photoshop Elements re-centers the pattern on the pointer each time you stop and resume painting.

Use an opacity of less than 100% to allow certain features—such as the shadows from the trees—to remain intact as you paint with the pattern. Since the surface over which you are painting in this case is essentially featureless, you don't need 100% opacity to hide it.

To pick the pattern, click the Pattern drop-down list in the center of the options bar, then choose the pattern you want:

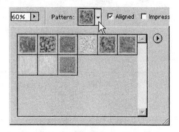

The triangle at the right edge of the pattern list displays a palette menu for the patterns:

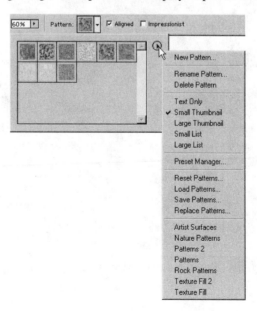

As with any other palette menu, you can rename or delete a pattern; specify how you want to view the patterns (Text Only, Small Thumbnail, and so forth); load, save, or replace the collection of patterns; work with patterns in the Preset Manager; and choose a set of patterns from those provided with Photoshop Elements (Artist Surfaces, Nature Patterns, and so on).

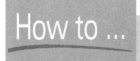

Create a New Pattern

Photoshop Elements comes with many preset patterns, but you can create your own. Here is how you do that:

1. Choose an area of an image that is suitable for use as a pattern. The area should include a repeating pattern of a reasonable size (large patterns can become hard to manage). Ideally, the left edge of the pattern area should be similar enough to the right edge that you don't see a strong discontinuity when the pattern is tiled. The same should be true of the top and bottom edges.

2. Select the Rectangular Marquee selection tool and select the area you want to convert to a pattern.

3. Choose Edit | Define Pattern. Photoshop Elements opens the Pattern Name dialog box:

4. Fill in a descriptive name for the pattern and click OK to add the pattern to the current set of patterns. You can see the new pattern defined at the end of the list:

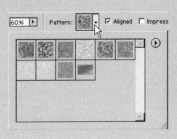

7

Part III

Apply Changes to Specific Parts of Your Photos

Chapter 8

Make Selections and Apply Changes

How to...

- Use the Marquee selection tools
- Use the Lasso selection tools
- Set the selection tools parameters
- Select everything in a given color
- Add to and subtract from the selection
- Sharpen a selected area
- Change the color of a selected area
- Apply a gradient to a selected area
- Fill an area with a pattern

You've looked at tools that allow you to apply a correction to an entire photo, such as adjusting the color, brightness, and contrast. You've also looked at tools for applying "touchups," such as burn, dodge, clone, smudge, and blur. However, many photos have problems that can be solved only by applying corrections to a specific area—and leaving the rest of the image alone. For example, a landscape might have the correct exposure for the field in the foreground, but the ocean and sky in the background may be overexposed, resulting in the loss of interesting details. The image shown in Figure 8-1 illustrates this problem. If you adjust the image to show the details in the background, the foreground area comes out too dark.

To correct a problem such as the one shown in Figure 8-1 (and a whole range of similar problems), you need to apply a brightness correction to the background only. To do so, you must select the problem area before applying the fix. When you select an area in Photoshop Elements, any work you do after making the selection results in changes only in the selected area.

> **NOTE** *It is important to remember that Photoshop Elements applies your corrections only to a selected area. It is quite disconcerting to choose one of the brush tools and start "painting" on your image, only to find that nothing is happening! If you discover that your changes don't seem to be working, choose Select | Deselect to remove any pre-existing selection.*

Photoshop Elements provides several selection tools so you can select the area you want to work on. You can configure these tools to change how they behave. You can also modify the selection by adding to it or subtracting from it until you have exactly the area you want in which to make the change.

FIGURE 8-1   There is no easy way to make an overall correction to this photo so that both the foreground and background are correctly exposed.

Once you have the area selected, you can apply corrections to that area. Technically, you can use *any* tool in a selected area, but there are a number of tools, which I will cover in this chapter, that really make sense to use *only* in a selected area.

You can copy a selection to the clipboard and either paste it back into the same image or into another image. Since copying and pasting also involves using layers, this subject will be covered in Chapter 9.

Make a Selection with the Selection Tools

Photoshop Elements provides four different types of selection tools: the Marquee selection tools, the Lasso selection tools, the Selection Brush, and the Magic Wand. The top three buttons in the left column of the toolbox are the Marquee tools, the Lasso tools, and the Selection Brush, in that order. The Magic Wand button is on the right side of the toolbox, second from the top.

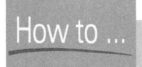

Soften the Edges of a Selection

One of the reasons you may want to select a portion of an image is to copy it and paste it into another image or into another portion of the same image (see Chapter 9). Photoshop Elements provides some options to soften the edges of the selection so that the border of the selected area is smooth when you paste it.

Your first option is to anti-alias the selection. This effect softens the color transition between the edge pixels in the selection and the background pixels of the image you are pasting into. Anti-aliasing is available for all the selection tools except the Rectangular Marquee tool and the Selection Brush.

The second option for softening edges is to use feathering. Feathering blurs the edges of the selected areas, and is available for all selection tools except for the Magic Wand and the Selection Brush. Feathering gives you increasing gradations of transparency in the selected image as you move closer to the edge of the image. For example, if you set Feather to 15 pixels in the options bar, the feathering effect begins 15 pixels from the edge of the selection, and reaches full transparency at the edge of the selected area. As you change the amount of feathering you apply, the selected area changes shape to approximate the feathered area, but you can't actually see the effect of the feathering unless you copy the selected area (choose Edit | Copy) and then paste the selected area (choose Edit | Paste). The effect is clearly visible here in this example, where I've copied a section of an image and pasted it into a new, empty document with lots of feathering.

> **NOTE** *As with any other Brush tool, you can use the hardness option with the Selection Brush. Remember that a low value of hardness adds soft edges to the brush strokes, approximating the same effect as feathering.*

There are two ways to apply feathering to a selection—before you make the selection or after you make the selection. To establish the amount of feathering prior to making the selection, set the Feather field in the options bar. To apply feathering to an existing selection, choose Select | Feather to open the Feather Selection dialog box, and enter the amount of feathering in the Feather Radius field:

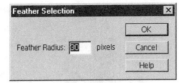

One last thing you should know about feathering. If you use a lot of feathering on a small selection, you may end up with a situation where the pixels in the selection are so faint that the edges of the selection are invisible. The selection then becomes non-selectable. Photoshop Elements will warn you of this situation with the following dialog box:

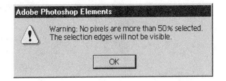

After clicking OK, the selected area will no longer be visible. You *can* still copy and paste the selected area, but you won't be able to click and drag it to a new location with the Move tool so it is of limited use. You are far better off reducing the amount of feathering or increasing the size of the selection (or both!).

Select with the Marquee Tools

Use the Marquee selection tools when the selection you need to make is either rectangular or oval. The Rectangular Marquee tool enables you to select a rectangular area of an image:

The Oval Marquee tool enables you to select an oval area of the image:

These tools give you three different styles to choose from, and each style affects how you perform the selection. To choose a style, pick it from the Styles drop-down list in the options bar. The three styles are:

Normal   Creates a selection by clicking and dragging with the mouse pointer. To click and drag so that the starting point remains the center of the selected area, make sure nothing else is selected (choose Select | Deselect if necessary), and hold down the ALT button as you click and drag.

Fixed Aspect Ratio   Maintains the specified height-to-width ratio while making the selection. To set the aspect ratio, enter a number in the Width and Height fields in the option bar. For example, to create a selection where the width is twice the height, enter **2** in the Width field and **1** in the Height field. Once you have specified the width and height, click and drag with the mouse to make your selection. The selection will be constrained to the specified aspect ratio.

Fixed Size   Creates a selection of the specified size. Type the width and height of the selection into the fields in the options bar. For both the width and height, you must specify a unit of measure of inches (in), pixels (px), or centimeters (cm).

 *To constrain the Rectangular Marquee tool to a square, or the Oval Marquee tool to a circle, make sure nothing is selected, and hold down the SHIFT key as you click and drag.*

Select with the Lasso Tools

If the area you need to select is neither rectangular nor oval, you can use one of the three Lasso tools to make your selection. They enable you to trace an area manually (Lasso tool), create a selection using straight lines (Polygonal Lasso tool), and create a selection by tracing an edge (Magnetic Lasso tool).

Use the Lasso Tool to Make a Manual Selection

To "trace out" an irregular area manually so that you can select it, choose the Lasso tool. Then follow these steps:

1. Move the Lasso tool to the beginning of the area you want to select.

2. Hold down the left mouse button and begin tracing the area:

3. Continue tracing the area until you have the selection completely defined.

4. Release the left mouse button. Photoshop Elements turns the area you defined into a selection:

 *Tracing out an irregular area takes a steady hand—one slip and you'll have to start over. If the area you want to select has a well-defined edge, you are better off using the Magnetic Lasso tool (discussed later in this chapter).*

Use the Polygonal Lasso Tool to Trace Straight Edges

If the area you want to select is defined by straight edges, you can quickly define the edges of the area using the Polygonal Lasso tool. After choosing the tool, follow these steps:

1. Move the Polygonal Lasso tool to the beginning of the area you want to select.

2. Click the left mouse button to define the beginning of the first line.

3. Move the mouse to the location where the line should end, and click again. This defines the line.

4. Continue moving the mouse and clicking to define a series of lines. Each line begins automatically where the last line ends, as shown in the illustration on the next page.

5. Use the Polygonal Lasso tool to define the last line, and double-click to automatically form a closed shape. Photoshop Elements connects the last point (where you double-clicked) to the starting point of the selection. You can also hold down the CTRL key while clicking to close the selection area.

8

You can constrain the line you draw to 45-degree angles by holding down the SHIFT key while defining a line.

Use the Magnetic Lasso Tool to Trace an Edge

Very often, the area you want to select has a well-defined edge. For example, look at Figure 8-2. The selected area contrasts sharply with the dark background. You might want to select the primary subject (as in this figure) so you can place it against a less-distracting background (a project I'll spend most of Chapter 12 discussing). The Magnetic Lasso tool is designed just for this purpose.

You can switch from the Polygonal Lasso tool to the Lasso tool temporarily. This is very handy if the shape you are trying to select has mostly straight edges, but has an irregular section that is *not* defined by straight edges. To switch to the Lasso tool, hold down the ALT key, then hold down the left mouse button and trace out the section as described previously. When you have traced the irregular section, release the ALT key and Photoshop Elements switches back to the Polygonal Lasso tool, enabling you to define the rest of the selected area with straight lines.

FIGURE 8-2   It is easy to select an object with a well-defined edge using the Magnetic Lasso tool.

To select an area with the Magnetic Lasso tool, choose the tool and follow these steps:

1. Click the edge of the area you want to select. This is your starting point.

2. Begin moving the tool along the edge. As you do, the selection "anchors" to the edge, and Photoshop Elements periodically provides a fastening point:

NOTE *You can provide your own fastening points at more frequent intervals by clicking anywhere you want to place a fastening point. This is handy if an area of the selection has a low contrast edge that Photoshop Elements is having trouble detecting.*

3. Continue tracing the edge until you are done. Double-click to finish and close the shape, as shown in Figure 8-2, shown previously.

TIP *If a fastening point is not properly situated along an edge, you can remove the point by pressing the DELETE key. Each time you press the DELETE key, Photoshop Elements removes the previous fastening point, which enables you to step backward along the edge and redo an area of the selection.*

You can temporarily switch to the Lasso tool or the Polygonal Lasso tool if you encounter a portion of the selection where the edge is not well defined, which may lead Photoshop Elements to misidentify the edge. To activate the Lasso tool so you can manually define a low-contrast edge, hold down the ALT key and drag the mouse with the left mouse button held down. You can also activate the Polygonal Lasso tool temporarily—just hold down the ALT key and move the mouse, clicking to define straight lines. In either case, once you release the ALT key, Photoshop Elements switches back to the Magnetic Lasso tool.

You can configure how sensitive the Magnetic Lasso tool is by adjusting the various parameters in the options bar. These parameters are:

Width The Magnetic Lasso searches for edges by starting at the location of the mouse pointer and searching the distance given by the width parameter. That is, the Magnetic Lasso detects edges only within the specified distance from the mouse pointer. You can set the width between 1 and 40 pixels (px).

TIP *To have the mouse cursor display the size of the width parameter, press the CAPS LOCK key after you choose a tool but before you click to begin the selection process. You can increase the width by one pixel while making your selection by pressing the] key. Pressing the [key decreases the width by one pixel.*

Edge Contrast The edge contrast controls how sensitive the Magnetic Lasso is to edges. If you use a high value, the tool detects only the edges that contrast sharply with the background. A low value enables the tool to detect lower-contrast edges. You can vary the edge contrast parameter from 1% to 100%.

TIP *If you find that the Magnetic Lasso tool is having trouble finding the edge in a low-contrast area, you can temporarily switch to one of the other Lasso tools (as described previously) or manually set fastening points in the problem area to force Photoshop Elements to trace the edge.*

Frequency   This parameter determines how often Photoshop Elements creates a fastening point. Higher values create more frequent fastening points anchoring the edge selection.

Pen Pressure   Checking the Pen Pressure check box enables you to control the width of the edge selection using pen pressure (assuming you are using a tablet and pen). Increasing the pressure increases the width; decreasing the pressure decreases the width.

You can minimize the amount of work you have to do to define a selection with the Magnetic Lasso tool. For an image with high-contrast edges, use higher width settings (20 to25 pixels) and edge contrast settings (15 to 20%), and trace the border roughly. On an image with soft edges, use lower width settings (3 to 5 pixels) and edge contrast (5%), and trace the border more precisely. This requires more work, but the results will be much more accurate. However, as with the Lasso tool, the lower the width and edge contrast setting, the steadier your hand needs to be. You may wish to use a tablet and pen instead of a mouse for very low settings of these parameters.

Make a Selection with the Selection Brush

The Selection Brush enables you to "paint" your selection. Once you've chosen the Selection Brush tool, set the brush type and size using the Brush drop-down palette and size control. Begin painting the area you want as your selection. For example, here is an image where it would be difficult to use one of the selection tools to make the selection. I began painting over the antlers, and each brush stroke added to the selection area:

You can stop at any point, change the brush style and size, and continue painting to define the selection.

To get an accurate picture of the selection you've created, choose Mask from the Mode drop-down list. This highlights the selected area. Switch back to the Selection Mode to continue creating your selection.

Select a Color with the Magic Wand

The Magic Wand tool enables you to choose an area (or all areas) of a given color. This can be very handy if you have a main subject against a single-color background (as you often do with studio portraits). For example, take a look at Figure 8-3. By simply choosing the Magic Wand tool and clicking the background, you select the entire background.

Another great use for the Magic Wand is to select an area of a given color (such as a piece of clothing), and change the color. I'll show you how to do this later in this chapter.

To select an area of a given color, choose the Magic Wand tool from the toolbox, position the tool over the color you want to select, and click. If you checked the Contiguous check box in the options bar, only adjacent areas of the same color are selected. If you clear the Contiguous check box, *all* areas of the selected color are selected, as shown in Figure 8-4.

8

FIGURE 8-3   Selecting a single-color background is easy with the Magic Wand tool.

FIGURE 8-4 Be sure you want to select all areas of the selected color when you clear the Contiguous check box.

Of course, this effect is *not* what I want in this portrait, since portions of the face and arms were also selected!

The Tolerance parameter in the options bar determines how similar a color must be to the selected color before it is included in the selection. A low value selects only colors that are very similar to the color you picked; higher values select a broader range of colors.

You can fine-tune your color selection with three specialized commands: Grow, Similar, and Smooth. You can actually use these commands with any selection, but they make the most sense when used with the Magic Wand. Be aware that the magnitude of the effect depends on the Tolerance option for the Magic Wand. Here is what the three commands do:

Grow Choose Select | Grow to include all adjacent pixels that fall within the tolerance range specified by the Magic Wand Tolerance option. A higher level for tolerance includes a broader range of colors.

Similar Choose Select | Similar to include all pixels (including non-adjacent pixels) that fall within the tolerance range specified by the Magic Wand Tolerance option.

Smooth Smooth helps you clean up stray pixels left inside or outside a color-based selection. Choose Select | Modify | Smooth and specify the sample radius in the resulting Smooth Selection dialog box. Once you have selected the sample radius, Photoshop Elements looks at each pixel in a range on each side of the pixel. The size of the range is specified by the sample radius. For example, if you enter 10 pixels for the sample radius, Photoshop Elements checks a square that is 21 pixels high and 21 pixels wide (10 pixels above and below, 10 pixels left and right). If most of the pixels in the range are selected, any unselected pixel is added to the selection. On the other hand, if most of the pixels are *not* selected, any selected pixel is removed from the selection. By carefully adjusting the tolerance by small amounts, you can include missed pixels or exclude pixels that should have been left out.

Modify a Selection

It can be difficult to select the exact area you want in one try. For example, you might want to select two areas that are not adjacent so you can later apply a correction. Or, you might need to add a small area at the edge of an existing selection because the Magnetic Lasso "missed" that area and left it out of the selection. Fortunately, Photoshop Elements enables you to modify a selection to include exactly what you want.

Add, Subtract, and Intersect Selections

8

Photoshop Elements provides options in the options bar (see Figure 8-5) to add to a selection, subtract from a selection, and create a new selection from the intersection of two selected areas.

Add to a Selection

When you add a new area to an existing selection, the resulting selected area includes both areas. For example, I created the two non-adjacent areas in Figure 8-6 by first selecting the area on the left, and then adding the area on the right to the selection.

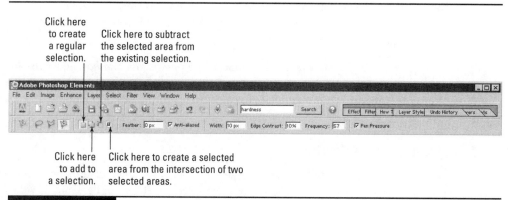

FIGURE 8-5   Use the tools in the options bar to control how you create selections.

FIGURE 8-6   Create a selection from two non-adjacent areas by adding the second area to the initial selection.

To add a new area to an existing selection, follow these steps:

1. Choose a selection tool and select the initial area.

2. Select the Add to Selection option in the options bar.

3. Create the second selected area.

When you are done, both areas are part of the selection (as shown previously in Figure 8-6). You can continue adding areas to the selection by following this procedure as many times as you like.

Instead of clicking the Add to Selection option, you can hold down the SHIFT key while creating the second selected area. When you press the SHIFT key, the selection tool displays a small plus sign (+) to denote you are adding to the selected area.

Subtract from a Selection

When you subtract an area from an existing selection, the resulting area does not include any overlap between the second area and the original selection. This can be handy if your initial selection included too much information, which often happens with the Magnetic Lasso tool. It is even more handy when you need to "cut out" an area before applying a correction. For example, Figure 8-7 displays an old photograph that is badly in need of help. The roof area needs to be darkened and color-enhanced, but I don't want to apply these same effects to the dark skylight. So, I just selected the entire roof and subtracted the skylight area.

To subtract an area from an existing selection, follow these steps:

1. Choose a selection tool and create the initial selected area.

2. Select the Subtract From Selection option in the options bar.

3. Create the second selected area.

When you are done, the overlapping area is removed from the initial selection. As with adding to a selection, you can continue subtracting areas by following this procedure as many times as you want.

NOTE   *Instead of clicking the Subtract From Selection option, you can hold down the ALT key while creating the second area. When you press the ALT key, the selection tool displays a small minus sign (−) to denote you are subtracting from the selected area.*

8

Risa in Toul–600dpi.jpg @ 33.3% (RGB)

FIGURE 8-7   Cut out an area from a selection before applying a correction.

Create a Selected Area from an Intersection

When you create an intersection of a new area and an existing selection, the resulting area consists of just the overlapping area.

To create an intersection selection, create an initial selection, choose the Intersect With Selection option, and create the second area. When you are done, the overlapping area is the only selected area.

 *You can also hold down the ALT and SHIFT keys while creating the second area. While holding down these two keys, the selection tool displays a small x to denote you are creating an intersection with the selected area.*

Invert a Selection

It can often be easier to select what you *don't* want from an image than to select what you *do* want. For example, as mentioned earlier in this chapter, it is quite simple to use the Magic Wand to select a single-color background in a studio portrait. Once you have made this sort of selection, it is easy to invert the selection so that everything *except* what you originally selected becomes the new selection. Thus, in my example, the subjects of the photo become the new selection, leaving out the single-color background. You could then follow the instructions in Chapter 12 to copy the main subjects and place them against a more interesting background.

To invert your selection, simply choose Select | Inverse.

Expand or Contract a Selection

You can increase or decrease the size of a selected area. This can be handy if you find that the selection isn't quite the right size when you apply a correction or copy and paste it. This is especially true if you use feathering, since it is hard to predict what size to make the selection until you actually copy and paste it—and see the resulting "fade-out" around the edges.

 *Increasing or decreasing the size of the selection does not affect the image— only the boundaries of the selection.*

To expand the selection, choose Select | Modify | Expand to open the Expand Selection dialog box, and enter the amount to expand the selection by in the Expand By field. The dialog box (along with the selected area) is visible in Figure 8-8.

FIGURE 8-8   To make the selected area larger, enter the enlargement amount in the Expand Selection dialog box.

Click OK, and Photoshop Elements expands the selected area:

Contracting a selection works pretty much the same way. Simply choose Select | Modify | Contract, enter the amount in the Contract Selection dialog box, and click OK.

Select a Border

You can convert a selection to the border of the selection. The border is automatically anti-aliased to soften the edges. To create the selection border, choose Select | Modify | Border, and enter the width of the border in the Border Selection dialog box:

Click OK to create the border selection, which you can see here after I copied the selected area and pasted it into a new image:

Add a Border with Stroke

Adding a hard-edged border to a selection can be very useful. For example, if you select a rectangular portion of an image with the Rectangular Marquee tool, you can then frame the area, as shown in Figure 8-9.

To create this type of border, follow these steps:

1. Select the portion of the image you want to add a border to.

2. Choose Edit | Stroke. This opens the Stroke dialog box:

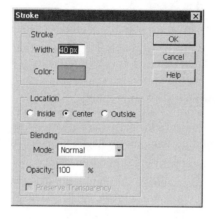

8

FIGURE 8-9   Frame a selection with the Stroke tool.

3. In the Width field, choose the width of the frame. You can set the width in pixels (px), inches (in), or centimeters (cm).

4. Click the Color rectangle to open the Color Picker, and pick the frame color. Then click OK to close the Color Picker.

5. From the Location area, choose one of the radio buttons to place the frame inside the selection (Inside), outside the selection (Outside), or centered on the selection (Center).

6. Choose the blending mode from the Mode drop-down list. The modes are identical to those discussed in Chapter 5.

7. Set the opacity from invisible (0%) to fully opaque (100%).

8. Click OK to create the border.

Move the Selection

You can change the location of the selection outline. Thus, if you find that the selection doesn't quite align with the item you are trying to select, move the selection outline in one of these two ways:

Use the mouse   You can move the mouse pointer inside the selection outline, where it turns into the Move tool automatically. Click and drag the selection to its new location.

Use the arrow keys   You can make fine adjustments to the selection location using the arrow keys. Each press of an arrow key moves the selection one pixel in the appropriate direction. Holding down SHIFT while pressing an arrow key moves the selection outline 10 pixels.

   *If you have a tight fit around an object you want to select, expand the size of the selection (Select | Modify | Expand) before moving it. By doing so, you can move the selection and still include the entire object you wanted to select.*

Cut and Move the Selected Object

You can cut and move a selected object in one step. Hold down the CTRL key while clicking and dragging the selection. The area that formerly contained the selected object is drawn in the background color, and the selected object remains selected in its new location, as shown in the following illustration.

Copy and Move the Selection

You can copy and move the selected object in one step as well. First, switch to the Move tool. Hold down the ALT key while clicking and dragging the selection. Each time you perform this action, you create a new copy of the selected object, which you can drag to its target location. Figure 8-10 shows two copies of a seascape. The left one shows only a lonely sea bird; the right one shows a whole flock of them sitting on the water. All I did was use the Magnetic Lasso to select the bird, and then duplicated it over and over again.

Reuse Selections by Saving and Loading

Selecting the exact area you want to work on can be a chore. In addition, you may need to go back and forth between selected areas, making corrections in each area until the overall image is to your liking. Clearly, reselecting each area to make further corrections is not only inefficient, but it is also difficult to get the exact same area selected on subsequent tries (perhaps missing a portion of one edge). Fortunately, Photoshop Elements provides a much easier way to go about doing this. You can save a selection definition and load it again later. Once you reload a selection definition, you can apply corrections to the selected area.

As an example, the shot of the Las Vegas Strip shown in Figure 8-11 has some real problems. The sky is overexposed, the buildings in the medium foreground are a little underexposed, and the replica of the Eiffel Tower is *very* underexposed. Oh, yeah—the balloon (just to the right of the center of the picture) could use some sharpening and brightening. As you can see, selecting specific items like the Eiffel Tower will be difficult—so you are going to want to do it only once.

FIGURE 8-10   Add more objects to an image easily by copying and moving the selection.

The first step is to select the area you want to correct. For example, I'll select the sky portion of the image first.

To save the selection, choose Select | Save Selection. This displays the Save Selection dialog box:

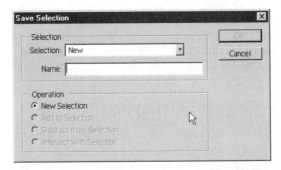

Fill in a descriptive name for the selected area and click OK to save the selection. If you choose New from the Selection drop-down list, you can only save a new selection. However, if you choose an existing saved selection from the Selection drop-down list, Photoshop Elements provides the following options for combining the new selection with the previously saved selection:

Replace Selection   Replaces the previous contents of the selection with the newly selected area.

FIGURE 8-11   I've selected the sky portion of this image so I can correct it.

Add to Selection   Adds the currently selected area to the saved selection. Thus, when you reload the selection, the selected area will consist of the previously selected area and the newly selected area.

Subtract from Selection   Subtracts the currently selected area from the saved selection. If there is no overlap between the areas, the saved selection is unchanged.

Intersect with Selection   Modifies the saved selection to include only the intersection between the previously saved selection and the current selection.

Once you have saved each selection area (in my case, sky, buildings, Eiffel Tower, and balloon), you can load the selection by choosing Select | Load Selection to open the Load Selection dialog box:

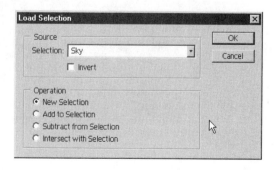

If you choose the default option (New Selection), any existing selection is replaced by the newly loaded selection. However, if you already have a selection active when you choose to load another one, you can choose one of the other options to add, subtract, or intersect the loaded selection with the current selection. You can also load the inverse of a selection by checking the Invert check box.

If you are not saving a file as a Photoshop Elements (psd) file, make sure you finish all your work with saved selections before closing the image. "Saved" selections are lost (and will have to be recreated if you need them again) when you close the image, unless you save the image as a Photoshop Elements (psd) file.

Apply Effects to Selected Areas

Now that you understand how to create selections and limit your work to just the selected area(s), you can explore some of the more advanced corrections that Photoshop Elements makes possible. These corrections make the most sense when applied to a limited area, rather than to a whole image.

Blur the Background

When an entire photograph is in sharp focus, a busy background can distract the eye from the main subject. To combat this effect, you can blur the background a little bit, leaving the main subject sharply focused. To accomplish this, follow these steps:

1. Open an image and select the main subject. In this example, I got good results using the Magnetic Lasso tool:

2. Invert the selection so that everything *except* the main subject is selected by choosing Select | Inverse.

3. Choose one of the Blur filters (Filter | Blur). The best control is with Gaussian blur or Smart blur. I used Gaussian blur in this example:

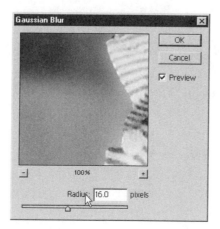

4. Set the radius for the Gaussian blur, and click OK to blur the background, leaving only the subject in sharp focus:

Gaussian blur quickly blurs a selection by an adjustable amount. You can select the radius, which determines how far the filter searches from a pixel to find dissimilar pixels to blur. The amount of applied blur falls off as you move away from a sharp edge according to a bell-shaped curve.

Smart blur is another good choice for blurring wide areas. In addition to the radius, you can set the threshold (how different pixels have to be before the filter blurs them) and the quality. The three levels of quality (low, medium, and high) specify the "fineness" of the blur calculations. High quality (as you would guess) creates a finer (and less obvious) blur, but takes longer to calculate and apply the effect.

Change the Color of an Object

Changing the color of an object can be fun and useful. For example, the picture of buoys floating on the water off the Oregon coast that is shown in Figure 8-12 was more interesting when the buoys were different colors (they all started out orange).

FIGURE 8-12   Changing the colors of similar objects can make an image more interesting.

Another good example of when it might be good to change an object's color is when a white shirt stands out too much in a photo.

To correct this situation, follow these steps:

1. Select the item whose color you want to change. I selected the light-colored shirt that was jarring to the eye. I actually made the selection in two steps. The first step selected the entire shirt, including the tie. I then held down the ALT key and selected just the tie, removing it from the selection, as shown in Figure 8-13.

2. Choose Enhance | Adjust Color | Hue/Saturation to open the Hue/Saturation dialog box.

3. Adjust the Hue, Saturation, and Lightness sliders to change the color of the offending object. Figure 8-14 shows the less-jarring result.

You can also achieve a similar effect using the Replace Color command. After selecting the area, choose Enhance | Adjust Color | Replace Color. This opens the Replace Color dialog box:

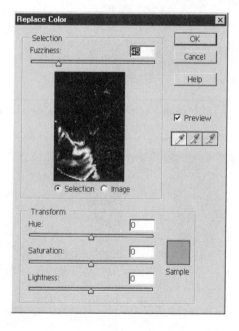

8

Follow these steps to change the color of the selected area:

1. Set the fuzziness by typing in a value or using the slider. This sets how similar a color must be to the color you select in order to be affected by the Replace Color command. If you select just the area you want to change, it doesn't matter too much what you set the fuzziness to. A good value to begin with is around 40.

2. Make sure you choose the Selection radio button. This option shows you, in a rectangle above the radio buttons, the area that contains the color you are going to replace.

FIGURE 8-13   The item I want to change is now selected.

FIGURE 8-14   Your eye doesn't automatically gravitate toward my bright white shirt.

3. Use the Eyedropper tools to pick the color(s) you want to replace. The left-most Eyedropper tool selects a single color. The middle eyedropper, with the plus sign (+), adds colors to the affected area. The right-hand eyedropper, with the minus sign (−), subtracts colors from the affected area.

4. Use the Hue, Saturation, and Lightness controls to set the replacement color. The sample rectangle shows you the color you have chosen.

5. Click OK to replace all the colors you selected (in step 3) with the color you chose in step 4.

Use Brightness/Contrast to Fix an Area

It is not unusual for a section of a photo to need drastic changes and serious corrections. For example, Figure 8-15 shows an image that is in pretty good shape, except for a couple of flowers near the right edge of the image that caught the flash, leaving that portion of the photo severely overexposed. The bright white area overpowers the rest of the picture. You *could* crop this section out, but this bunch of flowers in the foreground gives the picture depth, and removing them would be a shame. Further, since you can see *some* details in the flower petals, the damage is repairable.

8

FIGURE 8-15   A picture with interest and depth—and a really ugly flash reflection.

To correct this image, follow these steps:

1. Select the portion of the image you want to correct. I actually selected the first white area of the flowers only, and added the second white area to it, leaving me with just the two white areas to work on.

You may want to use the techniques discussed in the previous section to add a yellow tint to the white area, making the flowers even less distracting.

2. Choose Enhance | Adjust Brightness/Contrast | Brightness/Contrast to open the Brightness/Contrast dialog box:

3. Reduce the brightness to take the edge off the white flare, and bump up the contrast a bit to bring out the details in the petals. The result is visible in Figure 8-16.

Use the Paint Bucket to Fill an Area

The paint bucket is a tool you can use to fill an area with either the foreground color or a pattern. As described in Chapter 5, you can configure the paint bucket to set the blending mode (in the Mode drop-down list), opacity, and tolerance (how closely a color must match the selected color in order to be replaced), whether the fill is anti-aliased (by using the Anti-aliased check box), and whether the fill is limited to adjacent areas (by using the Contiguous check box). You can further limit the range of the paint bucket by selecting an area prior to using the paint bucket.

To fill an area with the foreground color, select Foreground from the Fill drop-down list in the options bar. Click the color in the image that you want to replace.

FIGURE 8-16   The reduction in the intensity of the white makes this a better picture.

8

Don't forget that you can click the foreground color at the bottom of the toolbar to open the Color Picker and choose a different foreground color.

Of somewhat more use is the ability to fill an area with a pattern. For example, take a look at Figure 8-17. The sky shows no detail due to a strong overcast. To correct this situation, you could fill the sky with a blue pattern or even a cloud pattern.

If you do want to use a cloud pattern, you'll have to create one yourself, as Photoshop Elements doesn't include one.

To fill an area with a pattern, select Pattern from the Fill drop-down list. You can then pick the pattern you want from the Pattern palette (click the Pattern drop-down list to display the palette). Click the area you want to fill with the pattern—the result is visible in Figure 8-18. Note that in the example image, I used the Magnetic Lasso tool to limit the effect to just the sky area, as the paint bucket had a tendency to "spill over" into the ocean portion of the image. You can lower the tolerance to control the spill-over, but small areas of the sky might not get filled in.

FIGURE 8-17   You can use a pattern fill to correct this featureless sky.

FIGURE 8-18   This image now has a much more interesting sky.

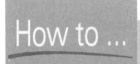

Perform a Fill with the Fill Command

Photoshop Elements enables you to perform a fill using the Edit | Fill command. Unlike the paint bucket, you must make a selection *before* doing the fill or the fill will cover the entire image. Choosing Edit | Fill displays the Fill dialog box:

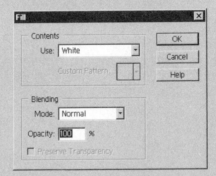

The first step is to choose what you want to use for a fill. The options in the Use drop-down list are:

Foreground Color   Fills with the foreground color.

Background Color   Fills with the background color.

Pattern   Fills with a pattern. Pick the pattern you want from the Custom Pattern drop-down list (palette). You can use the palette menu to change how patterns are displayed, as well as load new sets of patterns.

Black   Fills with black.

50% Gray   Fills with a medium gray.

White   Fills with white.

In the Blending portion of the dialog box, choose the blending mode (from the Mode drop-down list) and the opacity. Click OK to fill the selected portion of the image.

Use the Gradient Tool to Recolor an Object

The Gradient tool enables you to apply gradients of color to an image. You can easily achieve a surreal effect on water, or simulate a sunset, as shown in Figure 8-19.

To apply a gradient, select and configure the gradient, then click and drag a line across the area to which you want to apply the gradient. The portion of the selected area across which you drew the line is rendered by using the gradient. Depending on the type of gradient you selected, the area outside where you drew the line gets either the gradient's starting color or the gradient's ending color. For example, if you choose a linear blue-yellow-green gradient and draw a line from top to bottom, the area above the starting point of the line is blue, while the area below the ending point of the line is green:

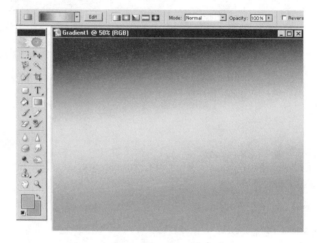

If, instead, you chose a radial gradient, the area where you drew the line is rendered in a radial gradient, and the area outside the line is green:

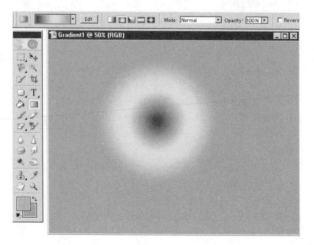

FIGURE 8-19   Although this picture was shot in mid-afternoon, I was able to apply sunset colors using the Gradient tool. A color version of this image is provided in the color section of this book.

You have a great deal of control in how you apply a gradient (and even more control if you build the gradient yourself, as discussed later in this chapter). You can choose the gradient color scheme, the type of gradient, the blending mode, and opacity (as with other tools), and whether to apply dither and the transparency mask.

Select a Gradient

Once you have chosen the Gradient tool from the toolbox, click the down-arrow alongside the gradient palette to display it. Then choose the gradient to use:

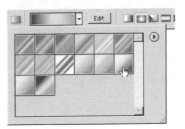

As with other palettes, you can use the palette menu (click the arrow button in the right border of the palette) to change how gradients are displayed, load new sets of gradients, replace the current set of gradients with a new set, reset the gradients to their defaults, and open the Preset Manager. You can also select a gradient and rename it (by choosing Rename Gradient) or delete it (by choosing Delete Gradient).

Select the Gradient Type

Photoshop Elements enables you to use five different types of gradients: linear gradient, radial gradient, angle gradient, reflected gradient, and diamond gradient. You choose the type of gradient by clicking one of the five icons alongside the Edit button in the options bar. Figure 8-20 shows samples of each type of gradient.

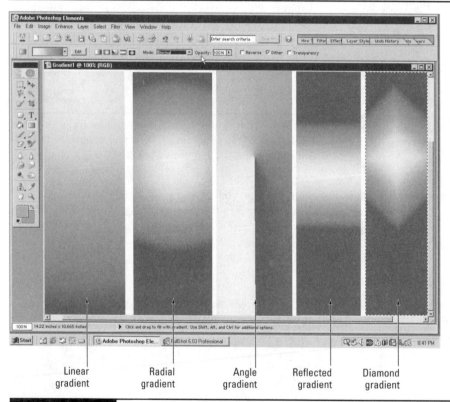

| Linear gradient | Radial gradient | Angle gradient | Reflected gradient | Diamond gradient |

FIGURE 8-20 Samples of each of the five types of gradients.

Set the Gradient Check Boxes

Photoshop Elements provides three check boxes to fine-tune how the Gradient tool works. They are:

Reverse   When this option is selected, the effect of the gradient is reversed. For example, if you select a blue-to-green gradient and check the Reverse check box, Photoshop Elements will render the gradient green-to-blue.

Dither   When this option is selected, dithering is used to smooth color gradient transitions and avoid noticeable banding.

Transparency   A gradient is actually defined by two masks. The *color mask* defines where the start and end color for each color transition is located in the gradient, and how the start color transitions into the end color. The *transparency mask* defines the start and end points for opacity in the gradient. That is, you can set an opacity start point at the beginning of the gradient that is 75% opaque, fading to a middle opacity point that is 50% opaque, and then increasing to 100% opaque at the opacity end point. You can set as many of these opacity points as you wish, varying the opacity up and down across the entire gradient. By checking the Transparency check box, Photoshop Elements will use the transparency mask, varying the opacity of the gradient according to these instructions. If you clear the Transparency check box, the transparency mask is ignored. Note that the transparency mask is in addition to the setting of the Opacity control in the options bar. That is, if you set the opacity in the transparency mask to be 50% opaque, setting the Opacity control in the options bar to 100% will still provide only 50% opacity. On the other hand, if you set the Opacity control in the options bar to 50%, the overall effect will be 25% opacity.

Use the Gradient Map to Recolor an Object

You can apply a "grayscale" gradient by using the gradient map. The effect of this gradient is quite different from the Gradient tool. The gradient map applies the gradient to the selected area, replacing the existing colors with the gradient colors according to the brightness of the original colors. Bright colors are replaced with colors from the right end of the gradient, while dark colors are replaced by colors from the left end of the gradient. For example, the sky scene in Figure 8-21 was replaced using a yellow-pink-purple pastel gradient, resulting in a deep evening sky because the original bright sky was replaced with the purples at the right end of the gradient. Of course, I'll probably want to do something about the bright sunlight shining off the water!

FIGURE 8-21   A bright sky becomes evening with the appropriate gradient.

To use the gradient map, choose Image | Adjustments | Gradient Map. This opens the Gradient Map dialog box:

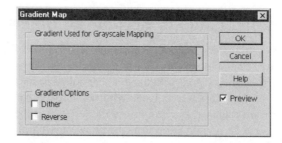

From this dialog box, you can select the gradient to use by making a selection from the Gradient Used For Grayscale Mapping, as well as choose whether to use dithering (by checking the Dither check box) or to reverse the gradient (by checking the Reverse check box).

Create a Smooth Custom Gradient

Although Photoshop Elements provides a wide variety of gradients, you may find that you need to build your own. To create your own smooth gradient, follow these steps:

1. Choose the Gradient tool and click the Edit button in the options bar. This displays the Gradient Editor dialog box, as shown in Figure 8-22.

2. Make sure the gradient type is set to smooth and choose an existing gradient as the starting point. You can pick one of the gradients available in the Presets area of the dialog box, or load a new set of gradients by clicking the Load button and choosing a gradient file to add to the list of available gradients. As with other palette-type tools, you can use the palette menu to pick a set of gradients to load or replace, reset the list of available gradients to the defaults, and change how the gradients are displayed (Small or Large thumbnail, small or large list, or text only).

3. Set the smoothness by typing a number (between 0 and 100) into the Smoothness field or using the Smoothness slider control. This quantity controls how smoothly the colors blend together in the gradient.

8

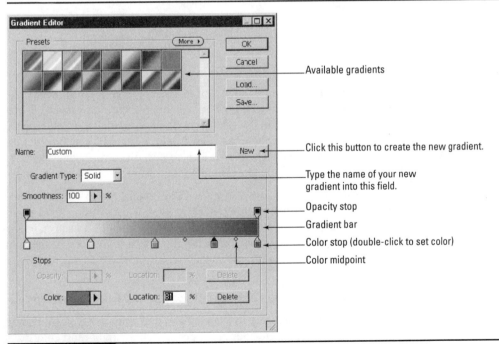

FIGURE 8-22   Build a new gradient using the Gradient Editor dialog box.

If you want to start your gradient "from scratch," remove the color stops and opacity stops from the gradient. To do so, click and drag a stop away from the gradient bar, or click a stop and then click the Delete button. You can't delete all the stops; you must leave at least two color stops and two opacity stops.

4. Position the left-most color stop by clicking and dragging it or typing a number (between 0 and 100) into the Location field. The gradient begins at the position of the left-most color stop. Thus, if you don't position the color stop at the left end of the gradient bar, everything to the left of the color stop will be the color you specify in the next step. You can see this situation here (the left-most color stop is positioned about a third of the way from the left end of the gradient bar):

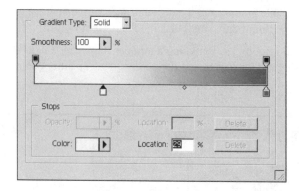

5. Specify the color of the left-most color stop. There are three ways to specify the color. The first way is to move the mouse pointer over the image (it turns into an eyedropper) and click the color you want to use. The second way is to click the Color rectangle or double-click the color stop, choose the color from the Color Picker, and click OK to return to the Gradient Editor. The third way is to click the arrow alongside the Color rectangle and choose either the foreground or color from the drop-down menu.

6. Add any intermediate color stops you want. For example, if you want the gradient to go from red to yellow to orange, you'll need an intermediate color stop (the left stop is red, the intermediate stop is yellow, and the right stop is orange). To add an intermediate color stop, position the mouse pointer below the gradient bar and click. Use the instructions in step 4 to set the location of the intermediate color stop, and the instructions in step 5 to set the color.

7. Continue adding intermediate color stops to add any additional colors to the gradient.

8. Position the right-most color stop by clicking and dragging it or typing a number into the Location field. The gradient ends at the position of the right-most color stop. Thus, if you don't position the color stop at the right end of the gradient bar, everything to the right of the color stop will be the color of the right-most color stop.

9. Use the instructions from step 5 to set the color of the right-most color stop.

10. For each pair of color stops, set the position of the color midpoint. Photoshop Elements displays each color midpoint as a small diamond below the gradient bar when you click a color stop. The color midpoints indicate the point at which the gradient is an even mix of the two color-stop colors. To position the color midpoint, click and drag the midpoint or type a number into the Location field. Here is what the gradient bar looks like with a red-yellow-orange gradient:

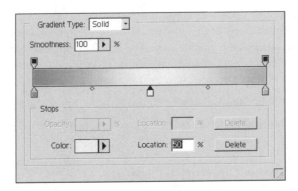

8

11. Position the left-most opacity stop by clicking and dragging it, or typing a number into the Location field. The Opacity gradient starts at the left-most opacity stop. Thus, if you don't position the opacity stop at the left end of the gradient bar, everything to the left of the opacity stop will have the opacity you specify in the next step.

12. Specify the opacity of the left-most opacity stop. You can either type a number into the Opacity field, or use the Opacity slider control. If you specify an opacity that is less than 100%, Photoshop Elements displays a checkerboard grid "showing through" the color to simulate the opacity:

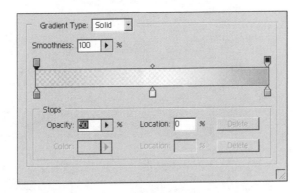

13. Add any intermediate opacity stops you want. For example, if you want the opacity to go from 100% (on the left) to 50% (in the middle) and back to 100% (on the right), you'll need an intermediate opacity stop set to 50%.

14. Position the right-most opacity stop by clicking and dragging it or typing a number into the Location field. The Opacity gradient ends at the position of the right-most opacity stop. Thus, if you don't position the opacity stop at the right end of the gradient bar, everything to the right of the opacity stop will be the opacity of the right-most opacity stop.

15. Use the instructions from step 12 to set the opacity of the right-most opacity stop.

16. For each pair of opacity stops, set the position of the opacity midpoint. Photoshop Elements displays each opacity midpoint as a small diamond above the gradient bar when you click the opacity stop. The opacity stops indicate the "halfway point" in opacity between the two opacity stops. To position the opacity midpoint, click and drag it, or type a number into the Location field.

17. Select the text in the Name field, and type the new name of your gradient into the field.

18. Click the New button to create the new gradient.

Create a Noise Custom Gradient

You can use the Gradient Editor dialog box to define a noise gradient. A noise gradient is a gradient that contains randomly distributed colors that fall within the range of colors you specify. To define a new noise gradient, choose the Gradient tool, click the Edit button to display the Gradient Editor, and choose Noise from the Gradient Type drop-down list:

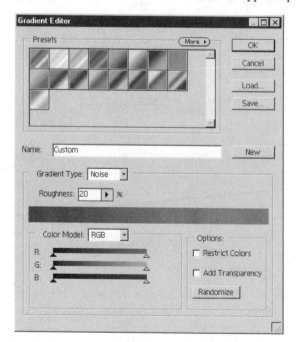

Set the following parameters in the Gradient Editor dialog box to achieve the result you want:

Roughness Adjust the roughness to control the amount of noise in the gradient. At low levels of roughness, the transitions between colors are relatively smooth. At high levels of roughness, the color transitions are more jarring. The previous graphic showed a low level of roughness; this one shows a much higher level:

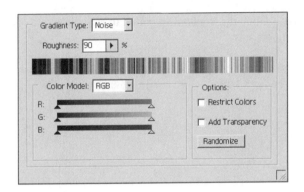

Color model Set the color model you want to use from the Color Model drop-down list. Choose RGB to specify the range of colors to include in the gradient using red, green, and blue. Choose HSB to specify the range of color to include in the gradient using hue, saturation, and brightness. Depending on which color model you choose, Photoshop Elements provides either controls for setting red, green, and blue (RGB); or hue, saturation, and brightness (HSB).

8

It is much easier to specify the gradient using HSB because you normally want to limit the gradient to a specific set of hues (such as blues), and allow the gradient to vary across saturation and brightness for those hues.

Specify the color range Each of the three bars in the Color Model section of the dialog box has two controls that determine the range of allowed colors in the gradient. Drag the black pointer and the clear pointer to limit the range. For example, here is a gradient that is limited to blue hues (H), a wide range of saturation (S), and just the bright colors (B):

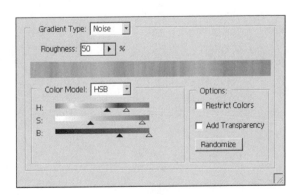

Restrict colors   Check the Restrict Color check box to use only muted colors—that is, to tone down the amount of saturation in the gradient colors.

Add transparency   By default, the colors in a noise gradient are fully opaque (although you can adjust the opacity of the gradient when you apply it to an image). However, if you check the Add Transparency check box, a random amount of transparency is added to the gradient.

Randomize   Click the Randomize button to step through a variety of randomly generated gradient patterns.

Once you have the noise gradient specified the way you want, specify the name in the Name field and click the New button to create the gradient.

Chapter 9

Create and Manage Layers

How to...

- Create new layers
- Understand the different kinds of layers
- Manage layers with the Layers palette
- Turn layers on and off
- Vary the layer opacity
- Link and group layers
- Control layer effects with a mask
- Build a mask using a gradient
- Manually modify a mask

When you first bring an image into Photoshop Elements, it consists of a single layer—the image you see on the screen. Up to this point in this book, I have been making changes to this single layer—touching it up with the Brush tool, changing the brightness and contrast, adjusting the color, and so on. Provided you don't undo a change, a change becomes permanent when you save the file. For example, if you select the sky in an image, decrease the brightness, and save the result, you have no way to return to the original state of the image.

Understand What Layers Can Do

The layers feature enables you to apply corrections and add objects to an image without changing the base image. Each layer is an independent part of the picture, and you can make adjustments to a layer without affecting other layers or the original image (which I will now refer to as the *background*). In my example, I can create a layer that applies a brightness and contrast correction to just the sky portion of the image. I can hide the layer in order to view the original image (background), fine-tune the brightness/contrast correction as much and as often as I want, and adjust the opacity of the layer to increase or decrease the effect. I can then save the file as either a Photoshop Element file (PSD) or a TIFF file, and the next time I open the file, the layers are still there, ready for me to use. Figure 9-1 shows the image I am discussing. Note the Layers palette, which shows two layers—the background (original image) and a layer for the brightness/contrast adjustment.

A good way to think about layers is as sheets of clear plastic, stacked on top of each other. Where there is no image *on* a layer (or the layer is less than 100% opaque), you can see "down" through the layer to the layers (including the background) below. This is illustrated by Figure 9-2, where the objects present on various layers stack up to form the entire image. You can change the stacking order to change the composition.

FIGURE 9-1   A landscape with the sky adjusted using a layer.

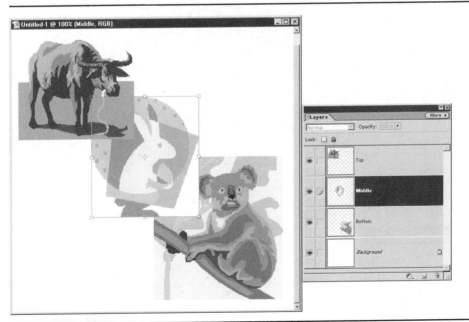

FIGURE 9-2   The overall image is a combination of the objects on all the layers.

You can also mask the effect of a layer. That is, you can specify that a correction layer (such as the brightness/contrast correction in Figure 9-1) applies to only a portion of the image. If you look closely at the layer thumbnail for the top layer in Figure 9-1, you can see a white area that is the shape of the sky, and a black area that is the shape of the foreground. Masking the effect of layer allows the correction to apply to just the white area—the sky—and hides the effect for the black area (the foreground).

View and Use the Layers Palette

The Layers palette (see Figure 9-3) is your "control panel" for working with layers. You can do most of what you need with layers by using the Layers palette, including creating and deleting layers, rearranging them, and adjusting their properties. You can also use the Layers menu to perform many of these tasks. I'll cover what these operations are throughout the rest of this chapter.

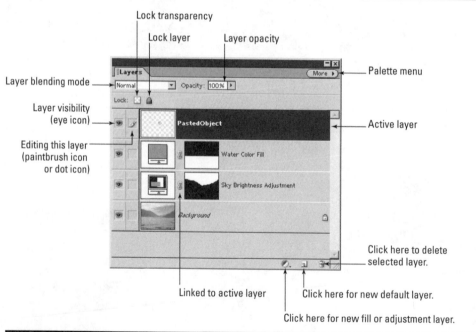

Use the Layers palette to work with layers.

Modify Layer Opacity

You can control the opacity of each layer, from invisible (0% opacity) to fully opaque (100% opacity) by using the Opacity control in the Layers palette. The opacity of the layer interacts with the opacity of any object on the layer. For example, if you create an object layer that has an opacity of 50%, then place an object on the layer that has an opacity of 100%, the object will have a total opacity of 50% because that is all the layer can handle.

The Opacity control is grayed out and unavailable if you are working with the background layer, since the background layer is always fully opaque (100% opacity).

Modify the Layer Blending Mode

In Chapter 5, we discussed the blending modes you can use when modifying an image using one of the brush tools. The full range of these blending modes is available when working with layers—just choose the mode you want from the drop-down list in the upper-left corner of the Layers palette:

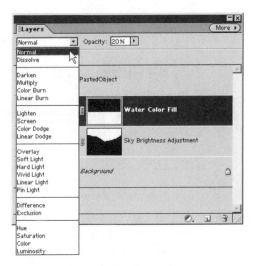

Thus, you can create a color fill layer, set it to a low opacity, and choose a subtle blending mode such as soft light.

The blending Mode drop-down list is unavailable if you are working on the background layer, since the background is the starting point for blending with other layers.

Change Layer Visibility

It can be helpful to hide or show the effects of a layer temporarily. For example, you might want to adjust the brightness on an adjustment layer without the color tint of a low-opacity color fill layer. The far-left column (layer visibility) for each layer controls whether the layer is visible. If the eye icon is visible, the layer is visible. If the eye icon is hidden, the layer is not visible. To change the visibility of a layer, simply click the layer visibility control to turn the eye icon on or off.

ALT-click the eye icon to show just that layer. ALT-click again to turn on the visibility of all layers.

Lock or Unlock a Layer

You can protect the contents of a layer from accidental modification by locking the layer. When a layer is locked, a small lock icon appears on the layer in the Layers palette:

There are two levels of lock protection: transparency lock and full lock.

Transparency lock   When a layer's transparency is locked, you can only paint or edit those areas of the layer that already contain pixels. You can, therefore, change the color of an object, but you cannot add a new object to the layer. To toggle the transparency lock, check or clear the Lock Transparency control in the Layers palette. Photoshop Elements displays a hollow lock in the layer when the transparency is locked.

Full lock   When a layer is fully locked, you cannot edit the layer, change the opacity or blending mode, move the image, delete the layer, or apply a layer style to the layer (see Chapter 10). You *can* change the stacking order of a locked layer. Photoshop Elements displays a solid lock in the layer when the layer is fully locked.

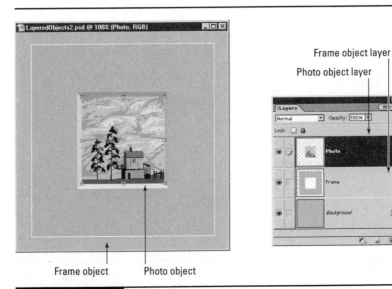

Frame object layer

Photo object layer

Frame object   Photo object

FIGURE 9-4   A photograph and its frame are actually two separate, stacked layers.

Rearrange the Layer Stacking Order

As mentioned earlier, the order of the layers is important. For example, here is an image that contains a colored background layer and two objects. Initially, the landscape object is positioned above the frame object. You can see how that looks in both the image and the Layers palette in Figure 9-4.

We can rearrange the stacking order of the two layers, but not the background. If, for example, you position the frame layer above the photo layer, you can immediately see the difference, as in Figure 9-5. The frame now hides the photo.

The easiest way to change the stacking order of layers is to click and drag a layer in the Layers palette:

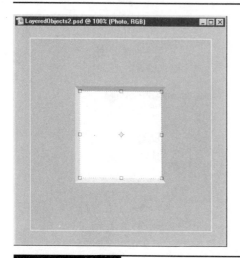

FIGURE 9-5 Changing the order of the layers changes how the image looks.

When the highlighted line appears in the desired position relative to the other layers, release the mouse button.

You can also change the stacking order by using the Layer | Arrange submenus. Choose the layer you want to move up or down, and then one of these menu items:

Bring to Front Makes the selected layer the top-most layer.

Bring Forward Moves the selected layer up one layer in the stacking order.

Send Backward Moves the selected layer down one layer in the stacking order. However, the selected layer cannot move behind the background; the background is always the bottom layer.

Send to Back Makes the selected layer the bottom-most layer except for the background layer.

 *You cannot change the stacking order of the background layer; it is always the bottom layer.*

Choose the Layer to Work On

You can work on only one layer at a time—the layer you are working on is referred to as the active layer. The easiest way to choose the active layer is to click it in the Layers palette. As was shown in Figure 9-3, the active layer is highlighted, and also displays a paintbrush icon (for object layers) or a dot icon (for adjustment or fill layers) in the second column from the left.

Another way to select a layer is to use the Move tool, provided you have checked the Auto Select Layer option in the options bar. When you click an item, the layer that contains the item automatically becomes the active layer. For example, I had the background layer set as the active layer. I then clicked the photo object, which automatically made the layer containing it the active layer:

If you have many objects stacked on top of each other, it may be difficult to use the Move tool as described previously to select the object and its layer. In this circumstance, you have yet another way to choose the active layer—choose the Move tool and right-click an object to display the context menu. The context menu displays a list of all layers that contain pixels at the clicked location. All you need to do is choose the layer you want from the context menu:

Rename a Layer

However you create a layer, Photoshop Elements provides a default name for the layer. The default name is usually something fairly uninspired, like Layer 1 or Color Fill 1. It is advisable to name the layers to indicate what they do, or to give an indication of their purpose. You have three ways you can rename a layer. The first way is to choose Layer | Rename Layer. This opens the Layer Properties dialog box, where you can type the layer name into the Name field:

Another way to rename the layer is to use the Layers palette. Right-click the layer's name in the Layers palette and choose Rename Layer or choose Rename Layer from the palette menu. Either of these actions opens the Layer Properties dialog box where you can type in a new layer name. Finally, you can double-click the name of the layer to make it editable, and type in the new name.

Group Layers Together

You can group layers together to allow the bottom-most layer (called the "base layer") to provide a mask for the other layers in the group. That is, the base layer defines the visible boundaries of all layers in the group. All layers in the group take on the blending mode and opacity of the base layer. For example, the background is filled with a color, the second layer contains a solid-color-filled oval, and the layer above it contains a photo. If you then group the photo layer with the oval layer, only the portions of the photo that overlay the oval would be visible, as shown in Figure 9-6.

 *You can group layers only if they are adjacent to each other in the Layers palette. As you group layers, the bottom-most layer is set automatically as the base layer.*

To group layers, you can use any of the following methods:

- Select a layer and choose Layer | Group With Previous. Once layers are grouped, you can ungroup them by selecting one of the grouped layers and choosing Layer | Ungroup.

- Hold down the ALT key and move the mouse pointer over the intersection between the two layers you want to group. The mouse pointer turns into two overlapping circles (see the illustration on the following page); click to link the two layers.

Adjusting color cast for your images can easily create a whole new look (see Chapter 4 for more details on color cast).

This image was taken through tinted glass and shows a strong color cast.

The color cast was removed by clicking an area that should have been white after choosing Enhance | Adjust Color | Color Cast.

Repairing a badly faded, damaged photograph is
well within your reach with Photoshop Elements.

This original photo, shown here before
any modification, is badly faded and
has apparently lost much detail.

After using layers along with color and brightness adjustments, I restored most of the
original brightness of this image.

You can apply effects to particular areas of images to greatly change their look. As shown here, you can apply a gradient and control which part of the image is affected using the available selection tools.

This peaceful beach scene could look much more interesting if it had been shot later in the day.

A transparent gradient was applied to just the selected sky section to make the modified sky look like it was shot at sunset.

You can use color tints and the Brightness/Contrast adjustment layer tools to make a picture taken in the morning look like it was taken in the late afternoon light instead.

The colors in this photo are biased toward blue because of the morning light.

The sky is darker and the landscape colors are now warmer. Each layer effect (darkened sky and tinted landscape) was limited to the appropriate area with a mask on that layer. The Fill Color layer uses a low opacity to limit the amount of color.

You can add effects to specific portions of images to change the time of day, the weather and other details. In these images, a snowstorm was added against a tinted sky where the original image showed only a snowcapped peak using layer styles. Snow was applied to the whole image as well as a Gray/Green for the sky, and masking was used to control the portions of the image affected.

This original image shows a snow-covered peak —if only it had been snowing at the moment I took the picture this could be more visually interesting.

Now the image shows a tinted darkened sky (with pink clouds) on a layer, and a Brightness/Contrast layer with a Snow layer style adds the look of a snowy day. Brrrr.

You can add interesting effects to any of your photos using feathered selections, fills, and layers, and can create a vignette of a portrait as shown here.

The original picture could benefit from a vignette to highlight the subject.

Using the Oval Marquee with a lot of feathering, I selected the subject, inverted the selection, and filled the result with a color.

In this image, I added a custom shape to its own layer, CTRL-clicked the shape to create a selection, inverted the selection, switched to the background, and filled the selection.

After selecting with the Oval Marquee (with feathering) and inverting the selection, I created a Brightness/Contrast layer and darkened the edges of the image.

The Filter Gallery, part 1

The original portrait.

Adding texture with the Texturizer filter set to Canvas.

The same portrait with the background converted to Conté Crayon.

Applying Paint Daubs to a woodsy scene.

A Spanish vegetable market modified with the Crystallize filter.

Applying Underpainting to an
image of the Norfolk docks.

Rough pastels applied to the same image.

The Filter Gallery, part 3

Applying Solarize gives an eerie glow to a scene.

The same image with the Stained Glass filter.

And one last trick with this image: the Difference Clouds filter.

NOTE *Repeat this action to ungroup a pair of layers.*

■ When you first create a layer, check the Group With Previous Layer check box in the New Layer dialog box (see the following section for more details).

9

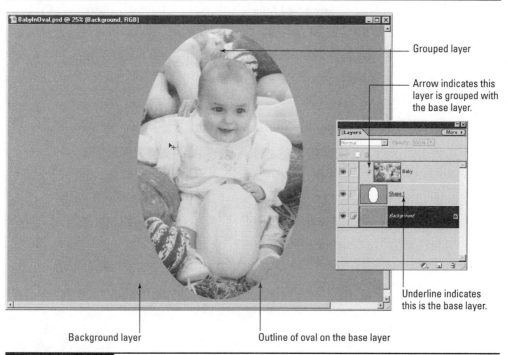

Grouped layer

Arrow indicates this layer is grouped with the base layer.

Underline indicates this is the base layer.

Background layer   Outline of oval on the base layer

FIGURE 9-6   The base layer masks the rest of the grouped layers.

Delete a Layer

Occasionally, you'll get a layer you don't need anymore. To get rid of a layer, you can:

- Right-click the layer and choose Delete Layer from the shortcut menu.
- Click and drag the layer to the trashcan icon in the Layers palette.
- Select the layer and click the trashcan icon in the Layers palette.
- Select the layer and choose Delete Layer from the palette menu.
- Select the layer and choose Layer | Delete Layer.

If you decide you no longer need hidden layers (click the eye icon to hide a layer and make it invisible), you can delete all hidden layers in one operation. Choose Delete Hidden Layers from the Layers palette menu.

You can also delete a set of linked layers, as described in "Link Layers Together to Control Them as One," later in this chapter.

Duplicate a Layer

It can be handy to duplicate an existing layer. For example, you might create a Hue/Saturation layer masked for the top portion of an image, then duplicate the layer, modify it slightly (perhaps to compensate for an underexposed foreground), and mask it for the bottom of the image.

To duplicate a layer, you can do any of the following:

- Right-click the layer and choose Duplicate Layer from the shortcut menu.
- Select the layer and choose Duplicate Layer from the palette menu.
- Select the layer and choose Layer | Duplicate Layer.

Photoshop Elements displays the Duplicate Layer dialog box:

Fill in the name of the duplicate layer in the As field. You can add the duplicate layer to any open image by choosing the filename from the Document drop-down list. You can also choose New from the Document drop-down list and fill in the name of a new document to create and add the layer to.

Copy a Layer to a New Image

If you create a layer you want to use in another image, you can copy the layer from the original image to the new image. To do so, open both images in Photoshop Elements and click the source image to select it. Follow either of these two steps:

Drag and drop from the Layers palette   Click and drag the layer you want to copy from the Layers palette of the source image to the target image.

Drag and drop the layer   Click and drag the contents of the source layer (it helps if you have the bounding box turned on) from the source image to the target image.

If the source image and the target image have different resolutions, the pasted data retains its original pixel dimensions. The pasted layer can be too large or too small in the target image. Thus, it is best to use Image | Resize | Image Size to adjust the resolutions of the two images so they match.

9

Create New Layers

Before you can work with layers, you must create them. There are three types of layers you can build: adjustment layers, fill layers, and object layers. In addition, you can convert the background layer to a "regular" layer, giving you more flexibility.

If you want to limit the effect of a layer to a specific area, select that area prior to creating the layer. Doing so creates a mask. This topic is covered in detail in "Use a Mask to Control Layer Effects," later in this chapter.

Create a New Fill Layer

A fill layer (as the name implies) enables you to create a layer that you can fill with a solid color, a gradient, or a pattern. In the case of a solid color or pattern layer, the layer hides everything underneath it unless you reduce the opacity.

To create a new fill layer, choose Layer | New Fill Layer, then select one of the three types of fill layers from the submenu. Alternatively, you can click the Create New Fill or Adjustment Layer button at the bottom of the Layers palette (it looks like a half-filled circle), then select one of the top three options:

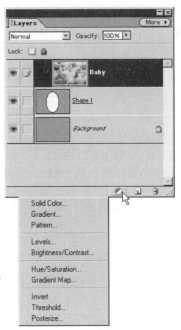

If you create a layer using the Layer menu, Photoshop Elements displays the New Layer dialog box, shown in Figure 9-7.

From the New Layer dialog box, you can set the basic properties of the layer, including the name, blending mode (from the Mode drop-down list), and opacity. You can also check the Group With Previous Layer check box to group this new layer with the previous layer you created.

Once you click OK to close the New Layer dialog box, Photoshop Elements provides the dialog boxes you need to set the properties specific to the layer. For example, you can set the fill color for the color fill layer. The specifics of creating each new type of fill layer is covered in the next few sections.

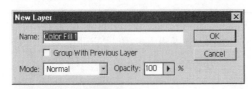

FIGURE 9-7   Use the New Layer dialog box to fill in basic layer properties.

NOTE   *If you create a layer using the Create New Fill or Adjustment Layer button, Photoshop Elements skips the New Layer dialog box, giving the layer a default name and proceeding straight to the Properties dialog box for that layer type.*

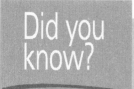

Once you create a layer, you can change how the layer works. In the Layers palette, double-click the Layer thumbnail to reopen the dialog box you used to configure the layer in the first place. You can also select Layer | Layer Content Options. For example, if you double-click on the Layer thumbnail for a solid color fill layer, Photoshop Elements reopens the Color Picker so you can choose another color. If you can't see the Layer thumbnail, choose the Palette Options command from the Layers palette menu, and then choose any thumbnail option other than None.

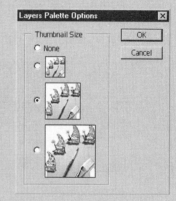

You can change the layer content altogether by choosing Layer | Change Layer Content and choosing the new layer type from the submenu. Thus, if you want to change a solid color layer to a gradient layer, it is easy to do so.

Create a New Solid Color Fill Layer

Once you create a solid color fill layer, Photoshop Elements displays the Color Picker so you can choose the fill color. This is the standard Color Picker, in which you can specify a color using the Color bar and Color field; the Hue, Saturation, and Brightness (HSB) fields; or the Red, Green, and Blue (RGB) fields.

Create a New Gradient Fill Layer

Once you create a gradient layer, Photoshop Elements displays the Gradient Fill dialog box:

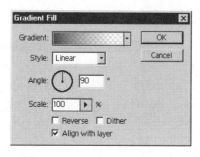

Working with a gradient fill layer is very similar to using the Gradient tool. Almost all the options you used with the Gradient tool appear in the Gradient Fill dialog box. You can choose a gradient by clicking the Gradient drop-down list. This displays the Gradient palette, which works exactly as we discussed previously.

The Style drop-down list presents the same gradient types available for the Gradient tool: linear, radial, angle, reflected, and diamond. You can adjust the angle of the gradient by either modifying the Angle icon (click and drag the line in the circle) or typing an angle into the adjacent field.

The Scale option enables you to set the size of the gradient. A small scale value limits the gradient to a small part of the layer, filling the balance of the layer with either the beginning color or the ending color of the gradient. A large scale value fills more of the layer with the gradient. For example, here are linear gradients with a small scale value (on the left) and a large scale value (on the right):

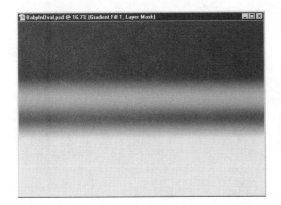 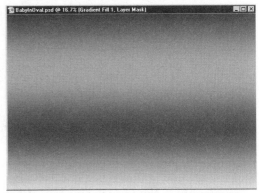

The three check boxes enable you to reverse the gradient (Reverse), dither the gradient to avoid banding (Dither), and scale the gradient to the size of any bounding box you create (Align with Layer). That is, say you create a rectangular selection (with the Rectangular Marquee) prior to creating the layer. If you check Align with Layer, Photoshop Elements scales the gradient to fit in the rectangle. If you *don't* check this check box, the gradient will be sized to fit the entire image—but you'll see only the portion that fits inside the rectangular mask.

Create a New Pattern Fill Layer

Once you create a pattern fill layer, Photoshop Elements displays the Pattern Fill dialog box:

Working with a pattern fill is very similar to using the paint bucket with a pattern. You can choose the pattern from the pattern palette that appears when you click the pattern drop-down list. The Scale option enables you to set the size of the pattern by scaling the pixels in the pattern.

The Link With Layer option is interesting, but only has an effect if you use a selection tool to create a mask in the layer. If you check the Link With Layer check box and then use the Move tool to drag the masked pattern around the layer, the pattern moves as if it is part of the shape. If you don't check the check box, the masked shape appears to scroll over a fixed background pattern. Of course, the pattern is no longer aligned to the shape if you do this. To realign the pattern to the shape so that the pattern starts at the upper-left corner of the shape, click the Snap To Origin button.

Create a New Adjustment Layer

Adjustment layers enable you to correct color, brightness, and contrast without impacting the image itself. The corrections reside in the layer, and you can adjust the strength of the adjustment by varying the opacity, as well as temporarily turning off the visibility of the adjustment layer. If you change your mind about making the adjustment—or want to start over—simply delete the adjustment layer, and the adjustment goes with it. You don't need to mess with undo, or reload the original image and start over. In fact, layers are so powerful in this regard that I never make corrections to an image without using adjustment layers.

To create an adjustment layer, select Layer | New Adjustment Layer and choose one of the seven types of adjustment layers from the submenu. Or, you can click the Create New Fill or Adjustment Layer button at the bottom of the Layers palette (it looks like a half-filled circle), then select one of the bottom seven options:

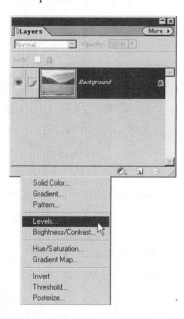

As with fill layers, when you create an adjustment layer using the Layer menu, Photoshop Elements provides the New Layer dialog box as shown in Figure 9-7. It enables you to name the layer, group it, set the blending mode, and the opacity.

The adjustment layers use controls that you've explored already. For example, the Levels adjustment layer enables you to use the Levels dialog box (discussed in Chapter 4) to make brightness and contrast corrections.

For more information on using the dialog boxes for these adjustment layers, see Chapter 4.

The adjustment layers you can use are:

Levels   Enables you to use the Levels dialog box to adjust input and output levels on each color (red, green, and blue) and the combination of colors. You can independently adjust the shadows, highlights, and midtones, as well as expand or compress the tonal range.

Brightness/Contrast   Enables you to use the Brightness/Contrast dialog box to adjust the brightness and contrast.

Hue/Saturation   Enables you to use the Hue/Saturation dialog box to either adjust all colors (Master) or each of the colors in the color wheel (red, yellow, green, cyan, blue, and magenta). For the selected color, you can change the color (hue), change the amount of color (saturation), and change the lightness.

Gradient Map   Enables you to use the Gradient Map dialog box to choose a gradient for grayscale mapping.

Invert   Inverts the image—that is, turns a positive into a negative:

Threshold   Enables you to use the Threshold dialog box to render the image in pure black and white.

Posterize   Enables you to use the Posterize dialog box to specify the number of available levels in each color channel.

Create a New Layer from the Background

The main image (such as a digital photo you've brought into Photoshop Elements) is normally the background layer. However, there are significant limits to what you can do with the background layer. Because it is always the bottom-most layer, you can't erase parts of it to transparency. You also can't change the blending mode (it is always Normal), and you can't change the opacity (it is always 100%). These limits can cramp your creativity. For example, you want to erase a blank part of the sky, and place a pattern layer underneath the background layer. You can't.

What you *can* do is convert the background layer to a regular layer. After you do that, you can rearrange, erase, and customize the layer just like any other layer. To convert the background layer into a regular layer, either double-click the background layer in the Layers palette or choose Layer | New | Layer From Background. Either way, Photoshop Elements displays the New Layer dialog box. From here you can name the layer, and set the blending mode and opacity. When you click OK, the background layer is converted into a regular layer.

> **TIP**   *If you want to erase the background layer to transparency, simply pick the Background Eraser tool and click the background layer. Photoshop Elements automatically converts the background layer to a regular layer and performs the erasure.*

> **NOTE**   *To convert a layer into the background layer, select the layer and choose Layer | New | Background From Layer. This menu option is not available if there is already a background layer.*

9

Create a New Layer Using Cut and Paste

You can create new layers when you cut or copy an item to the clipboard and then paste it back into the same image or another image. For example, in Figure 9-8, I copied the orange floats and pasted them back into the image, creating a number of layers, each one with a single pasted float on it.

To place an item on the clipboard, select the item using one of the selection tools, and use either Edit | Copy, Edit | Cut, or Edit | Copy Merged. Copy and Cut place the selection from the currently active layer only, and Copy Merged makes a merged copy of all the layers in the selected area.

To paste the contents of the clipboard, use either Edit | Paste or Edit | Paste Into. Paste creates a new layer containing the item.

FIGURE 9-8 Copy and paste items to create new layers containing the pasted objects.

Paste Into works differently. The pasted selection is visible only within the selected area of the target layer. To use Paste Into, follow these steps:

1. Copy the selection to the clipboard.

2. Switch to the layer you want to paste the item into. In this example, the layer already contains an item that had been pasted previously.

3. Select an area in which the item will be visible. In this example, I used the Rectangular Marquee to select the area, and turned off the background to make the results more visible:

4. Make sure the target layer is selected, and choose Edit | Paste Into. The selection is pasted into the layer as a floating selection.

5. Switch to the Move tool, and drag the selection. Any part of the selection that falls outside the selected area becomes invisible. For example, here I have dragged the float partially outside the original rectangular selection area, which is no longer visible:

6. Once you have the selection positioned properly, deselect the pasted image by clicking outside of it. This groups the selection with any other shapes present on the layer. If you leave part of the pasted object outside the originally selected area when you deselect the object, that portion of the object will never be visible:

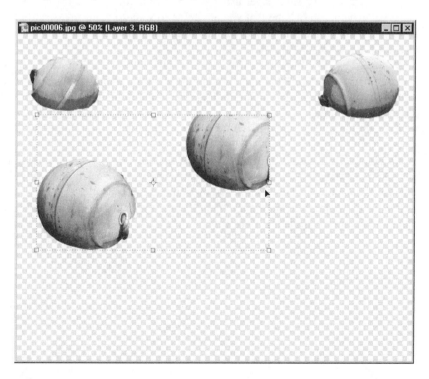

9

If you have the Show Bounding Box option of the Move tool checked, you can see the bounding box that surrounds the items that have been pasted into a layer (it was visible in the last illustration). You can click inside the bounding box and drag the contents to a new location.

 *The bounding box also displays "handles," the small squares located at the corners and in the middle of each side. As we will see in Chapter 11, you can click on one of these handles to activate the Transform tool and stretch, shrink, distort, or rotate the contents of the bounding box.*

Manage and Manipulate Layers

Photoshop Elements provides controls for managing your layers. The controls include linking layers together, merging layers to reduce the size of the file, and simplifying layers to enable editing.

Link Layers Together to Control Them as One

As I mentioned in the previous section, you can move groups of objects as a single object if you paste them into the same layer using Paste Into. Of course, this requires some planning— that is, knowing ahead of time that you are going to want to manage a specific set of objects together. You also can't change your mind and decide to manage the objects on a single layer individually or in smaller groups.

A much more flexible alternative is to link layers together. The first step is to copy and paste items into separate layers, as discussed previously. Next, you link the layers you want to manage together. Finally, click and drag one of the items in a linked layer. All the items in all the linked layers move when you move the selected item. If you decide you need to move one of the objects on a linked layer independently of the other objects, simply unlink its layer.

An example is Figure 9-9, which shows the float picture with three layers (in addition to the background). Each layer contains one float, and I've made each one a different color (via Enhance | Adjust Color | Hue/Saturation) to highlight the layers.

I chose Layer 1 and linked Layer 2 and Layer 3 to it. As you can see in Figure 9-10, the bounding box now encircles all three floats.

Float on Layer 3

Float on Layer 2

Float on Layer 1

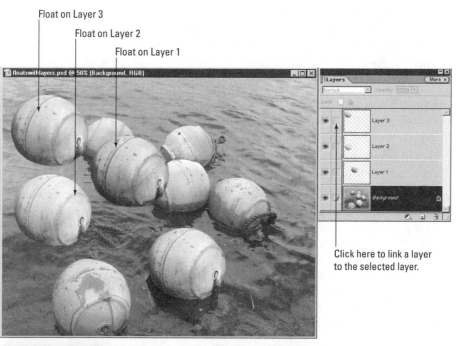

Click here to link a layer
to the selected layer.

FIGURE 9-9   Each different-colored float is on a different layer.

9

FIGURE 9-10   A bounding box encircles all selected layers.

I can then click and drag them together as a single unit.

To link a layer to the selected layer, click in the second column from the left (as indicated in Figure 9-9). The chain link icon indicates that the layer is linked. To unlink a layer, simply click in the second column again, removing the chain link icon.

Once you have linked layers together, you can perform operations on the linked layers as a set. Here is what you can do:

Group linked layers   You can group a set of linked layers by choosing Layer | Group Linked. The bottom-most layer in the linked set becomes the base layer, providing the boundaries for all the other layers in the linked set.

Delete linked layers   You can discard an entire set of linked layers in one operation by choosing Delete Linked Layers from the Layers palette menu.

Merge linked layers   You can convert an entire set of linked layers into a single layer by choosing Merge Linked from the Layers palette menu or Layer | Merge Linked. If you merge multiple layers containing objects, the result is a single layer that contains all the contents of the linked layers. This operation reduces the number of layers, thus making the resulting file smaller. However, there are a couple of caveats to keep in mind. First, if you merge two adjustment layers together (for example, a Hue/Saturation layer and a Brightness/Contrast layer), you can no longer change the layer's adjustment properties. Likewise, if you merge an adjustment layer and an object layer, you can no longer change the adjustment properties, although you *can* still click and drag the object in the layer.

Reduce the Number of Layers

It's easy to go overboard when creating layers, resulting in a complex image that actually gets more difficult to manage. You've already seen how you can merge linked layers together to reduce the number of layers. You can also merge all visible layers, merge two adjacent layers, or remove all layers from the image. Figure 9-9 shows the example I'll use to illustrate merging layers.

Merge All Visible Layers

You can merge all visible layers (including the background layer) into a single layer. To do so, hide all layers you *don't* want to merge by clicking the eye icon to turn it off. Then choose Merge Visible from the Layers palette menu or Layer | Merge Visible. In the example shown on the following page, I hid the background layer and Layer 3, and merged Layers 1 and 2 into a single layer.

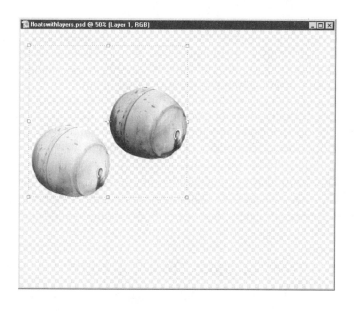

Merge Adjacent Layers

When two layers are adjacent to each other in the Layers palette (as Layers 1 and 2 are in our example), you can merge the upper layer into the lower layer. Simply select the upper layer, and choose Merge Down from the Layers palette menu or Layer | Merge Down.

Remove All Layers

The ultimate layer removal is to remove them all (called "flattening"), leaving you with only the background layer containing the contents of all the removed layers. Here is what it looks like when an image is flattened:

Flattening reduces the size of the file to a minimum by removing all layers. In addition, most file formats (such as the popular JPEG format) do not support layers, so if you try to save a layered file to one of these formats, Photoshop Elements requests your permission to flatten the image first. (You must agree or you can't save the image in that format.) Only the Photoshop (PSD, PDD) and TIFF (TIF) files support layers.

 *Flattening the image discards all hidden layers (those that are not showing the eye icon in the Layers palette). Make sure to unhide all your layers before flattening the image unless you really want to discard the hidden layers.*

 *Unless you are absolutely, positively sure you are never going to need the image layers again, save the flattened file under a different filename, keeping the original (with its layers) available for future modifications.*

Simplify Layers to Make Them Editable

When you create a fill layer (solid color, gradient, or pattern), you can't modify your image by painting on the layer. For example, you can't use the Red Eye brush, Clone Stamp, or Pattern Stamp. And, if you try to use the Brush, Pencil, or Gradient tools, or Image Adjustments such as Invert, Posterize, or Threshold commands, you are actually modifying the layer's *mask*, and *not* the painting on the layer itself. (For more on masks, see "Use a Mask to Control Layer Effects," later in this chapter.) Any filters you apply are also applied to the mask and not to the layer itself.

To paint on or apply a filter to a fill layer, you must first *simplify* the layer. Simplifying the layer converts it to a raster image, and essentially provides a layer that you can paint on just like the background layer.

To simplify a layer, choose Simplify Layer from the Layers palette menu, or select Layer | Simplify Layer.

 *Simplifying a layer so you can paint directly on the layer is very important for Type layers (see Chapter 16) and Shape layers (see Chapter 13). These two kinds of layers are not created using the normal tools for creating new layers (fill layers and adjustment layers). Instead, Photoshop Elements creates a Type layer or a Shape layer automatically when you select one of the type tools or one of the shape tools from the toolbox.*

Sample from All Layers with the Brush Tools

Certain tools sample data as part of their operation. These tools include the Magic Wand, Smudge, Blur, Sharpen, and the Clone Stamp. By default, these tools sample only from the active layer. For example, if you choose the Smudge tool, select an object layer, and click and drag in an area where there is nothing on that layer (that is, you can see the background "through" the object layer), no changes are visible. If, however, you perform a smudge on an area where there are pixels in the selected layer, you will see the smudge effect, as shown in Figure 9-11.

All of the sampling tools have a check box option in the options bar called Use All Layers. Normally, this check box is cleared—as it was in the last example. However, you can check this check box to force the sampling tools to sample pixels from *all* layers, not just the active layer. Not only does checking this option enable you to do things like smudge on the active layer using sampled pixels from another layer (such as the background layer), but it also enables you to sample from one layer and paint on another using the Clone Stamp. This can be very handy because the changes made using the Clone Stamp are then localized to a layer and do *not* affect the background image. Thus, if you change your mind, you can simply discard the modified layer and start over.

Smudge here on the active layer produces a smudge.   Click here to sample all layers.

Smudge here on the background while it is not the active layer produces nothing.

FIGURE 9-11   Using a sampling tool (such as Smudge) produces a result only where the active layer has pixels.

Area where effect of layer is masked.

This dark area represents
the masked area.

Mask thumbnail in
Layers palette.

FIGURE 9-12   Applying a mask to a layer allows you to control where the layer
effects are applied.

Use a Mask to Control Layer Effects

By default, the effects of a fill layer or an adjustment layer are applied to an entire image. For
example, if you create a Brightness/Contrast layer, the entire image is brightened or darkened
to reflect the layer settings. However, that may not be what you want. If the sky is the only
thing that is too bright, you will want to apply the brightness/contrast correction to the sky
only. To limit the effects of a layer to a certain area, you must create a mask. For example,
Figure 9-12 shows an image in which a solid color fill (blue) has been applied with a moderate
opacity so you can still see the background image. You can see a portion of the image where
the color tint has *not* been applied. This area has been masked using one of the techniques I
will cover shortly.

Create a Mask with the Selection Tools

The easiest way to create a mask that limits the effects of a layer is to make a selection *before*
creating the layer. If an area is selected when you create the layer, the effect of the layer is
applied to the selected area only, and masked (not applied) to the balance of the image. For

example, you have an image where the top portion is too bright (overexposed). You want to apply a brightness correction (or perhaps a Levels correction) to just the upper portion of the image. To do so, select only the upper portion using any of the selection tools (or a combination of the tools). Then create the correction layer. As you can see in Figure 9-13 (look at the thumbnail of the mask in the Layers palette), the upper portion of the mask thumbnail is white, indicating the area where the effect of the layer will be applied. The balance of the mask thumbnail is black, indicating the area where the layer will have no effect on the image.

> **TIP** *If the area to which you want to limit the layer is fairly rectangular (such as the entire upper portion of an image), use the Rectangular Marquee selection tool. If the area is irregular but well defined—such as a bright sky against hills or trees—use one of the Lasso selection tools or the Magic Wand.*

Modify a Mask with the Brush Tools

As we saw in the previous section, the mask thumbnail represents masked areas of the layer as black (areas where the layer effect is ignored), and unmasked areas of the layer as white. This is because the layer mask is actually a grayscale image. Where the mask image is black, the effect of the layer is hidden. Where the mask image is white, the layer has its full effect. In areas where the image is a shade of gray, the layer effect is partially applied, depending on the shade of gray. The lighter the shade, the more the layer effect is applied.

9

FIGURE 9-13   The brightness correction will be applied only to the top (selected) portion of this image, as indicated by the mask thumbnail.

You can modify a mask using the Brush tool. Simply select the tool and the layer, and begin painting. As noted, painting in any shade of gray (or black or white) modifies the amount of the layer effect. If you paint in a color, the brightness of the color determines the amount of the layer effect applied.

You can set the brush colors to white (foreground) and black (background) by clicking the Set Current Colors to Black and White button in the lower-left corner of the toolbox. To swap the colors so that the foreground is white and the background is black, click the Switch Foreground and Background Colors button. This button is located just above the upper-right corner of the two color swatches at the bottom of the toolbox.

For example, if you paint in a very dark blue, most of the layer effect will be masked. I created Figure 9-12 using the Brush tool and painting the masked area using black.

If you want to see only the grayscale mask for a layer, ALT-*click the mask thumbnail in the Layers palette.* ALT-*click the mask thumbnail again to revert to the regular view.*

Using one of the brush tools to modify a mask provides several advantages over creating a mask using only the selection tools. The first advantage is that you can "fine-tune" the edges of the selection. If the selection included too much information around the edges—or left out something that should have been included—you can pick a small brush, set it to black (to mask out something) or white (to include something), and simply "paint in" the correction. That is what happened in Figure 9-14. I used the Magnetic Lasso to select the overexposed area at the top of the image before creating the adjustment layer. However, some of the tips of the branches on the left (which were included in the selected area) should be left out of the brightness correction.

After I created the brightness/contrast layer, I used a small brush set to black and painted out the leaves, removing them from the effect supplied by the mask:

I also used a small brush set to white to add the layer effect to the areas between the branches where the layer mask held back the decreased brightness of the layer. You can see these bright areas between the branches in the previous illustration.

These parts of the trees are inside the selected areas.

FIGURE 9-14   The mask created by the selection included too much information around the edges.

Another advantage to using a Brush tool is that the break between the masked area and the unmasked area (or between two areas with different masks) may be too abrupt, showing a distinct line. This is especially true for Brightness/Contrast and Hue/Saturation adjustment layers. This problem is visible in Figure 9-15. If you look closely, you can see the break between the sky and the water.

To feather the change, you can choose a brush, set it to gray and a low opacity, and carefully apply gray to the interface:

 FIGURE 9-15   The abrupt change between the upper and lower portions of the image is a problem.

 Set the brush to use a moderate amount of fade (under the More Options button in the options bar), and drag from the masked part of the image (the lower part in the example) to the unmasked part of the image. This applies less and less gray as you move from the masked to the unmasked part of the image, feathering the abrupt change.

The final advantage to using a Brush tool on a mask is that you can adjust small portions of the unmasked part of the image. For example, if you brighten a patch of water that contains reflected sunlight, you may over-brighten the sparkling light. To avoid this problem, apply the adjustment layer correction, then choose a gray brush, zoom in on the portion of the image with the reflected sunlight, and mask part of the effect so that the sunlight is no longer so bright.

NOTE   *You could, of course, also burn in the reflected sunlight before applying the correction, but by using only layers, you can change your mind or make further adjustments to the brightness whenever you like.*

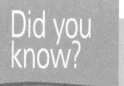

You can modify a layer mask by using the selection tools and brush tools directly on a layer. To mask a portion of an adjustment layer after you add the layer, select the layer and create a selection with the selection tools. Because you selected the adjustment layer first, the selection is actually located on the adjustment layer. Then, for example, you can adjust the layer mask by selecting the paint bucket, and filling the selected area with black. You can also choose Image | Adjustments | Invert to switch the "normal" color of the mask (white) to black. Doing this, would, of course, swap where the layer effect is applied. The formerly masked area would get the layer effect, and the affected area would return to its unadjusted state because it is now masked.

Apply a Gradient Mask

One of the best ways to mask off part of an image from the effect of an adjustment layer is to use a gradient. A gradient that goes from black to white masks part of the image, allows the layer effect to work fully in another part of the image, and provides a gentle transition between the two. Figure 9-16 shows a skyline where the sky is too bright for the foreground scenery. In addition, although this picture was taken at mid-day, I wanted it to have the warm tint of late afternoon.

9

FIGURE 9-16   The sky is too light, the foreground just right—what will I do to fix this sight?

Here is how I went about fixing this image:

1. To apply a yellow-orange tint to the hillsides and water, I created a color fill layer by choosing Layer | New Fill Layer | Solid Color. I called the layer "Afternoon Sun" then I set the mode to Color Burn and the opacity to 44%, and clicked OK to create the layer.

2. I set the color in the Color Picker to the following values: R=251, G=194, and B=89. Then I clicked OK to set the color of the layer.

3. Since I didn't want the yellow tint to affect the upper part of the picture, I chose the Gradient tool to create a mask. I clicked the Set Current Colors to White and Black button. That left me with the foreground color set to white and the background color set to black.

4. Next, I needed to apply the gradient. The foreground to background gradient normally works well to mask a color tint effect, but in this case the transition from white to black takes place over too wide a range—I couldn't cut off the yellow tint at the top of the houses and trees without having it spill over into the sky too much. To fix this, I clicked the Edit button in the options bar to create a custom gradient. I added a new foreground color stop at about 55%, and dragged the color midpoint located between the new color stop and the background color stop (the one at the far right) very close to the new color stop (at about 15%), creating a fairly abrupt transition:

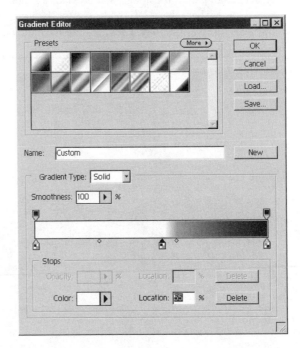

5. I named the transition and clicked OK to create the custom transition.

6. To apply the transition, I moved the mouse pointer to the bottom of the image and held down the SHIFT key to constrain the gradient to 45-degree angles. While still holding down

the SHIFT key, I held down the left mouse button, and dragged the mouse pointer straight up, ending the drag near the top of the image. I positioned the transition of the gradient to apply the yellow tint to just the lower portion of the image (houses, trees, and lagoon) and left the sky out.

7. The sky is still too bright for the late afternoon yellow tint. To fix this, I'll add an adjustment layer to correct the brightness. I chose Layer | New Adjustment Layer | Brightness Contrast. I named this layer "Darken Sky," left the mode set to normal and the opacity to 100%, and clicked OK to create the layer.

8. I set the brightness down to make the sky look like late afternoon—about 30—in the case of this image. Of course, this darkened the balance of the picture too much, but I'll correct that in the next step. I clicked OK to apply the brightness correction.

9. To mask the effect of the layer from the lower portion of the image, I chose the Gradient tool from the toolbox. From the Gradient picker (drop-down list), I chose the foreground to background gradient.

10. Holding down the SHIFT key, I held down the left mouse button and dragged the mouse straight down from the top of the image. It took a little experimentation to find the gradient ending point, but I got the effect that I wanted: the dark sky (the full layer effect) transitioning to a light foreground (where the gradient masked the effects of the adjustment layer). The result is shown Figure 9-17.

9

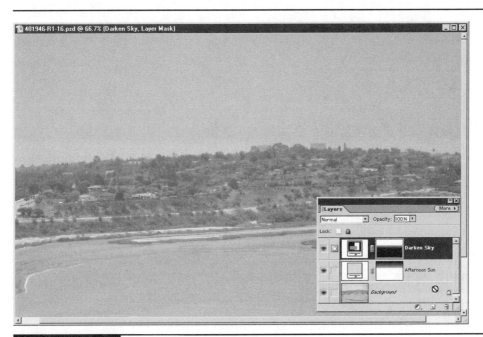

FIGURE 9-17 A picture taken at midday now looks like it was taken in late afternoon.

Did you know?

You can adjust the background portion of a foreground-to-background gradient by dragging. For example, after applying the gradient in step 6, you can select the Move tool and choose the layer to which the gradient had been applied ("Afternoon Sun" in my example). As you can see in Figure 9-18, Photoshop Elements displays an outline of the dark portion of the gradient. You can reposition the entire gradient by clicking and dragging the "bull's-eye" in the middle of the outlined area. You can also adjust the breakpoint between the white lower section and the black upper section by dragging the sizing handle located in the middle of the lower border.

Click and drag this sizing handle to adjust the breakpoint
between the dark and light sections of the gradient.

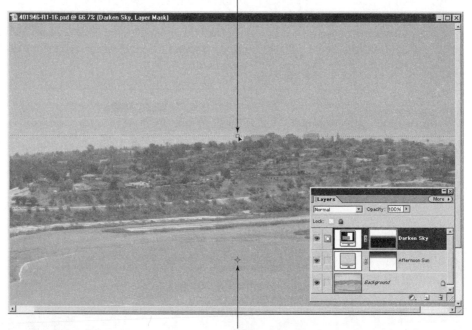

Click and drag here to move the entire gradient.

FIGURE 9-18   Click and drag the lower sizing handle to adjust the breakpoint in the gradient.

Chapter 10

Customize Layers with Layer Styles

How to...

■ Choose a layer style

■ Build up multiple layer styles

■ Customize layer styles

■ Copy layer styles

In Chapter 9, you learned to use the power of layers. But, you're not done yet. Photoshop Elements includes a feature called "layer styles." Need to add a beveled border to a selection? Just click. Need to add a drop shadow to a selection on a layer? Click again. Want to create the reflection of a selection in water? Or add fog? Or turn a peaceful summer scene into a raging snowstorm? Or add a sunset sky? Layer styles let you add these effects and many others easily. Further, you can customize many of the effects. For example, you can set the size of a drop shadow *and* the angle of light. You can also build up multiple layer styles to achieve the effect you want.

Set a Layer Style

To add a layer style to a layer, the first thing you must do is create the layer. For example, here is the by-now famous "floats" picture with one of the floats copied and pasted back into the image, creating an object layer:

The next step is to open the Layer Style palette, shown in Figure 10-1. From here you can choose and apply a layer style.

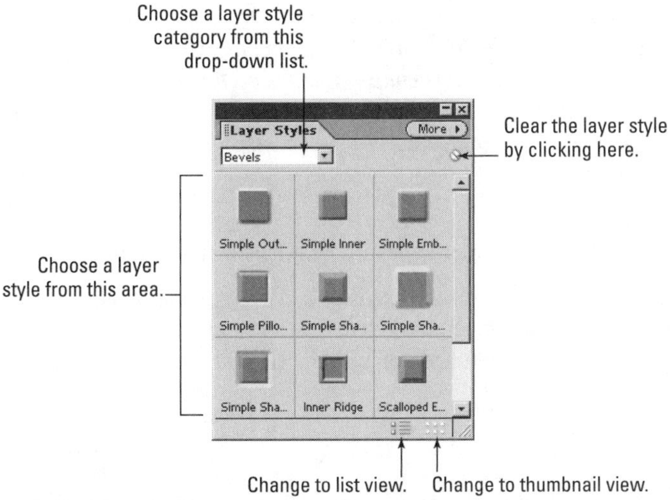

Choose a layer style
category from this
drop-down list.

Clear the layer style
by clicking here.

Choose a layer
style from this area.

Change to list view.   Change to thumbnail view.

FIGURE 10-1   Select a layer style using the Layer Style palette.

NOTE   *Although many examples in this chapter use individual objects that have been pasted into an Object layer (creating the layer), you can apply a layer style to any type of layer, including fill layers and adjustment layers. For example, if you create a brightness/contrast adjustment layer, and apply a Snow layer style, everything visible through the layer will have the Snow layer style. Applying a layer style to an entire image this way makes lots of sense for styles like Color Burn, Snow, Rain, and Fog, as you'll see in "Create Useful Digital Effects with Layer Styles," later in this chapter.*

10

Apply a Layer Style Using the Layer Style Palette

From the Layer Style palette, you pick both a style category and a style. You choose the style category from the drop-down list in the upper-left corner of the Layer Style palette. Once you have selected a category, the styles belonging to that category are available in the main area of the palette. Simply clicking the layer style adds that style to any existing layer styles. You can also click and drag the layer style from the Layer Style palette to the layer in the image.

If you want to replace all the existing styles with the newly selected style, hold down the SHIFT key while choosing the layer style or while dragging the layer style onto the layer.

You can switch between viewing the available layer styles as thumbnails or as a list by making a selection from the palette menu. To view the layer styles as a list, choose List View. To view the layer styles as thumbnails (the way they are displayed in the various illustrations in this chapter), choose Thumbnail View. You can also choose the type of view by clicking one of the icons in the lower-right corner of the Layer Style palette, as indicated in the callouts for Figure 10-1.

The categories are:

Bevels   Adds a variety of beveled border styles to the edges of layer content.

Drop Shadows   Adds a drop shadow to the items in a layer. You can control the lighting angle and style of the shadow (hard edge, soft edge, outline, and so forth). For example, if the lighting is coming from the upper left and you chose a High style, the drop shadow would look like this:

Inner Glows   Adds a glowing edge to the inside edge of the items in a layer.

Inner Shadows   Adds a shadow along an inner edge. The shadow appears along the edge *facing* the light, which is somewhat counterintuitive. For example, if the light source were in the upper left, an inner shadow would look like this:

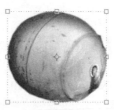

 *The exception to the inner shadow rule is the reverse shadow style of the Inner Shadow. This style places a shadow on the selection everywhere except along the edge facing the light.*

Outer Glows   Adds a glowing edge to the outside edge of the items in a layer. For example, here is the blue ghost style of Outer Glows:

Visibility   Enables you to make the layer contents visible (Show), invisible (Hide), or partially visible (Ghost).

Complex   These are a set of complex effects that are of limited use with digital photography. You can take the layer contents and turn them into molten gold, diamonds, or a rivet, give them a pepper or salt border, or a chrome border, make them look like a cactus, and add many other effects.

Glass Buttons   Turns the layer contents into (can you guess?) glass buttons. The various styles include a multitude of colors.

Image Effects   Contains a lot of interesting and useful effects that I will explore in much greater detail later in this chapter. This group includes such styles as rain, snow, water reflection, and fog.

Patterns   Applies patterns to the items in a layer. Some of these patterns can produce useful effects. The patterns include denim, stone, stucco, copper, asphalt, fiberglass, brick, dried mud, and smoke. These styles are most useful as background patterns, applied to a fill or adjustment layer. Here is one of our floats lying on a bed of dried mud:

Photographic Effects   Duplicates some other effects, such as Inner Shadows and Bevels. Other styles in this category include various color tints, and turning the layer contents into negatives.

10

Wow Chrome   Overlays the layer contents with one of several chrome-based effects. I've never used these with digital images.

Wow Neon   Replaces the items in a layer with a neon-like border of orange, green, purple, or blue.

Wow Plastic   Replaces the items in a layer with what looks like one of several colors of translucent plastic.

Once you've applied a layer style, the layer displays the Layer Style icon (f) in the Layers palette:

Adjust the Layer Style Settings

You can adjust the various parameters that control layer styles by either double-clicking the Layer Style icon, or by choosing Layer | Layer Style | Style Settings. Either way, Photoshop Elements displays the Style Settings dialog box:

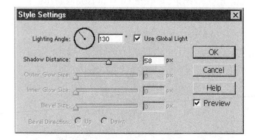

Only applicable options are available in this dialog box. For example, if you are not using a Bevels layer style, the Bevel Direction option is grayed out. If you have added multiple layer styles (such as Drop Shadows and Inner Glows), then multiple options are available in the Style Settings dialog box.

Set the Lighting Angle

The Lighting Angle option sets the angle at which light-sensitive styles are applied to the layer contents. For example, here is a drop shadow applied with the lighting angle set to 30 degrees:

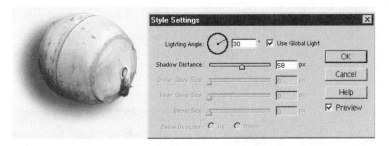

Here is the same drop shadow applied with a lighting angle of 140 degrees:

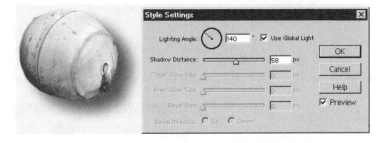

The light shines from the direction of the outside circle toward the center.

If you check the Use Global Light check box, each layer has the same lighting angle. Essentially, this gives a global light source for all layer styles, regardless of which layer the style is on. If you don't check the Use Global Light check box, you can set the lighting angle separately for each layer. However, even if you don't check the Use Global Light check box, the lighting angle is the *same* for all the styles on a given layer. For example, if you use both the drop shadow and inner shadow on the same layer, the lighting angle applies to both styles because they are applied to the same layer.

To set the lighting angle, click and drag the line inside the circle, or type a value into the field.

If you need to use a different lighting angle for a drop shadow and inner shadow that is applied to the same object, create two copies of the object and place them on different layers. Make sure they overlay each other so you can see only one instance of the object, and then apply the inner shadow to the top layer containing the object and the drop shadow to the lower layer containing the object.

10

Set the Shadow Distance

To set the shadow distance, drag the control or type a value into the field.

For a Drop Shadows style, the Shadow Distance option specifies the distance between the items in the layer and the bottom edge of their shadows. Increasing the distance creates a larger drop shadow.

For an Inner Shadows style, the Shadow Distance option specifies the size (thickness) of the inner shadow, except for the Reverse Shadow style. With the Reverse Shadow style, increasing the shadow distance *decreases* the size of the shadow. For example, here is a Reverse Shadow with the shadow distance set to 25 pixels:

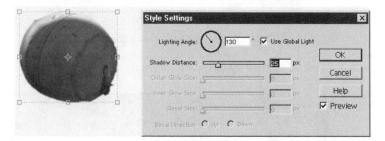

In comparison, here is the Reverse Shadow style with the shadow distance set to 100 pixels.

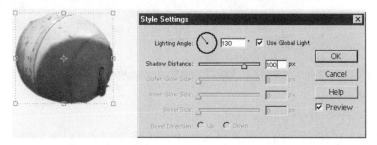

 *As with the lighting angle, you can apply different shadow distance settings to an object on a layer by creating two copies of the object (each on its own layer) and overlaying them on the two layers. Just remember to apply the inner shadow (if you use one) to the object on the top layer.*

Set the Outer Glow Size

To set the outer glow size, drag the control or type a value into the field.

This option sets the size of the glow that emanates from the outside edges of the layer content.

Set the Inner Glow Size

To set the inner glow size, drag the control or type a value into the field.

This option sets the size of the glow that emanates from the inside edges of the layer content.

Set the Bevel Size and Direction

To set the bevel size, drag the control or type a value into the field. To choose the bevel direction, pick either the Up or the Down option. An Up bevel means that the bevel starts low at the edge and gets higher as the effect moves away from the edge. A Down bevel starts high at the edge and gets lower as the effect moves away from the edge.

Scale the Layer Style

You can control the size of all the layer styles with a single command: choose Layer | Layer Style | Scale Settings to open the Scale Layer Effects dialog box:

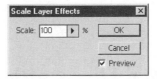

When you change the Scale—either by typing in a percentage or dragging the slider control—you change the size of everything in one shot. For example, if you applied a drop shadow, bevel, and inner glow, increasing the scale has the same effect as increasing the shadow distance, bevel size, and inner glow size in the Style Settings dialog box.

10

You can temporarily hide all the layer styles on all layers. This can be handy if you want to get back to the unmodified layers without throwing away the layer styles you may have spent a fair amount of time building. To hide all the layer styles temporarily, choose Layer | Layer Style | Hide All Effects. To redisplay the layer styles, choose Layer | Layer Style | Show All Effects.

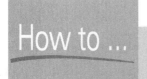 **Copy, Paste, and Clear Layer Styles**

Although layer styles are easy to create and apply, you may end up spending a lot of time getting them exactly right. For example, you might combine a drop shadow (carefully tuned for size) with a sun-faded photo effect (from Image Effects) and fog (also from Image Effects). Once you get a set of layer styles that work well for you, you can reuse them so you don't have to build them from scratch. To do so, select the layer that contains the styles you want to reuse in the Layers palette, and choose Layer | Layer Style | Copy Layer Style. Select the layer to which you want to reapply the set of layer styles, and choose Layer | Layer Style | Paste Layer Style. Note that this action replaces any existing layer styles on the target layer.

If you change your mind about a set of layer styles, you can remove them altogether. To do so, choose Layer | Layer Style | Clear Layer Style.

Create Useful Digital Effects with Layer Styles

As mentioned earlier, the Image Effects category of layer styles contains a number of useful effects you can use to quickly customize a digital photograph. Some of the effects are similar to the Enhance menu options.

Use Color Burn

The Color Burn layer style darkens the existing colors of the layer. This is a "quick and dirty" effect, as you have none of the controls you have with the Enhance | Adjust Color | Hue/ Saturation, nor can you modify the effect using the Layer Style settings.

Use Color Fade

Like Color Burn, this layer style enables you to apply a quick fix without much control. The Color Fade layer style comes in three variations:

Color Fade—Horizontal   Applies the color fade with more faded color at the right edge of the objects in the layer. The original color is maintained at the left edge of the layer contents.

Color Fade—Vertical   Applies the color fade with more faded color at the bottom edge of the objects in the layer. The original color is maintained at the top edge of the layer contents.

Colorful Center   Applies the color fade around the edges of the layer contents. The original color is maintained in the center of the layer contents.

Use the Fog Layer Style

Applying fog to an image can make it look really eerie. For example, Figure 10-2 shows a shot of a forest path in mid-afternoon.

To make it look like a foggy morning, I followed these steps:

1. I added a brightness/contrast adjustment layer by choosing Layer | New Adjustment Layer | Brightness Contrast. I named the layer "Fog" and left the brightness and contrast settings at their default values.

NOTE   *I could have converted the background to a layer and then applied the layer style to that layer. But that would have prevented me from performing some of the adjustments I will do later.*

IMG_0389.JPG @ 50% (RGB)

FIGURE 10-2   I'll shroud this bright forest path with fog.

10

FIGURE 10-3   The fog has settled in on this forest path.

2. I then added the Fog layer style by choosing Image Effects from the drop-down list in the Layer Style palette and clicking the Fog style.

3. The full effect of the Fog layer style hides too much, so I'll reduce the amount of fog by adjusting the layer opacity to 90%. It is this flexibility you would lose if you applied the Fog layer style directly to the background (after first converting it to a layer). The result is shown in Figure 10-3.

Use the Rain Layer Style

Applying rain to an image—especially a dark image—can really improve the "gloomy" feel of a photo. For example, Figure 10-4 shows a dark, overcast day, with a wooden boardwalk going off into the distance.

To add rain to this image, simply add an adjustment layer and choose the Rain layer style from the Image Effects category. You can adjust the opacity of the layer after applying the layer style if you wish, although I didn't find that necessary. Figure 10-5 shows the result.

FIGURE 10-4   A dark and gloomy day…

FIGURE 10-5   …now even gloomier with rain.

One of the possible shortcomings of Figure 10-5 is that even though it is raining, the boardwalk doesn't look wet. To fix this, I can select the boardwalk with the Magnetic Lasso and apply a filter (see Chapter 15) to the boardwalk section of the image. In this case, the Ripple filter (choose Filter | Distort | Ripple) works well to give a "wet look" to the boardwalk. I set the amount to 105% and the size to Medium to give the result you can see here:

Use Snow to Turn Summer into Winter

I live in California, so I don't see snow very often. But it's easy for me to add snow to an image. For example, Figure 10-6 shows a scene shot on a bright, clear day.

FIGURE 10-6   A bright, sunny day

By adding a brightness/contrast adjustment layer and then adding the Snow layer style (from Image Effects), the image now looks like it was shot in a driving snowstorm:

Somewhat more of a challenge is the image shown in Figure 10-7. A recent snowstorm had blanketed everything, but I wanted to make the shot look like it had been shot *while* the snow was still falling. I could have added an adjustment layer and the Snow layer style, but there is a problem—the sky is too blue and bright for anyone to believe there was really a blizzard!

Follow these steps to add a blizzard to this photo:

1. Choose the Magnetic Lasso tool and select the sky portion of the image. It is not really possible to get a clean selection, not only because the trees at the right edge are very complex, but also the contrast between the peak and the sky is pretty low. But I'll fix all that shortly.

2. Create a new adjustment layer by selecting Layer | New Adjustment Layer | Brightness/ Contrast. Name the level "Sky" and adjust the brightness down to –100 to darken the sky. The sky is now too dark, but because of this it is easy to see where the mask we created needs touching up:

10

FIGURE 10-7   A snowy landscape, but no blizzard. Some layers and layer styles can help here.

3.   Zoom in on any problem areas that need cleaning up. For example, here is a section near the top of the hill where the sky mask accidentally included part of the hill:

4. Switch to a small brush (I used the Hard Round 5 pixel brush) and choose black as the foreground color. The easiest way to do this is to click the Set Current Colors To Black And White button in the lower-left corner of the toolbox, then press the x key to switch the foreground and background colors.

5. Select the Sky layer in the Layers palette, and touch up the mask to exclude the portions of the mountaintop that shouldn't be affected by the changes you'll make to the sky.

6. You may need to switch to black and touch up the edges of the sky mask. I also wanted to keep the pink clouds that were obliterated by the sky mask, so I painted over those clouds with a black brush, masking the effect of the mask and bringing the clouds back. Doing this also hides the fact that the pink clouds show through the branches of the trees at the right side of the image.

7. Zoom out until you can see the image (choose View | Fit On Screen) to see the result so far, as shown in Figure 10-8.

FIGURE 10-8 The sky portion is masked and I'm ready to apply the first layer style.

8. Double-click the layer thumbnail for the Sky layer and adjust the brightness back to about –25 to darken the sky part of the image to a more reasonable value. You'll notice right away that the sky is still too blue.

9. Switch to the Layer Style palette and choose the Photographic Effects category. Apply the Gray Green Tone style. This darkens the sky and makes it look quite threatening.

10. Create a new adjustment layer (Layer | New Adjustment Layer | Brightness/Contrast) and call it "Snow." If you wish, you can set the brightness to –20 to darken everything a bit, but I found that leaving the layer set to the default of 0 actually worked better once I applied the Snow layer style.

11. Choose the Snow layer style and apply it to the snow layer. You can experiment with the intensity of the snowstorm by varying the opacity of the snow layer. You can also vary the effect by choosing a different mode for the snow layer. For example, the Dissolve mode creates a more intense snowstorm of smaller snowflakes than the Normal mode. Multiply mode makes the whole effect gloomier by darkening the image and reducing the color intensity. The result for Normal mode is shown in Figure 10-9.

FIGURE 10-9   With two layers, each containing a layer style, the calm, quiet image was turned into a raging blizzard.

Chapter 11

Transform and Rotate Part of an Image

How to...

- Rotate a selection
- Rotate a layer
- Skew or distort a selection
- Adjust the perspective and reference point
- Scale part of an image

In Chapter 3, I discussed flipping an image to reorient it. Photoshop Elements can do much more than flip an entire image, however. Using the items in the Image menu, you can flip and rotate selections *and* layer contents. You can also change a shape by skewing, distorting, or scaling the shape. You can change the perspective, and pick the reference point—the fixed point around which the operations are performed. Using these tools, you have the ability to completely change how a shape or layer looks. For example, you can take the float picture, select the floats and paste them into layers, rotate and scale each layer, add drop shadows (layer styles), and even produce some three-dimensional effects on the floats. Figure 11-1 shows a sample of what you can achieve.

FIGURE 11-1   You can go nuts rotating, scaling, and skewing shapes. And I did.

Flip and Rotate Layers

If you create an object and paste it into a new layer, you can reorient the contents of the layer using the options in the Image | Rotate menu:

Free Rotate Layer   Enables you to rotate the contents of a layer. The mouse pointer turns into a bent, double-headed arrow. To perform the rotation, hold down the left mouse button and drag:

NOTE *Once you are done with the rotation, click the Commit Transform check mark in the options bar, or click the Cancel Transform symbol (a circle with a line through it) to undo the rotation. There are many more options available for rotating a layer or shape, and these are covered later in this chapter.*

11

Layer 90 Degrees Left   Rotates the layer contents 90 degrees counterclockwise.

Layer 90 Degrees Right   Rotates the layer contents 90 degrees clockwise.

Layer 180   Rotates the layer contents 180 degrees. That is, the layer contents face the opposite direction after the rotation. For example, a layer with objects facing up will have those objects facing down after applying this command, while a layer with objects facing left will have those objects facing right after applying the command.

Flip Layer Horizontal   Flips the layer contents around a vertical axis, creating a mirror image. That is, imagine a line through the layer contents from top to bottom. Flip Layer Horizontal rotates the layer contents around this line, so that if the contents were facing right initially, they would be facing left after the rotation.

Flip Layer Vertical   Flips the layer contents around a horizontal axis, creating a mirror image. That is, imagine a line through the layer contents from left to right. Flip Layer Vertical rotates the layer contents around this line, so that if the contents were facing up initially, they would be facing down after applying the command. Figures 11-2 and 11-3 show the before and after views of Flip Layer Vertical.

FIGURE 11-2 The layer contents before using Flip Layer Vertical…

FIGURE 11-3 …and after using Flip Layer Vertical.

Flip and Rotate Selections

You can reorient a selection, whether that selection is on the background or on an object layer. Of course, if the selection is on the background, it leaves a transparent "hole" around the edges. If the selection is on an object layer, it leaves a hole through which you can see the layers beneath. For example, here I copied and pasted a set of the floats using the Rectangular Marquee, creating a new object layer with a rectangular section containing a float. I then selected one of the floats and rotated it, giving me the result you can see in Figure 11-4. Notice you can see the white background layer around the edges of the rotated object.

FIGURE 11-4   You can rotate or flip any selection.

When you have an active selection, the Image | Rotate submenu contains the following submenus: Selection 90 Degrees Left, Selection 90 Degrees Right, Selection 180, Flip Selection Horizontal, and Flip Selection Vertical. These submenus work identically to the similar submenus I discussed for layers in the previous section, except, of course, they operate on the selection instead of on the layer.

If you don't want to leave a hole when you rotate or flip a selection, use either the Rectangular Marquee (for flipping) or the Oval Marquee (for flipping and rotating) to select the area to be flipped or rotated. While making the selection, constrain the rectangle to a square or the oval to a circle by beginning the selection and then holding down the CTRL key.

11

Perform a Transform

You can transform either the contents of a layer or a selection by changing its size, rotating the shape or layer, skewing it, or distorting it. You can also adjust the perspective, giving a flat object a three-dimensional look. Transform gives you the opportunity to fix some pretty major mistakes!

Regardless of which transform you choose, the options bar provides the same options for you to use, as shown in Figure 11-5. Because these options are available at all times, you can actually choose one type of transform, and then perform an entirely different transform. For example, you could choose to perform a rotation, but actually scale the image by entering values in the Set Horizontal Scale or Set Vertical Scale fields.

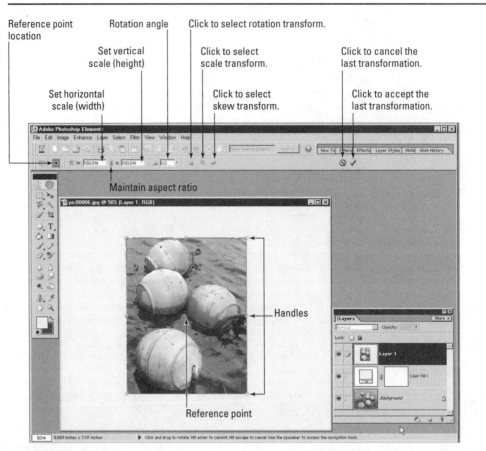

Reference point location

Rotation angle

Click to select rotation transform.

Set vertical scale (height)

Click to select scale transform.

Click to cancel the last transformation.

Set horizontal scale (width)

Click to select skew transform.

Click to accept the last transformation.

Maintain aspect ratio

Handles

Reference point

FIGURE 11-5   You can specify parameters for many types of transforms in the options bar.

Regardless of which transform you perform, you must either accept or reject the transformation before proceeding to other operations. To accept the transformation, click the Commit Transform check mark at the right end of the options bar (or press ENTER). To reject the transformation, click the Cancel Transform icon or press the ESC key.

Did you know?

Once you have chosen to perform a transform, you can perform additional different transforms by selecting one of the transformation icons on the options bar. For example, after you are done performing a scaling transform, *but before clicking the Commit Transform check mark*, you can click the Skew Transform icon and skew the object. You can keep switching between transforms, and end by choosing either the Commit Transform or the Cancel Transform icon to accept or reject the entire set of transformations.

Scale Part of an Image

Scaling the contents of a layer or a selection means changing the size of the item. For example, if you double the size of an item, it could be said that you scaled the item by 200%. For example, here is the original image:

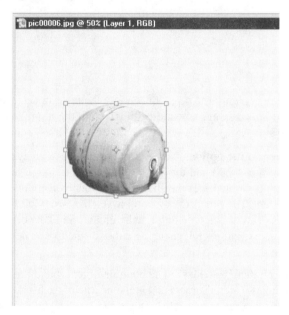

11

And here is the image after it was scaled by 200%, maintaining the aspect ratio (the ratio of the width to the height):

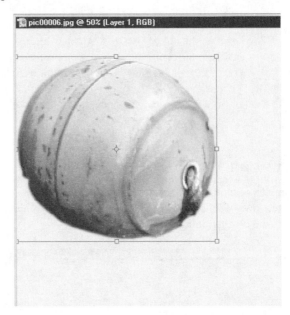

To scale layer contents or a selection, choose the layer or select an item, then choose Image | Resize | Scale. This displays a bounding box around the item. You can then change the size in one of two ways:

Enter values on the options bar   Enter the scale percentage in the Set Horizontal Scale field (adjacent to "W") and the Set Vertical Scale field (adjacent to "H"). A percentage greater than 100% increases the size of the item; a percentage less than 100% reduces the size of the item. The Small Link icon between the two scale fields is the Maintain Aspect Ratio toggle. Turn this toggle on to maintain the ratio between the height and width. If the Maintain Aspect Ratio is *on*, changing either of the two scale fields automatically changes the other field.

Use click and drag to resize   The bounding box around the item contains small squares (called "handles") at the corners and in the middle of each side. To resize the layer contents or selection using the mouse, click one of the handles, hold down the left mouse button, and drag. To maintain the aspect ratio, hold down the SHIFT key while dragging.

NOTE   *When you resize by clicking and dragging with the mouse, you can maintain the aspect ratio by turning on the Maintain Aspect Ratio toggle in the options bar. But this only works if you click and drag a corner handle. If you click and drag one of the side handles, Photoshop Elements does not maintain the aspect ratio, and automatically toggles off the Maintain Aspect Ratio.*

Normally, when you scale an image, the handle you click and drag moves, but the opposite handle remains anchored in place as scaling takes place. For example, if you click and drag the lower-right corner up and left, the upper-left corner does not move, so the item shrinks, and the center of the resulting object has moved up and left. You can see that here, where I decreased the size of the object. To make it more obvious, I drew a crosshair on the white fill layer, and reduced the opacity of the float layer slightly so you can see the crosshair through the float. The following illustrations show the shape before the transform (on the left) and after the shape is scaled to about 75% of its original size (on the right):

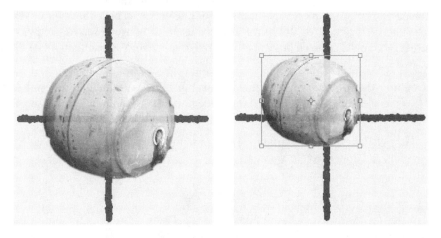

However, if you have set the reference point to the middle of the bounding box, you can hold down the ALT key to get a different scaling effect—when you drag one handle, the opposite handle moves as well, essentially scaling the object *without* moving the center. For example, if you click and drag the lower-right corner up and left, the upper-left corner (its opposite) moves *down* and *right* by the same amount. You can see this variation here, where I decreased the size of the object, but the center of the object remained right where it was before the transform:

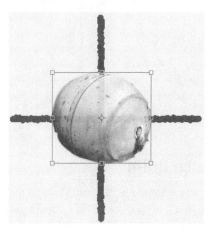

11

When you scale using the Set Horizontal Scale and Set Vertical Scale fields in the options bar, the center of the object does not move—that is, you get the same effect as dragging a handle with the ALT key held down.

Rotate Part of an Image

You can rotate the contents of a layer or a selection either clockwise or counterclockwise. If you specify a positive angle, the item rotates clockwise; a negative angle rotates the item counterclockwise. To rotate layer contents or a selection, choose the layer or select an item, then choose Image | Free Rotate Layer (for a layer) or Image | Free Rotate Selection (for a selection). This displays a bounding box around the item. You can then rotate the item in one of two ways:

Enter the rotation angle in the options bar   Type a value into the Set Rotation field to rotate the item. A value from 0 to 180 degrees rotates the item clockwise, and a value from 0 to –180 degrees rotates the item counterclockwise.

Use click and drag to rotate   The mouse turns into a bent, double-headed arrow. Simply click and drag to rotate the item:

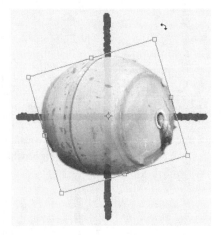

To constrain the rotation to 15-degree increments, hold down the SHIFT key while rotating with the mouse.

Set the Reference Point

By default, when you rotate an image, it rotates around the center point because the default *reference point* for rotation is the center of the bounding box. However, you can change the point around which a rotation occurs. For example, you can choose to rotate the image around the upper-left corner of the bounding box.

You can identify the reference point by its distinct appearance—a circle with crosshairs. The reference point is visible in the center of each bounding box in previous illustrations in this chapter, including Figure 11-5, where it is identified with a callout. To change the reference point, use the Reference Point Location control near the left end of the options bar (visible in Figure 11-5). Click one of the white dots to move the reference point to one of the handles that corresponds to that point in the bounding box—or click the middle white dot to move the reference point to the middle of the bounding box. For example, to move the reference point to the upper-left corner handle, click the upper-left corner dot in the Reference Point Location control. As you can see here, the reference point is now located in the upper-left corner:

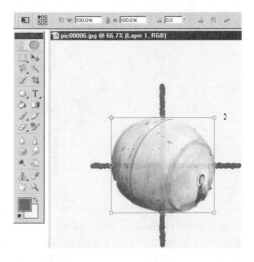

If you now rotate the shape, it rotates around the upper-left corner, giving a very different effect from rotating around the center:

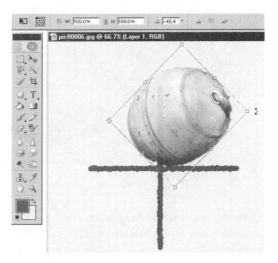

11

Skew Part of an Image

Skewing typically refers to slanting an object in such a way that a rectangle ends up as a parallelogram. For example, if I start with a square bounding box on a layer (containing one of the floats) and skew this image, it would look like this:

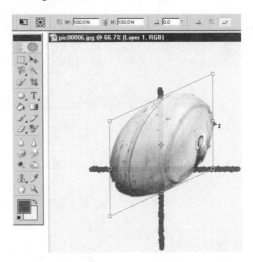

To skew an item, select Image | Transform | Skew. Move the mouse pointer over one of the side handles (it becomes a double-headed arrow) and drag the handle to skew the item. The previous image shows what happens when you drag the right or left handle; this next image shows what happens when you drag the top or bottom handle:

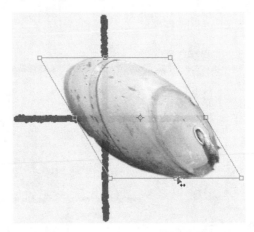

The two previous images illustrate the normal way of skewing an object—the side you drag moves (either up/down or left/right), but the opposite side remains where it is. However, if you have set the reference point to the middle of the bounding box, you can hold down the

ALT key to get a different skewing effect—when you drag one side, the other side moves in the opposite direction, essentially skewing *around* the reference point. For example, if you click and drag the right side *down*, the left side moves *up* by the same amount:

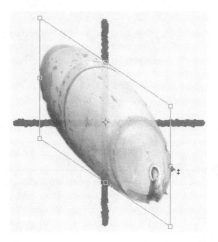

Distort Part of an Image

Skew, Rotate, and Scale apply very specific changes to layer contents or a selection. Distort enables you to freely distort the bounding box (and its contents). Using Distort is easy. Choose Image | Transform | Distort, and then click and drag any handle in the bounding box. For example, if you click and drag the upper-right corner of the bounding box *out*, you might get something like the image on the left. If you drag the corner *in*, you might get something that looks like the image on the right.

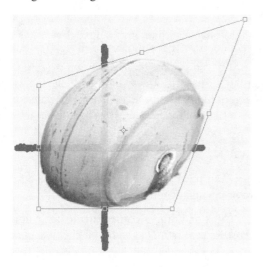
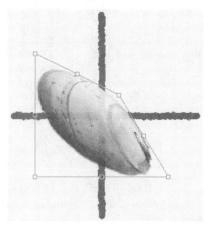

11

Distort behaves differently depending on which handle you click and drag—and which direction you drag it in. Table 11-1 summarizes this behavior.

Handle Dragged	Direction	What Happens
Any corner	Any direction	Distorts shape
Left/right side	Left or right	Scales shape left or right
Left/right side	Up or down	Skews shape
Top/bottom side	Up or down	Scales shape up or down
Top/bottom side	Left or right	Skews shape
Center reference point	Any direction	Moves shape

TABLE 11-1   The Effects of Using Distort on a Bounding Box

Apply Perspective

The idea of adjusting perspective is to either add or remove the distortion that occurs when a flat image attempts to represent something that has depth. A pair of examples should help illustrate the effects of perspective. Figure 11-6 shows a church that was shot from the ground, looking up. Now, I *know* that the spires of this church actually point straight up. The fact that they seem to be pointing toward a common point somewhere off the top of the image is an example of the type of distortion I am talking about. Although a certain amount of this perspective distortion give a feeling of depth, too much just looks silly.

The point at which the imaginary lines drawn through the church spires would meet is called the "vanishing point." The closer the vanishing point is to the tops if the spires, the more distortion is present, as is apparent in Figure 11-6. The farther away the vanishing point is located, the less distortion. If the lines never meet—that is, the vanishing point is at infinite—then no perspective distortion will be present. However, there will not be a feeling of depth to the image.

To adjust perspective, choose Image | Transform | Perspective. Then, drag a corner handle to adjust either the left/right perspective or the up/down perspective:

Adjust the left/right perspective   Click and drag a corner handle up or down. The Perspective transform controls the corners together. That is, if you click the upper-right

FIGURE 11-6   Depth distortion effects are clearly visible in this photo.

corner and drag it down, the lower-right corner is automatically moved up to match. This gives the effect of a vanishing point to the right of the image. Here is an uncorrected image, which shows little depth:

11

And here is the same image with the right edge expanded and the left edge contracted to heighten the effect of the perspective:

Adjust the up/down perspective   Click and drag a corner handle left or right. Again, the Perspective transform controls the corners together. That is, if you click the upper-right corner and drag it right, the upper-left corner automatically moves left to match.

In both cases, Photoshop Elements also stretches the image to fit the new dimensions. For example, by adjusting the perspective of Figure 11-6, you can achieve the result you see in Figure 11-7.

Here is how I created Figure 11-7:

1. I first turned the original image background into a layer. This is because the Perspective transform will leave holes where I need the sky color to show through. Thus, I really need the background layer to be a solid color fill layer. To turn the background into a layer, I chose Layer | New | Layer From Background. I named the new layer "Church" and clicked OK.

2. I used the Eyedropper tool (from the toolbox) to sample a portion of the sky near one of the spires, where I knew the major hole would appear. This made the foreground color the sampled blue from the sky.

3. I chose Layer | New Fill Layer | Solid Color to build the solid color fill layer I wanted to use as the background. I called this layer "Sky Fill" and clicked OK to create it. I then simply clicked OK in the Color Picker because the default fill color is the foreground color I set in step 2.

FIGURE 11-7 By dragging the upper corners out (away from the center), perspective distortion is decreased.

4. I converted the solid fill layer into the background by choosing Layer | New | Background From Layer. This gave me a Layers palette that looked like this:

5. I chose the Magnetic Lasso, selected the Church layer, and created a selection that included both the spires. I was careful to include all the details at the top of the spires, and cut off the selection at the ledge at the bottom of the spire, as shown in Figure 11-8.

NOTE *I chose to select the spires rather than just apply perspective to the whole image because I didn't want any of the lower portion of the building distorted by the Perspective transform. I used the Selection Brush around the edges to ensure that none of the spires was left out of the selection.*

FIGURE 11-8
The portion of the image for which I want to adjust the perspective is now selected.

6.   I chose Image | Transform | Perspective to make the bounding box visible, and dragged the edges of the canvas to enlarge it enough so that I could change the perspective:

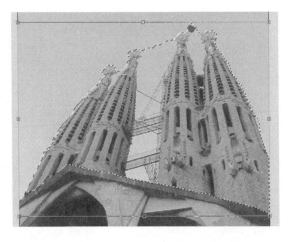

7. I clicked the upper-right corner handle, and dragged it to the right, with the following result:

8. The last step was to click the Commit Transform check box to complete the perspective transformation.

And where are those holes I mentioned earlier? You can't see them because of the fill layer behind the Church layer. But if I turn off the fill layer, you can see where the holes would have been:

11

As previously discussed, you only get the perspective effect if you click and drag a corner handle. If you click and drag a side handle, you get the same effect as Skew.

In the previous sections, I discussed the various menu options you must use to select a transform. For example, to scale an image, you choose Image | Resize | Scale. But there is a much quicker way to put Photoshop Elements into Transform mode if you can see the bounding box. Simply click one of the handles of the bounding box. If you do, Photoshop Elements reacts as if you had chosen Free transform (Image | Transform | Free Transform). You can now use all the options and perform all the same operations as you can for Free Transform.

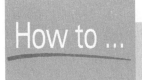

Use Free Transform to Modify a Layer or Shape

The last type of transform you can use is Free transform. As its name implies, once you select Image | Transform | Free Transform, you can scale, rotate, skew, distort, or apply perspective to layer contents or a selection. Here is how you use Free transform:

Scale   To scale an object, click and drag any handle in the bounding box.

Rotate   To rotate an object, move the mouse pointer outside the bounding box. The mouse pointer turns into a bent, double-headed arrow. Click and drag to rotate the contents of the bounding box.

Skew   Hold down both the SHIFT and CTRL keys, then click and drag the side handles. To skew the shape up or down, click the right or left handles and drag up or down. To skew the shape left or right, click the top or bottom handles and drag left or right.

Distort   Hold down the CTRL key, and click and drag any handle to distort the contents of the bounding box.

Perspective   Hold down SHIFT, ALT, and CTRL, then click and drag a corner handle. To adjust perspective left or right, click a corner handle and drag it up or down. To adjust perspective up or down, click a corner handle and drag it left or right.

Chapter 12

Add Objects and Change Image Backgrounds

How to...

- Add an object to a photo
- Change an area using layers and masks
- Change an area using the Clone Stamp
- Change the background of an image

In Chapter 7 you saw how you can use the Clone Stamp tool to remove objects from a photograph. In this chapter you will see examples of more sophisticated changes. For example, how do you get two people into the same photograph when one of you has to hold the camera?

Another common procedure is the need to replace a portion of an image with something more interesting. Many of the images in this book show a rather featureless sky. Adding dramatic clouds to the sky can enhance the photograph considerably.

Finally, some photos may have unique subjects—such as a doctor holding the first baby he or she delivered, or someone receiving an award. Such images are often shot without regard to composition or background—the idea was to take the picture before the moment was gone. In such cases, you may need to change the background entirely.

Add an Object to an Image

Placing an object into a photograph that wasn't there before can be tricky—but rewarding. For example, Figure 12-1 shows a photograph of me standing in a gazebo at the Marriott in Newport Beach. My wife took the picture, and because we didn't have a tripod, a remote release, or a friendly stranger nearby, she couldn't be in the picture with me.

What I needed to do was find a picture of her with similar lighting, and then copy and paste her into the photo. I did find one, taken just a few minutes later at the same hotel, but there was size problem. When I did a trial copy and paste, she came out too large in the picture with me. I had two choices for resizing her to fit.

The first was to use one of the selection tools to select her from the image she was in and paste her into the target picture (with me) as a new layer. From there, I could choose Image | Resize | Scale, turn on the Maintain Aspect Ratio toggle, and drag to resize her. However, this option distorted her image enough that you could tell it had originated in another photo. The effect was especially noticeable around the edges of the selection.

FIGURE 12-1   The starting point for a romantic picture. Just me, so far...

A more satisfactory solution was to resize her original image *before* transferring her to the new image. To do so, I chose Image | Resize | Image Size to open the Image Size dialog box:

By experimenting, I discovered that I needed her image to be 80% of the size of the original. I chose "percent" as the unit in the Pixel Dimensions area (for both width and height), and set the width to 80% (which automatically set the height to 80% as well). Photoshop Elements resampled the image when I clicked OK, applying an algorithm to resize the entire image and minimize distortion.

The next step was to zoom in on my wife's image and select her. I used the Magnetic Lasso, with the edge contrast set very low—just 5%. This was necessary because the difference in contrast between her head and the background is almost non-existent in places. Even with the low edge contrast setting, I had to go back and adjust the selection, removing extraneous areas from the selection by setting the selection mode to subtract the new selection from the original selection. The result looked like the illustration shown below on the left.

I then copied her image and pasted it into the gazebo picture with me (shown below on the right), positioning her so that her head came up to my shoulder—right where it is in real life. Notice that she appears to be standing on top of the flowers because the layer she is on is in front of the background layer (which contains me and the flowers, among other things).

To fix the problem with the flowers, I reduced the opacity of the layer she is on to about 60% so I could see where the flowers should go through her image. I then followed these steps to correct the problem:

1. I chose the Clone Stamp tool from the toolbox.

2. I selected the background layer in the Layers palette.

3. While holding down the ALT key, I chose the clone source from the background layer. I was very careful to pick a spot that was readily identifiable—in this case, one of the white flowers in the flowerbed.

4. After switching to the layer my wife's image was on, I began painting with the Clone Stamp, covering the sections of her feet that should not have been visible.

5. I reset the opacity of the layer my wife was on to 100%, and the result is visible in Figure 12-2.

FIGURE 12-2 We are now standing together in this peaceful garden scene.

12

Add a Dramatic Sky to a Photo

Many of my photos could benefit from replacing the featureless blue sky with a more dramatic sky—perhaps a sky with large, threatening clouds. You can use one of three techniques to make this happen. Which technique works best depends on the original image.

Add a Dramatic Sky to a Photo with the Magic Eraser

If the original image contains a featureless sky with a complex obstruction (such as the tree branch in Figure 12-3), the Magic Eraser may be the easiest way to replace the existing sky.
Here is how I added a cloudy sky to this image:

1. The first thing I did was to remove the existing sky. I used the Magnetic Lasso to select the sky portion of the image, including the tree. This limits the changes I will make to just the sky, since some of the shades of blue in the sky also show up in the roof of the building.

2. I chose the Magic Eraser, and set the opacity to 100%, tolerance to 30, and cleared the Contiguous check box. I then clicked a few times in the sky area, not only erasing the sky to transparency, but also converting the background layer to a regular layer.

FIGURE 12-3   A good photo, but it could be better with a more eye-catching sky.

FIGURE 12-4   The cloudy sky shows behind the building and through the branches of the tree.

3. I then opened the image containing the cloudy sky I wanted to use, and chose Select | All to select the entire image. I could have also selected just a portion of the sky, but in this case, that wasn't necessary.

4. I copied the image containing the cloudy sky to the clipboard (Edit | Copy), then switched to the target image and pasted the image in as a new layer (Edit | Paste).

5. The new layer appeared in front of the layer containing my image, so I clicked and dragged the new layer in the Layers palette to place it below the layer containing my image. The result is visible in Figure 12-4.

Add a Dramatic Sky to a Photo with a Mask

If the original image contains no obstructions that would make creating a mask difficult (as in Figure 12-5), you can use a mask to replace the existing sky.

To replace the sky in this image by using a mask, follow these steps:

1. Use a selection tool to select just the sky portion of the image.

FIGURE 12-5   It is easy to select the sky portion of this image so you can replace it with something better.

 *Use the Magnetic Lasso tool to select the line between the horizon and the sky. Then, switch to the Lasso tool by holding down the left mouse button and the ALT key, and trace the edges of the image.*

2. Save the selection for later use by choosing Select | Save Selection to open the Save Selection dialog box. Give the selection a name (I called mine "Sky") and click OK to save the selection.

3. Create a new fill layer for the sky by choosing Layer | New Fill Layer | Solid Color. Fill it with any color you want (I used a moderate gray), as you won't be keeping the color fill anyway. The new layer has a mask that allows you to modify just the sky portion of the image.

4. Open the image you want to use as the source of the dramatic sky, and use the Rectangular Marquee (or other selection tool) to copy the sky to the clipboard (Edit | Copy).

The image containing the sky should be at least as large (in terms of pixel count) as the image into which you want to add the sky. Otherwise, the sky will be too small when you copy it into your image. If the source image is too small, you can use Image | Resize to enlarge the pixel count so that it fits properly.

5. Select the fill layer you created in step 3 and simplify it so you can paint on it (or paste into it). To do so, select the layer and choose Layer | Simplify Layer.

6. Reapply the selection you made in step 2 to the fill layer by choosing Selection | Load Selection, choosing the selection you saved, and clicking OK. This gives you the intermediate result you see in Figure 12-6. The fill layer (with its gray fill) sits on top of the background and contains the sky selection so that any changes to the fill layer will be limited to the sky portion only.

7. Choose Edit | Paste Into. This pastes the sky section you copied in step 4 into the selected area of the simplified fill layer. The result is shown in Figure 12-7.

FIGURE 12-6   The new layer is ready to accept the sky you've chosen.

12

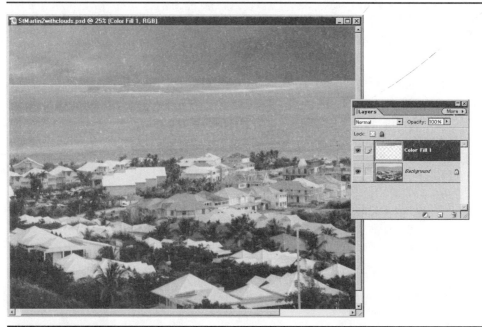

FIGURE 12-7   Your new sky is pasted into the fill layer.

Add a Dramatic Sky to a Photo with the Clone Stamp

One of the problems you might face when using masks is the appearance of a sharp break between a dark sky and a light landscape or seascape. One way around this problem is to use the Clone Stamp to transfer the sky from one image to another. By modifying the opacity of the Clone Stamp as you use it, you can gain fine control over how you blend the new sky with the existing image. Again, this works best when the target image doesn't contain any obstructions that would make creating a mask difficult.

To clone a sky from one image to another, follow these steps:

1. Use a selection tool to select just the sky portion of the image in which you will be replacing the sky.

2. Save the selection for later use by choosing Select | Save Selection to open the Save Selection dialog box. Give the selection a name (I called mine "Sky") and click OK to save the selection.

3. Create a new fill layer for the sky by choosing Layer | New Fill Layer | Solid Color. Fill it with a reasonable color. For example, if you are going to add a dark, cloudy sky into your original image, choose a moderate gray color so that if you clone information into that area with an opacity of less than 100%, the original color won't show through and ruin the effect.

4. Select the fill layer and simplify it (Layer | Simplify Layer). Apply the selection from step 2 to the fill layer by choosing Select | Load Selection, choosing the selection you saved, and clicking OK.

5. Open the image you want to use as your source for the sky.

6. Choose the Clone Stamp tool and pick a starting point in the source image by holding down the ALT key and clicking the sky portion of the image.

7. Switch to the target image, set the opacity of the Clone Stamp to 100%, make sure the Aligned check box is checked, and choose a square, hard-edged brush. To get access to square brushes, you'll need to choose Square Brushes from the Brushes drop-down list.

8. Begin painting near the top of the image in the selected sky portion:

9. As you move down in the sky, slowly reduce the opacity of the Clone Stamp, so that by the time the cloned sky reaches the boundary with the land or ocean, it is faded enough to feather gracefully. You'll want to be careful not to overlap the edges at lower opacities. Otherwise, you'll be able to see the overlaps.

Hold down the SHIFT key while painting with the Clone Stamp to limit your brush's movement to painting left and right (horizontally) only.

Figure 12-8 shows the final result.

FIGURE 12-8   The cloned sky has been added to the image, and the transition to the land or ocean is less abrupt than using a mask.

Change the Background of an Image

Figure 12-9 shows a classic example of a "shoot for the moment" photo. It was taken quickly, without regard for anything except the subject—a young doctor holding the first baby he ever delivered. But the background is about as ugly as it could possibly be. It contains distracting items as well as some bounce-back from a flash. There really isn't much that can be done to improve the existing background. So, I'll just replace it altogether.

Replace the Background Using Copy and Paste

The simplest way to replace the background is to copy the subject and paste it into another image—one containing a more attractive background. To replace the background in this way, follow these steps:

1. Select the subject using the Lasso tools. In this particular case, the selection is tricky because there is virtually no density difference between part of the subject's head and the dark background. You have to switch between tools to "eyeball" the section to get a good selection. You also need to be careful about the dark shadow behind the left arm caused by the flash.

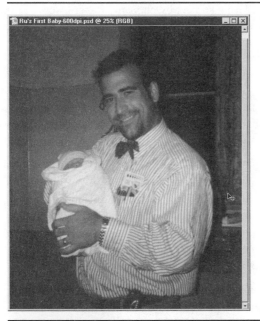

FIGURE 12-9   A great subject—and a really ugly background.

2.   Choose Edit | Copy to copy the subject to the clipboard.

3.   Open the image containing the background, and paste the subject into that image. This creates a new layer.

NOTE   *You'll probably have to clean up the selection once you paste it into the new image, as it will be very difficult to get a perfect outline of the subject under these particular circumstances. To clean up the picture, select the layer containing the subject, choose the Eraser tool and a small brush size, and carefully touch up the edges to remove extraneous pixels.*

12

Replace the Background by Creating a Layer Via Cut

Another method of replacing the background involves several Layer commands that haven't really been discussed until now. One such method is creating new layers by cutting. To replace a background with these layer tools, follow these steps:

1.   Select the subject using the Lasso tools. Save the selection by choosing Select | Save Selection, giving the selection a name, and clicking OK.

2. Create a new layer containing only the subject by choosing Layer | New | Layer Via Cut. The new layer (Layer 1) contains the subject only, with a transparent background, while the original background layer now contains the background with a "hole" where the subject used to be. You can see that here, where I turned off the new layer so you can see the background layer:

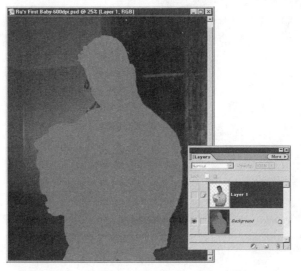

3. Choose Layer | New | Layer From Background, converting the background layer to a regular layer. Once you've done that, select the layer that *was* the background layer (Layer 0) and click the trashcan icon in the Layers palette to discard the layer. This leaves you with Layer 1, containing just the subject and a transparent background:

4. Open the image containing the background you want, and click and drag the background layer into the original image.

5. Either drag the new layer below the original layer, or choose Layer | New | Background From Layer to turn the new layer into the background. Either of these actions places the new layer behind the subject, giving the result you see here:

6. The subject is a little too dark for this brightly lit outdoor scene. To fix this, I chose the layer containing the subject and reloaded the selection I saved in step 1 by choosing Select | Load Selection, picking the saved selection, and clicking OK.

7. I added a Brightness/Contrast layer (Layer | New Adjustment Layer | Brightness/Contrast) and adjusted the brightness "up" to give it a more "outdoorsy look." The adjustment was applied only to the subject because the Brightness/Contrast layer contains a mask as a result of the selection I loaded in step 6. The result is much more balanced:

12

Replace the Background Using Layer Via Copy

You can replace the background by *not* replacing it at all and simply dragging the layer containing the subject to a photo that has a nice background. To do so, follow these steps:

1. Select the subject in the original photo.

2. Create a new layer containing just the subject by choosing Layer | New | Layer Via Copy. The result is the original background layer and a new layer (Layer 1) containing the subject only, with a transparent background:

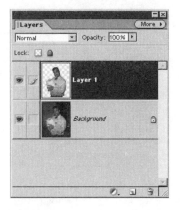

3. Open the image containing the background you want.

4. Click and drag Layer 1 from the original image into the target image. Here is the result:

5.   To lighten the subject, I have to reselect it (him). However, since I dragged the layer into a new image, even had I saved the selection, it would not be available in the new image. However, all I have to do is select the layer the subject is on in the Layers palette, and CTRL-click the thumbnail in the Layers palette. This selects all pixels in the layer, which selects the subject.

6.   I then added a new Brightness/Contrast layer (Layer | New Adjustment Layer | Brightness/Contrast) and adjusted the brightness to match the outdoors better.

12

Chapter 13

Add Simple Shapes to Your Image

How to...

- Choose a shape to add to an image
- Customize the color and size of shapes
- Move the shapes on the shape layer
- Skew, distort, and rotate shapes
- Fill the shapes with colors or patterns
- Fill shapes with gradients
- Apply layer styles to shapes

Photoshop Elements enables you to add vector shapes, such as squares, ovals, lines (with or without arrowheads), polygons, and custom shapes, to an image on their own layers. You can specify the properties of these shapes, including the fill (color or pattern). You can also apply layer styles to the shapes to further customize them. Vector shapes are useful for such things as adding a frame to an image, adding objects to an image (such as the stylized sun I added to Figure 13-1), and, in combination with type (see Chapter 16), adding annotations to an image (also visible in Figure 13-1).

FIGURE 13-1   Add shapes and annotations to an image using simple shapes.

To add a shape to an image, you must select the shape, customize its behavior, and click and drag in the image to define the shape.

Choose and Customize a Shape

The first step in adding a shape to an image is to pick the shape you want and customize the shape's properties.

Choose the Shape to Use

You can choose a shape from either the toolbox or the options bar.

To select a shape from the toolbox, click the Shape button in the toolbox (fourth button down on the left side). If the shape visible on the button is not the one you want to use, hold down the mouse button to display a list of available shapes. Then choose the shape you want from the list:

Once you have selected a shape, you can change shapes by making a selection from the options bar. All shapes are visible in the options bar—just click the type of shape you want. This is a very useful way to choose shapes when you want to draw several different types of shapes.

Here are the available shapes:

Shape Selection tool   Selects shapes you have already drawn and drags individual shapes to new locations.

Rectangle tool   Draws a filled rectangle. Pressing the SHIFT key while drawing the rectangle constrains it to a square.

Rounded Rectangle tool   Draws a filled, rounded rectangle. Pressing the SHIFT key while drawing the rounded rectangle constrains it to a rounded square. You can set the radius of the rounded corners by typing a value into the Radius field, along with the units (px, in, or cm) to specify the curvature of the corner in pixels, inches, or centimeters.

Ellipse tool   Draws a filled ellipse (oval). Pressing the SHIFT key while drawing the ellipse constrains it to a circle.

Polygon tool   Draws a filled polygon with the number of sides given by the Sides field in the options bar. Type in a number between 3 and 100 to specify the number of sides.

Line tool   Draws a filled line with the thickness (weight) given by the Weight field in the options bar. Type in a number and the units (px, in, or cm) to specify the weight in pixels, inches, or centimeters.

Custom Shape tool   Draws a filled custom shape. To choose the custom shape, click the Shape down-arrow in the options bar to display the Custom Shape palette:

 *As with other palettes, you can use the Custom Shape palette menu to change the display of the shapes (text, small thumbnail, large thumbnail, small list, large list) and to load other palettes of custom shapes. To load another palette of custom shapes, choose the palette of shapes you want from the palette menu.*

Figure 13-2 shows a sample of each type of shape detailed previously.

Customize Shape Behavior

I've already talked about how you can set certain properties of a shape, such as the weight of a line, the number of sides of a polygon, and the radius of a rounded rectangle. However, there are many more properties you can specify about a shape by clicking the small down-arrow alongside the Custom Shape icon in the options bar. For example, the options for the Rectangle tool are shown on the following page.

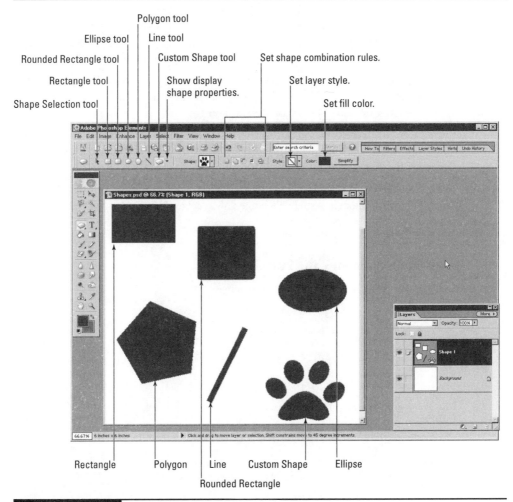

FIGURE 13-2   A sample of each type of vector shape.

13

Define Shape Behavior for Rectangles and Ovals

The properties available for the Rectangle, Rounded Rectangle, and Oval tools are very similar. You can set the following properties:

Unconstrained   Selecting this option applies no constraints to how you size the shape.

Square (Circle for the Oval tool)   This option constrains the rectangle to a square or the oval to a circle. This is the same effect you get if you hold down the SHIFT key when you draw the shape.

Fixed Size   Type the width (W) and height (H) into the fields. Once you have specified this option, each time you click the image, Photoshop Elements defines a new shape with the specified dimensions. You can specify the width and height in pixels (px), inches (in), or centimeters (cm). For example, to specify a width of 2 inches, type **2 in**.

Proportional   Type the ratio of the width (W) to the height (H) of the shape into the fields. For example, if you want the resulting shape to be three times as wide as it is high, type **3** into the Width field and **1** into the Height field.

From Center   When you check this check box, the point at which you click to start drawing the shape becomes the center of the shape. As you drag the mouse away from the center, the edges of the shape grow away from the center on both sides.

Snap to Pixels   This option is not available for the Oval tool. When you check this check box, Photoshop Elements snaps the edges of a rectangle or a rounded rectangle to the pixel boundaries.

Define Shape Behavior for Polygons

The shape properties of a polygon are shown here:

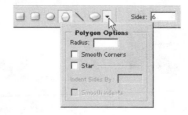

You can set the following properties:

Radius   You set the radius of the polygon in this field. Type in a value and the units (px, in, or cm) to set the radius in pixels, inches, or centimeters. The radius is measured from a vertex to the center of the shape.

Smooth Corners   You can round the vertices of the shape with this option. For example, Figure 13-3a shows a three-sided polygon (otherwise known as a triangle) with rounded corners.

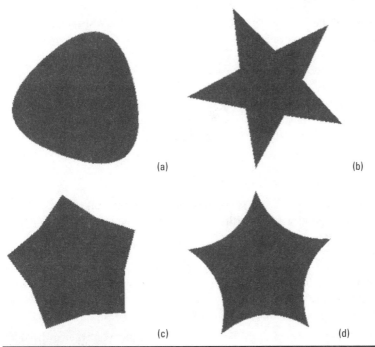

(a)   (b)

(c)   (d)

FIGURE 13-3   Customize shapes by modifying the properties of the sides and corners.

NOTE   *For polygons with more than six sides, rounding the corners basically leaves you with a circle.*

13

Star   If you check this option, you get a polygon with the specified number of vertices. However, the vertices are drawn like points on a star, with indents between them. For example, a five-sided polygon with the Star option checked is shown in Figure 13-3b.

Indent Sides By   This field becomes available only if you check the Star check box. Type in the amount of indent to use for the indented points of the star. For example, typing in **50%** sets the indents to half of the diameter of the polygon (as shown in the Star example in Figure 13-3b). Entering **10%** sets the indent to 10% of the diameter of the polygon. The results are shown in Figure 13-3c.

Smooth Indent   This field becomes available only if you check the Star check box. Checking this check box rounds the indented portion of the star (see Figure 13-3d), rather than having it come to a point, the way it did in the Indent Sides example in Figure 13-3c.

Define Shape Behavior for Lines

Other than the weight of the line and the color (discussed earlier), the shape properties for lines are used for defining arrowheads:

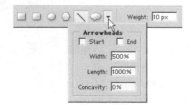

You can set the following properties for arrowheads on lines:

Start   Check the Start check box to place an arrowhead on the starting end of the line. The "start" of a line is the point where you first click to define the line.

End   Check the End check box to place an arrowhead at the end of the line. The "end" of a line is the point where you release the mouse button to finish defining the line.

Width   Type a value into the Width field to define the width of the arrowhead in percent of the line weight. For example, if you create a 20-pixel line and specify the width to be 200%, you'll get an arrowhead that is 40 pixels wide.

Length   Type a value into the Length field to define the length of the arrowhead in percent of the line weight. For example, if you create a 20-pixel line and specify the length to be 400%, you'll get an arrowhead that is 80 pixels long. Here is an example of a line that uses these parameters for weight, width, and length:

Concavity   The concavity determines the angle formed by the line that joins the back "points" of the arrowhead and the main line. If the concavity is zero, this angle is a right angle (90 degrees), and if the concavity is positive, this angle is acute (less than 90 degrees). However, if the concavity is negative, this angle is oblique (greater than 90 degrees). Figure 13-4 shows these three examples. Set the concavity in percent of the line weight.

Arrowhead with negative concavity
(between –1% and –50%)

Arrowhead with positive concavity
(between 1% and 50%)

Arrowhead with zero concavity

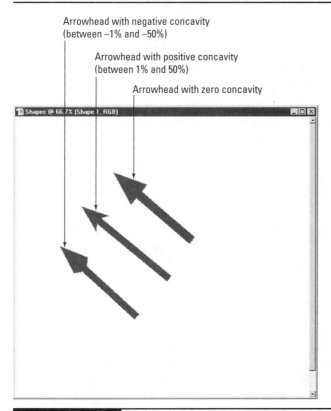

FIGURE 13-4   The effects of setting concavity on a line.

Define Shape Behavior for Custom Shapes

The shape behavior for custom shapes is similar to what you saw for rectangles:

You can set the following properties for custom shapes:

Unconstrained   Selecting this option applies no constraints to how you size the custom shape.

Defined Proportions   You can make the shape any size, but the originally defined proportions are maintained. For example, if you choose this option, you can't stretch the width of a custom arrow shape without also stretching the length.

Defined Size   This option specifies that the shape is automatically set to the size it was originally defined in the Custom Shape palette. Each time you click the image, Photoshop Elements creates the custom shape at the defined size.

Fixed Size   Type the width (W) and height (H) into the fields. Once you have specified this option, each time you click the image, Photoshop Elements defines a new custom shape with the specified dimensions. You can specify the width and height in pixels (px), inches (in), or centimeters (cm).

From Center   When you check this box, the point at which you click to start drawing the shape becomes the center of the shape. As you drag the mouse away from the center, the edges of the shape grow away from the center on both sides.

Work with Shapes

Now that you understand how to choose shapes and specify their properties, you can draw shapes in the image, change their properties, apply the transform tools (Scale, Skew, Distort, and so forth) to the shapes, apply layer styles, and use the fill tools to modify the shape fill properties.

Add Shapes to the Diagram

Once you have selected a shape from either the toolbox or the options bar, set the color and any other properties you want. Drawing the shape is easy—just click the image and drag to define the position and size of the shape.

With certain options—notably the Fixed Size or Defined Size options—you can't set the size of the shape when you first draw it. However, you can change the dimensions using the transform tools, as you will see later in this chapter.

The first time you draw a shape in an image, Photoshop Elements defines a new shape layer. Shape layers work pretty much like fill layers or adjustment layers. You can merge, link, and group shape layers, as well as rename, duplicate, or delete them. As with fill or adjustment layers, you must simplify a shape layer before you can paint on that layer.

When you merge shape layers, Photoshop Elements simplifies the resulting layer. This means you can paint on the resulting layer, but you can't add any more shapes to that layer, nor can you use the Shape Selection tool to select individual shapes to scale, rotate, or transform them. Essentially, the shapes on the layer are no longer individual objects that you can operate on. You can, however, operate on all the shapes as a single object using the techniques discussed in Chapter 11.

Once you have created the first shape (and its shape layer), you can add additional shapes to the image. The five buttons toward the middle of the options bar (indicated by the "Set shape combination rules" callout in Figure 13-2) determine how additional shapes interact with existing shapes. From left to right, the options are:

Create New Shape Layer   If you choose this option, each new shape appears on its own layer. This can make the image quite large, but since any fills you apply to a shape are applied to *all* shapes on the layer, placing the shapes on separate layers does give you the flexibility to modify the shapes individually. In addition, you have the freedom to place the shape layers in the stacking order you want.

If you need to move or apply the same transforms to shapes on different layers, link the layers. However, this does not work with fills (as discussed later in this chapter). You have to apply fills to individual layers regardless of whether the layers are linked.

Add to Shape Area   Any additional shapes you add are added to the selected layer and filled with the fill color. For example, here I had a layer with a rectangle on it, and I added an ellipse to the layer:

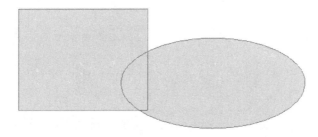

Subtract from Shape Area   When you add a new shape to the selected layer, the new shape is not filled and is not considered part of the shapes on the layer. In addition, any overlap between the new shape and the existing shapes is subtracted from the layer shapes.

13

For example, here I had a layer with a rectangle on it, and I added a rounded rectangle that partially overlapped the first rectangle. Both the rounded rectangle and the overlap area are *not* filled with color, indicating that they are not part of the shape:

Intersect Shape Areas   When you add shapes to the selected layer, *only* areas that overlap are filled and considered part of the shape on the layer. For example, here I had a layer with a rectangle on it, and I added a polygon that partially overlaps the rectangle. Only the overlap is filled, indicating that that is *all* that is considered as part of the shape:

Exclude Overlapping Shape Areas   When you add shapes to the selected layer, the overlapping area is not filled and is not considered part of the shapes on the layer. For example, the illustration on the following page shows what would happen if I had a layer with a rectangle on it, and then added a rounded rectangle that partially overlapped the rectangle.

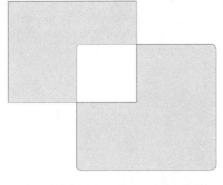

One of the trickiest parts of combining shapes on a layer is that you can actually change how shapes interact, even after you add the shapes. To do so, select the Shape Selection tool and click a shape. Photoshop Elements makes the shape combination tools in the options bar (except Create New Shape Layer) available. When you click one of the shape combination options, the combination rule for the selected shape *as well as all shapes that were on the layer when you added the currently selected shape* is adjusted to match the new selection.

For example, take a look at Figure 13-5. The three rectangles were drawn in order from upper left to lower right, and in each case, I used the Add to Shape Area option, giving the result you see—all three rectangles are fully filled.

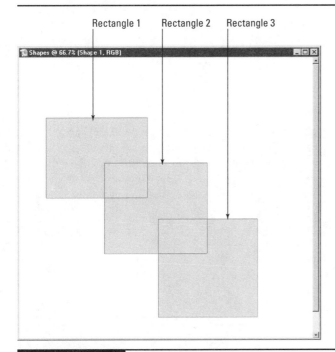

Rectangle 1   Rectangle 2   Rectangle 3

Shapes @ 66.7% (Shape 1, RGB)

FIGURE 13-5   Selecting rectangle 2 and changing the Shape Combination option changes how it interacts with rectangle 1.

13

I then chose the Shape Selection tool, selected the middle rectangle (rectangle 2), and chose the Exclude Overlapping Shape Areas option from the options bar. As you can see here, the result was that the overlapping area between rectangle 1 (upper left) and rectangle 2 is no longer filled, but the overlapping area between rectangle 2 and rectangle 3 (lower right) has not changed:

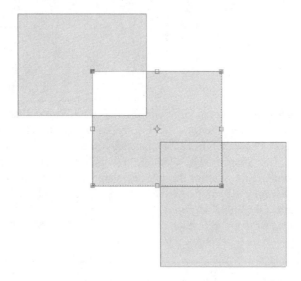

This is because rectangle 1 was already in the image at the time I drew rectangle 2, but rectangle 3 was *not*.

You can change your mind about having individual shapes on a layer. If you create a bunch of shapes on a layer and then decide that you'd really like them to be one shape, just click the Combine button on the options bar. This combines all the shapes into a single shape, so any operation you apply to one shape on the layer (such as moving or scaling) will be applied to all the shapes.

Choose a Layer Style

You can customize a shape layer by applying layer styles to the layer. When you apply a layer style, Photoshop Elements applies the style to all shapes on the layer. For example, here is a layer with multiple shapes to which I have applied a Drop Shadow layer style and Fire Inner Glows:

As I discussed in Chapter 10, first choose a category of layer style from the drop-down list in the Layer Styles palette, then choose the layer style itself from the thumbnails or list of styles. If you have applied a layer style to a layer, the Layer Style icon (a stylized "f") appears in the Layers palette. Double-click the Layer Style icon to open the Style Settings dialog box to set the shadow distance, outer and inner glow size, bevel size and direction, and lighting angle.

A Style drop-down list appears in the options bar next to the fill color. Clicking the arrowhead alongside the Style drop-down list displays the Layer Style palette:

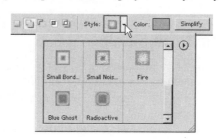

To choose a different category of style (for example, to switch from drop shadows to bevels), open the palette menu and choose the Layer Style category from the list:

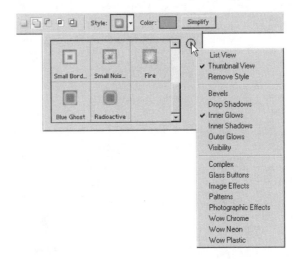

Some layer styles override the fill color of a shape. For example, if you apply Wow-Blue/Gray Swirl from the Wow Chrome layer style category, it doesn't matter what fill color you used—what you get is a chrome-tinted swirl. So, if you find yourself changing the fill color and not noticing any difference in the shape fill color, check the layer styles you've applied.

Move and Transform Shapes

Once you've placed one or more shapes on a layer, you can use the rotation, scaling, and transform tools (Free Transform, Skew, Distort, and Perspective) discussed in Chapter 11 to modify the shapes. You have two choices on how to apply these modifications—either to all the shapes on a layer or to individual shapes.

To apply rotation, scaling, or transforms to all the shapes on a layer, choose the Move tool from the toolbar. This action causes Photoshop Elements to display a bounding box around all the shapes on the layer, as shown in the illustration on the following page.

Then apply the modifications exactly the same way you did with the selections. For example, to scale the shapes, click one of the handles (small squares around the edges of the bounding box) and drag. Or, to skew all the shapes on the layer, you can choose Image | Transform | Skew, or (after performing some other transforms) click the Skew icon in the options bar. Here is a skew transform applied to a multi-shape layer:

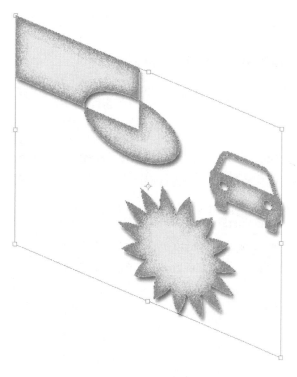

13

To apply rotation, scaling, or transforms to individual shapes on a layer, choose the Shape Selection tool from the toolbox or the options bar. Click the shape you want to modify to place a bounding box around that shape. Once the bounding box is visible, you can move, scale, rotate, or transform the shape. For example, here I have applied a perspective transform, affecting only a single shape in the shape layer:

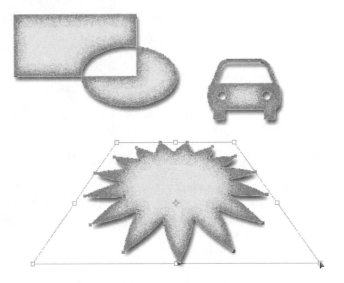

Change the Shape Fill Color

You can easily change the fill color for the shapes on a layer. There are three ways to do so: use the Color rectangle (Set Color for New Layer) on the options bar, use the Paint Bucket tool, or choose Edit | Fill.

Change the Shape Fill Color with the Color Rectangle

To change the shape fill color with the color rectangle, follow these steps:

1. Choose any shape (except the Shape Selection tool) so that the color rectangle is visible in the options bar.

2. Click the color rectangle to open the Color Picker.

3. Choose the new fill color from the Color Picker.

4. Click OK. Photoshop Elements changes the color of all shapes on the layer to the new color.

Change the Shape Fill Color with the Paint Bucket

To change the shape fill color with the Paint Bucket tool, follow these steps:

1. Select the layer containing the shapes you want to change in the Layers palette.

2. Choose the Paint Bucket tool from the toolbox.

3. From the Fill drop-down list in the options bar, choose either Foreground or Pattern to set the type of fill you want to perform.

4. If you chose Foreground, click the Foreground Color tool in the toolbox, choose the foreground color from the Color Picker, and click OK. If you picked Pattern, choose the pattern you want from the Pattern palette that appears when you click the down arrow adjacent to the Pattern drop-down list.

5. Move the Paint Bucket tool over any of the shapes in the layer and click. Photoshop Elements fills all the shapes with the selected color or pattern.

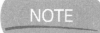

When filling shapes with the Paint Bucket, the Mode drop-down list is unavailable—you can fill the shapes only using the Normal mode; none of the other modes (such as Color Burn, Soft Light, and so forth) are available.

Using the Paint Bucket tool to fill shapes with a pattern causes Photoshop Elements to change the shape layer to a Pattern layer. Take a look at the Layers palette after you use the Paint Bucket tool. The shape layer has changed its name! It is now called "Pattern Fill" (followed by a number). Basically, Photoshop Elements has converted the layer content from a solid fill layer to a pattern fill layer. You can verify this—add a shape to an image to create a shape layer, then choose Layer | Change Layer Content. You'll find that the currently selected layer type in the fly-out menu (the checked menu item) is Solid Fill. Now check this same menu after using the Paint Bucket tool to fill shapes with a pattern. You'll find that the Pattern menu item is now checked. This suggests a way to return to a solid fill if you applied a pattern fill to the shapes—choose Layer | Change Layer Content | Solid Fill. This action causes the Color Picker to appear. Just choose the solid fill color you want, and the shapes are filled with that color.

13

Change the Shape Fill Color with Edit | Fill

You can change the shape fill color or convert to a pattern fill by choosing Edit | Fill. Follow these steps:

1. Choose the layer containing the shapes you want to change in the Layers palette.

2. Choose Edit | Fill to open the Fill dialog box:

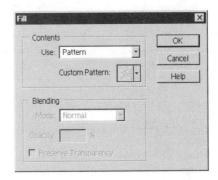

3. In the Contents section, choose the fill option you want to use from the Use drop-down list. Options include Foreground Color, Background Color, Pattern, Black, 50% Gray, and White.

4. If you chose Pattern from the Use drop-down list, choose the pattern you want to use from the Pattern palette. This palette appears when you click the down arrow alongside the Custom Pattern field. As with any other palette, you can use the palette menu to load a different set of patterns.

5. Click OK to apply the new color or pattern.

As with the Paint Bucket, Photoshop Elements changes the shape layer to a pattern fill layer.

The options in the Blending section of the Fill dialog box are unavailable when filling shapes. That is, you cannot vary the blending mode, opacity, or check the Preserve Transparency check box.

Fill Shapes with Gradients and Patterns

As you may have already begun to suspect, you can fill shapes with a pattern by converting the shape layer to a pattern layer yourself. Choose Layer | Change Layer Content | Pattern. This displays the Pattern Fill dialog box:

Choose the pattern you want from the pattern palette, adjust the scale and any other options if you wish, and click OK. Photoshop Elements applies the selected pattern to all shapes on the selected layer and converts the layer to a Pattern layer (as you can tell from the name of the layer in the Layers palette).

 *Once you've converted the layer to a pattern layer, you can still use the Paint Bucket tool or Edit | Fill to change the fill color/pattern of the shapes on the layer.*

An even neater effect is to fill shapes with a gradient. To do so, choose Layer | Change Layer Content | Gradient. This displays the Gradient Fill dialog box:

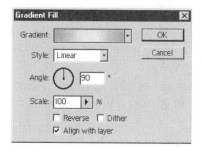

Click the down arrow to display the gradient palette, and select any other options you want, such as the gradient style, angle, and scale. Click OK to apply the gradient to all shapes on the selected layer and convert the shape layer to a gradient layer (as you can tell from the name of the layer in the Layers palette):

13

 *Unlike a pattern layer, once you convert to a gradient layer, you cannot use the Paint Bucket tool or Edit | Fill (or other paint tools) unless you first simplify the layer by choosing Layer | Simplify Layer.*

Use Shapes with Photos

The focus of this book is on how to use Photoshop Elements with digital photos. You can use shapes and layer styles to "dress up" photographs—beyond hokey, fake "suns" and annotations (see Figure 13-1).

Dress Up an Image with Thought Bubbles

The most obvious way to dress up photos is to add "thought bubbles," as I did in Figure 13-6. To achieve this effect, follow these steps:

1. Select the Custom Shape tool from the toolbox.

2. Click the Shape drop-down list to display the Shapes palette, and choose Talk Bubbles from the palette menu. Then choose one of the two thought bubbles from the available shapes in the palette.

3. Click and drag to add the thought bubble shape to the image, and change the fill color if necessary. (I set the fill color to an off-white beforehand, so I didn't need to modify the fill color.)

4. I then used a type tool (as detailed in Chapter 16) to add my "thoughts" to the image.

FIGURE 13-6   Combine an image, a custom shape, and some text to add "personality" to a picture.

The original thought bubble was facing the wrong way. That is, the bubbles were going off to the left, and I needed them to go off to the right as they are in Figure 13-6. To fix this, I selected Image | Rotate | Flip Layer Horizontal to reverse the orientation of just the thought bubble layer.

Of course, you can use "talk" bubbles for the same effect.

Build a Custom Sign

As you could tell from Figure 13-6, I was leaning on a sign that indicated I wasn't allowed to go off the trail and into the trees behind me. Of course this sign didn't work too well for the German tourists we encountered on this trail, who didn't speak English! That gave me the idea to transform the sign into something a little more "international," giving the result you can see in Figure 13-7. Here is how I did it:

1. The first step was to cover up the existing sign. I used the Eyedropper tool to set the foreground color to the same color as the sign by clicking the sign.

2. I used a rectangle shape to cover up the sign. I scaled the shape to the size of the sign, and rotated it slightly because the original sign was a little crooked.

FIGURE 13-7   "Don't go off the trail"—understandable in any language.

3. Making sure the Create New Shape Layer tool in the options bar was selected, I switched to the Custom Shape tool and chose the shape of the hiker from the Symbols shape palette.

4. I clicked the color rectangle and adjusted the fill color to a medium purple.

5. I clicked the Add to Shape Area tool in the options bar, and then chose the shape of the dog from the Animals shape palette. This placed the hiker and the dog on the same layer.

6. Using the Shape Selection tool, I placed the hiker and the dog in close proximity, and scaled each one until I got the size I liked—and one that fitted the sign.

7. I then switched to the Move tool so I could move both symbols at once, and dragged the symbols on top of the sign rectangle.

8. I switched back to the Create New Shape Layer tool in the options bar, and then chose the "Not" symbol from the Symbols shape palette.

9. I clicked the color rectangle and adjusted the fill color to a dark blue.

10. I switched to the Shape Selection tool, dragged the "Not" symbol on top of the sign (and the hiker/dog), and scaled it to fit.

11. The "Not" symbol covered up too much of the hiker and the dog, so I selected the layer containing this symbol and reduced the opacity to about 60%, allowing the hiker and the dog to show through. And there you have it!

Add a Frame to an Image

It is easy to add a frame to an image using shapes in Photoshop Elements. In fact, the Custom Shape tool includes an entire palette of frames:

The simplest way to add a frame is to choose a frame custom shape and create it in the image on its own layer. Here I applied one of the Wow Chrome layer styles to give it a metallic "look":

Of course, there are problems with this simple approach! The most obvious one is that the image shows through around the edges. Here is what I'll do to fix this problem:

1. Convert the background layer to a regular layer by choosing Layer | New | Layer From Background. The default name for the layer is Layer 0, and I used that name for the layer.

2. Choose the rectangle shape from the toolbox and drag a rectangle across the interior area of the frame, creating a new shape layer (called Shape 2), which gives you the result shown in Figure 13-8.

3. Drag Layer 0 (the former background) up in the Layers palette so that it is on top of the Shape 2 layer containing the rectangle.

13

FIGURE 13-8 Mask a photo to be visible only inside a frame using a simple shape.

4. Group Layer 0 with Shape 2 by choosing Layer | Group With Previous. This masks the photo, allowing only the portions that overlap the rectangle to show through:

The portions of the image outside the frame are now invisible.

Another approach to providing a frame is to blank out the areas of the image you don't want *before* you add the frame. Here is what I did:

1. I opened the picture I wanted to add a frame to, and selected just the subjects (see Figure 13-9a).

2. I inverted the selection, and chose Layer | New Fill Layer | Solid Fill. In the Color Picker dialog box, I chose the fill color as white (R, G, and B all equal to 255). This left me with the results shown in Figure 13-9b, in which the balance of the image is covered with the white fill.

3. I selected the Custom Shape tool from the toolbox, and chose the frame I wanted to use from the Custom Shape palette.

4. As the last step, I selected the Paint Bucket tool, set the fill to Pattern, and filled the frame with a custom pattern I had built from another picture of this same dog (see Figure 13-9c).

Did you know?

If all you want to do is create a rectangle around the edges of the picture, rather than use a fancy custom shape, there is a much easier way to do that. Follow these steps:

1. Select the subjects with the Rectangular Marquee tool.

2. Invert the selection, leaving everything *except* the subjects selected.

3. Create a new pattern layer, and choose the pattern for it in the Pattern Fill dialog box.

13

The final way to add a frame involves simplifying a fill layer and erasing a portion of it to allow the image to show through. Here is what I did:

1. I opened the image to which I wanted to add a frame (see Figure 13-10a).

2. I chose Custom Shape tool and added the frame shape to the image, sizing it to fit, as shown in Figure 13-10b.

3. I moved the mouse pointer over the shape layer in the Layers palette, held down the CTRL key, and clicked. This selected all the pixels on that layer—that is, the frame shape was now selected.

4. I chose Select | Inverse to select everything *except* the frame shape.

(a)

(b)

(c)

FIGURE 13-10 Add a frame, fill the outside, and punch a hole to allow the image to show through.

13

5. I chose Layer | New Fill Layer | Solid Color, clicked OK in the New Layer dialog box to accept the default name, and chose white as the fill color from the Color Picker dialog box. Then I clicked OK. This gave me a white fill layer with a mask where the frame shape was.

6. I simplified the fill layer so I could paint on it by choosing Layer | Simplify Layer.

7. Finally, I chose the Magic Eraser tool, made sure the Contiguous check box was checked, and clicked the center of the fill layer. This erased the center area, allowing the background image to show through, as shown in Figure 13-10c.

Part IV

Use Effects, Filters, and Text to Go Beyond the Darkroom

Chapter 14

Use Media Filters to Change the Look of Your Images

How to...

- Add a filter to an image
- Add artistic effects with filters
- Simulate different brush strokes
- Convert your photo into a sketch
- Modify the edges of an image
- Add texture to your image

Up to now, we have been using tools from the toolbox to make limited, mostly manual changes to an image. For example, we used the Clone Stamp to paint over a portion of an image to repair damage. But Photoshop Elements enables you to make large-scale, automated changes to an image as well. You can make an image look like it was painted on fabric (see Figure 14-1) or created with watercolors (see Figure 14-2). You can also distort images, change the lighting, sharpen images or blur them, add texture, stylize with contours or glowing edges (among others), and many other interesting effects. All of this is done with *filters*. Many of these filters have a set of controls so you can customize how they operate.

FIGURE 14-1   A portrait "painted" on burlap.

FIGURE 14-2   Sometimes, watercolors are more suited for the purpose than a photo. But who knows how to paint? You do!

In this chapter, I will focus on filters that enable you to make your image look like anything *but* a photograph. With these filters, you can simulate colored pencils, paint, torn paper, charcoal, crayons, and various textures. In addition, you can simulate various painting styles and even artistic techniques such as rubber stamping and bas relief.

Chapter 15 covers more advanced filters that let you perform powerful transformations such as simulating motion, moving pixels around any way you choose, and even manipulating your flat images in three dimensions.

NOTE   *Neither this chapter nor Chapter 15 covers every filter or every option. Many filters are not appropriate for use with digital photos because they create such massive changes that the image is no longer recognizable.*

TIP   *Many filters are very memory intensive and can take a while to apply. You can end up applying a filter only to decide you don't like the effect. To sample the effects of a filter, select a small but representative area of the image using the selection tools before applying the filter. Photoshop Elements applies the filter to only the selected area, so you can see how it looks before investing the time to apply the filter to the whole image.*

14

Choose a Filter to Apply to Your Image

To apply a filter to your image, I recommend making the Filters palette visible. You can drag it out of the palette area or choose Window | Filters:

Choose the Filter category from the drop-down list in the upper-left corner of the Filters palette. Once you do, the list of available filters for that category becomes visible in the palette. You can apply the filter to an image by dragging and dropping the filter onto the image, selecting the filter and clicking the Apply button in the palette or the palette menu, or double-clicking the filter in the Filters palette.

If you have checked the Filter Options check box and the filter has options (not all of them do), you have an opportunity to customize how the filter works immediately after you apply the filter. If you *don't* check the Filter Options check box, the filter is applied without giving you the opportunity to customize the parameters. For example, if you check the Filter Options check box and then apply the Mosaic filter (from the Pixelate category) to an image, you get the dialog box shown on the following page.

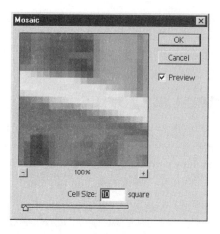

This is a fairly simple dialog box: all you can do is set the cell size by typing a value into the Cell Size field or using the slider. Some dialog boxes are far more complex (and we'll look at quite a few of them). All filter option dialog boxes have the preview square in the center of the dialog box. You can zoom in on the preview by clicking the plus sign (+) button, or zoom out by clicking the minus sign (–) button. You can also view a different part of the image by clicking and dragging inside the preview square. With some dialog boxes, you can move the mouse pointer over the portion of the image you wish to see (it turns into a small square) and click.

It may take a moment or two to display the contents of the preview square when you change the magnification. Photoshop Elements displays a flashing line under the preview size to indicate that it is still rendering the image.

Another way to apply filters to an image is to use the Filter menu:

14

To pick a filter from the Filter menu, choose the category from the items in the Filter menu, then pick the filter itself from the submenu that appears. If the filter allows customization via a dialog box, the menu item is followed by ellipses (…).

Understand Filter Categories

As mentioned earlier, filters are divided into categories. Each category contains multiple filters. Some filters are of little use when working with digital photographs, primarily because the results are too extreme. However, many of the filters can give you some attractive effects or provide a way to create surreal effects.

 *There are too many filters to cover each one in detail. Instead, I'll describe the basic categories and a few of the more useful filters.*

The most useful categories of filters are Artistic, Brush Stroke, Pixelate, Sketch, Stylize, Texture, Blur, Distort, Noise, Render, Sharpen, and three-dimensional filters. These types of filters provide you with ways to modify photographs and achieve attractive results without completely obliterating the image content.

Work with the Artistic Filters

The filters in the Artistic category produce effects that duplicate traditional media, such as a palette knife, fresco, colored pencil, poster edges, pastels, dry brush, watercolor, and others.

Add Texture with Underpainting

Figure 14-1 displayed an example of what you can do with the artistic Underpainting filter. Once you pick this filter, you have the opportunity to adjust a lot of parameters in the Underpainting dialog box, as shown in Figure 14-3.

In addition to picking the basic texture (such as Canvas, Burlap, Brick, or Sandstone) from the Texture drop-down list, you can adjust the level of detail (Brush Size), how much of the image area shows texture (Texture Coverage), the size of the texture (Scaling), how much the texture protrudes from the surface (Relief), and the direction of the light (Light Direction). This remarkable filter enables you to quickly give an image the look of having been rendered on fabric or other material.

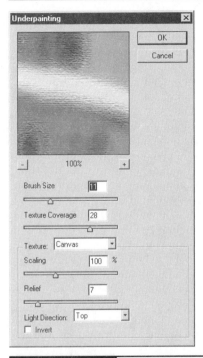

FIGURE 14-3   The many options in the Underpainting dialog box enable you to create exactly the result you want.

You can load a Photoshop Elements image to use as a texture as well. Using the same picture as the texture gives you an image that looks like it was shot through distorted glass. To load a texture, choose Load Texture from the Texture drop-down list, then pick the Photoshop Elements file to use as a texture.

Add Texture and Style with Rough Pastels

The Rough Pastels filter is similar to Underpainting. The image appears to be created with colored chalk on a textured background. The Texture controls (Texture, Scaling, Relief, and Light Direction) are identical to Underpainting. However, the brush controls are different. With Rough Pastels, you control the amount of detail with the Stroke Length and Stroke Detail controls/sliders. Larger values of Stroke Length tend to lose a little sharpness around edges and shadows. Small values of Stroke Detail preserve the original image well. Large values of Stroke Detail tend to accentuate the texture and introduce light areas to the image that are not in the original. This effect is visible in the preview area of the Rough Pastels dialog box, as shown in Figure 14-4.

14

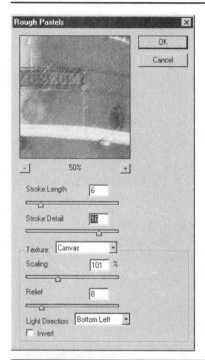

FIGURE 14-4   Use the options in the Rough Pastels dialog box to configure this filter.

Convert an Image to Colored Pencil

The Colored Pencil filter enables you to quickly make an image look like it was drawn in (can you guess?) colored pencil. Oddly, the default Paper Brightness setting is 0, making the paper black, and rendering light-colored areas (like Caucasian flesh tones) as black. Adjusting the paper brightness up to 45 provides a more accurate rendering of these tones, as shown in Figure 14-5.

The Pencil Width controls how visible the strokes are, as well as the amount of color in darker areas, like the hair and lips in Figure 14-5. The Stroke Pressure controls how dark the image is drawn.

Use the Cutout Filter to Simulate Paper Cutouts

Photoshop Elements makes it easy to simulate building an image from paper cutouts using the Cutout filter, as shown in Figure 14-6.

FIGURE 14-5   Convert a photo to a color pencil sketch with the Color Pencil filter.

14

FIGURE 14-6   Use the options in the Cutout Filter dialog box to configure this filter.

The No. Of Levels control indicates the number of levels of paper, *not* the number of colors. The more levels you use, the more detail you can preserve. Most detail is lost in the light-colored areas, so portraits of light-skinned people may require all the levels available (8) to preserve facial features.

Edge Simplicity controls how many colored areas are reproduced in the filtered image. A low value of Edge Simplicity matches the original image closely; a high value may leave you with ill-formed blobs!

Edge Fidelity controls how closely the edges match the original image. A low value (1) of Edge Fidelity leaves rough edges that only vaguely follow the outlines of the original image. A high value (3) of Edge Fidelity give you smoother edges that closely follow the original image.

Paint an Image in Fresco Style

"Fresco" refers to a style of painting that was popular in Italy in the Middle Ages. It was done by painting on freshly spread moist lime plaster with water-based pigments. This style primarily shows up on building murals, but is also seen in landscapes and some portraits. Fresco is a coarse style that uses a rounded brush, with the paint applied in dabs. The Fresco filter simulates this style of painting. You can set the brush size, detail, and texture:

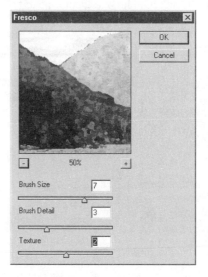

The parameters have the following effects:

Brush Size   Increasing the brush size makes the "dabs" larger, decreasing the apparent detail and also displaying more texture for a given value of the Texture control.

Brush Detail   Increasing the brush detail leads to sharper edges in the image.

Texture   Increasing the texture shows more of the rounded texture of the dabs in the image.

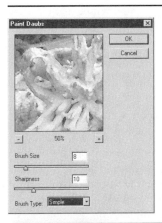 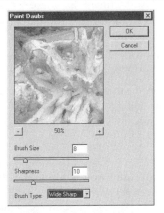

FIGURE 14-7   Using different brushes (such as Simple and Wide Sharp brushes) gives very different effects with the Paint Daub filter.

Create a Painting with Paint Daub

The Paint Daub filter enables you to quickly turn a photo into something that looks like it was painted, as shown in Figure 14-7.

Increasing the Brush Size reduces overall detail, and increasing the Sharpness highlights high-contrast edges. The brushes available in the Brush Type drop-down list affect the look of the image considerably. For example, the Paint Daubs filter on the left in Figure 14-7 uses the Simple brush type, while the filter on the right shows the Wide Sharp brush (one of my favorites).

Work with Brush Stroke Filters

The Brush Stroke filters are similar to the Artistic filters in that they simulate paint or other media, such as pencil hatching (Crosshatch), ink (Ink Outlines), or the Japanese style of painting with black ink on rice paper (Sumi-e). Here are some of the more useful styles for working with photos:

Angled Strokes   This filter repaints the image using diagonal strokes. The lighter areas are painted in strokes going in one direction (upper right to lower left), and darker areas are painted in strokes going in the other direction. The Direction Balance control determines the brightness level at which the strokes change direction. Stroke Length determines the length of the stroke—higher values of this quantity show less detail in the image. The Sharpness control determines how well you can see the strokes—higher values of Sharpness makes the strokes more visible (see Figure 14-8).

14

Spatter   This filter makes the image look like it was painted with a spatter airbrush. Personally, I think it looks like it is being viewed through frosted glass, but that's just me. The Spray Radius determines the level of detail—larger values lose much of the definition in the original image. Smoothness determines how much distortion the effect applies, especially around the edges. Very high levels make the effect almost unnoticeable.

Crosshatch   As mentioned earlier, this filter gives the impression of having drawn the image with a pencil while adding texture. The Stroke Length controls the amount of detail visible, while the combination of Sharpness and Strength controls how visible the crosshatch markings are (see Figure 14-8).

Sprayed Strokes   The Sprayed Strokes filter takes the original image and overlays it with paint strokes. You can set the direction of the strokes from the Stroke Direction drop-down list. As you make the strokes shorter (controlled with the Stroke Length control), you get more distortion of the original image. As you make the Spray Radius shorter, you get less of the effect of the spray (see Figure 14-8).

Work with the Pixelate Filters

The Pixelate filters change the look of your image by modifying groups of pixels by combining, averaging, or changing their shapes. But unlike the Artistic filters, most of the Pixelate filters produce such a drastic effect they aren't appropriate for use with photos. A few, however, are useful:

Pointillize   This filter changes the image into a pattern of dots, similar to the artistic method called Pointillism, in which artists created a painting by making lots of tiny dots (see Figure 14-9). The only control is the Cell Size. In general, only very small values (5 or less) produce anything recognizable as the original image.

Crystallize   This filter reduces the detail of the photo by grouping pixels together into polygon-shaped cells. Each cell is colored with the average of the pixels that Photoshop Elements grouped together to form the cell. The Cell Size control sets the size of the cells; lower values preserve more of the details of the image. The result when you set the Cell Size to 10 is shown in Figure 14-9.

Mosaic   Mosaic reduces the detail of the photo by grouping pixels together into square tiles. Each tile is colored with the average of the pixels that Photoshop Elements grouped together to form the tile. As with Crystallize, the Cell Size sets the size of the tiles—lower values preserve more of the details of the image. This filter does not work well on highly detailed images. The result when you set the Cell Size to 10 is shown in Figure 14-9.

Facet   The Facet filter groups similar-colored pixels into pixels of the same color. The effect essentially adds a certain blockiness to the image, and gives the impression that the image was painted rather than photographed. You have no control over the intensity of this filter—simply apply it as many times as you want, since the effect is additive. Figure 14-10 shows one of our beach scenes to which I applied the Facet filter six times. The effect is most noticeable in the light-color clouds and the edge of the water.

Fragment   This filter averages four copies of the pixels in the image and offsets the results. This is basically a fancy way of saying it blurs the heck out of the image. In addition, sharply defined spots are noticeable as showing up multiple times. There are no settings available to control the strength of the effect, although you can apply the filter multiple times. One use for this filter is to quickly blur a background, as shown in Figure 14-11.

 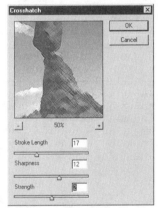 

FIGURE 14-8   The Brush Stroke filter dialog boxes (shown here for Angled, Crosshatch, and Sprayed Strokes) let you configure these filters.

FIGURE 14-9   The Pixelate filter dialog boxes (shown here for Pointillize, Crystallize, and Mosaic) let you configure these filters.

14

FIGURE 14-10   The Facet filter adds a square block look to an image.

FIGURE 14-11   Blur an image with the Fragment filter.

Apply Alternate Media to an Image with the Sketch Filters

The Sketch filters add texture to an image or can be used to make an image appear as if it was drawn in charcoal, pens, chalk, Conté crayons, or a combination of these tools. Only one of the sketch filters (Water Paper) preserves the original colors of the image. Most of the rest use a combination of the foreground and background color, and one (Chrome) ignores the color settings altogether. Many of the Sketch filters are appropriate for applying a stylized background to a portrait, as I did in the illustration on the following page.

Build a Color Image Using Water Paper

The Water Paper filter gives the appearance of having applied large dabs of paint onto a fibrous, wet paper. This causes the colors to flow and blend; the amount depends on the length of the fibers in the paper. To control the options for the Water Paper filter, use the options in the Water Paper dialog box:

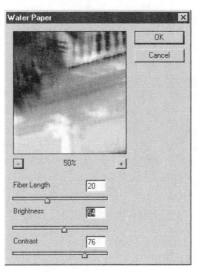

14

Here is what the options do:

Fiber Length   Use the Fiber Length to set the length of the paper fibers. Short fiber lengths give more intense color with visible smearing; long fiber lengths give a finer texture to the fibers and less smearing.

Brightness   This option adjusts the overall brightness of the image. Small changes in brightness have a large impact on the image.

Contrast   This option adjusts the overall contrast of the image.

Here is an example of using the Water Paper filter with the defaults for all the parameters:

Turn Your Image to Metal with the Chrome Filter

The Chrome filter turns your image into molten metal:

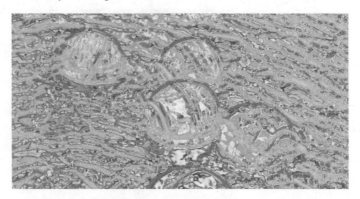

This filter is best used with images that don't contain a lot of very detailed areas, as the result can be a molten mess! To control this rather interesting effect, use the Chrome dialog box shown on the following page.

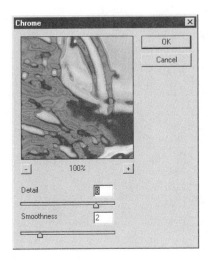

The two options are:

Detail   This option controls the amount of detail preserved in the final image. Too much detail actually detracts from the image, as Photoshop Elements attempts to render the detail using only shades of chrome.

Smoothness   This option controls the smoothness of the transition between the various shades of chrome in the image.

Render Images in Two Colors

The rest of the Sketch filters apply texture and various effects to render the image in a combination of the foreground color and background color. Most establish the balance between the foreground color and background color by analyzing the brightness of the colors in the original image, and provide some sort of control to enable you to modify that balance.

In general, these filters render the dark areas of the image in the foreground color, while the light areas are rendered in the background color. Thus, you'll probably want to choose a dark color for the foreground and a light color for the background.

14

These Sketch filters are:

Torn Edges   This filter is most effective for high-contrast images, especially landscapes. It gives the effect of an image built up from ragged, torn pieces of paper (see Figure 14-12). The Image Balance control enables you to balance the ratio of the foreground color to the background color. That is, increasing values of Image Balance cause lighter areas to be rendered in the foreground color. Increasing the value of the Smoothness control preserves more detail from the image and dithers the edges where the foreground and background colors meet. The Contrast control adjusts the overall contrast of the image.

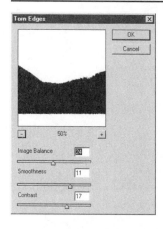
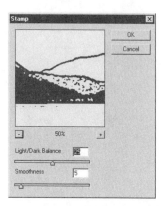
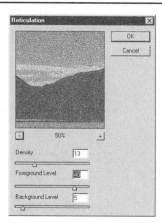

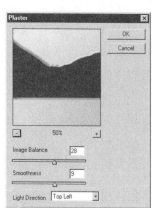
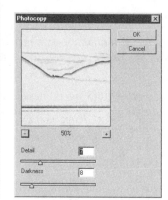
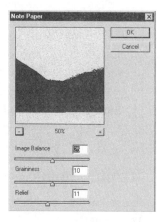

FIGURE 14-12   The first set of Sketch filter dialog boxes (Torn Edges, Stamp, Reticulation, Plaster, Photocopy, and Note Paper) let you configure these filters.

Stamp   This filter converts the image to what it would look like if it was made out of a rubber stamp (see Figure 14-12). This works best with images that are largely shades of two colors, such as black and white images or dark hills shot against a light sky. In general, sharp edges are raised in the stamp and rendered in the foreground color, and wide areas are recessed and rendered in the background color. The Light/Dark Balance control determines the width of the edges, as well as how much contrast must be present before an edge is defined. At low values of the Light/Dark balance, Photoshop Elements has a low sensitivity to contrast, so the edge must be very sharp before it is detected. At high values of the

Light/Dark Balance, Photoshop Elements has a high sensitivity to contrast, so even modest edges are detected. The Smoothness control determines how smoothly the transitions between raised and lowered parts of the stamp occur. At high values of Smoothness, narrow edges may disappear.

Reticulation   The Reticulation filter creates an image in which grain appears throughout, but the foreground color is prevalent in dark areas, and the background color is prevalent in light areas (see Figure 14-12). The Density control sets how much of the foreground grain appears in the light areas and how much of the background grain appears in the dark areas. Low values of density display a lot of foreground grain in the light areas, and little background grain in the dark areas. High values of density reverse this—you have very little foreground grain in the light areas and lots of background grain in the dark areas. The Foreground Level determines the brightness level at which the foreground color starts to appear. As you increase the value, lighter areas show the foreground color. The Background Level determines the brightness level at which the background color starts to appear. As you raise the value, darker areas show the background color.

Plaster   This filter creates an image that appears to be made from plaster, coloring the raised (dark) areas with the foreground color, and the recessed (bright) areas with the background color (see Figure 14-12). The Image Balance and Smoothness work just as they do for the Torn Edges filter. You can also pick the direction from which the light comes from the Light Direction drop-down list. The light direction has a substantial impact on both the brightness and the texture of the rendered image.

Photocopy   Ever copied a color photo on a black and white photocopier? Large areas of darkness tend to copy well only around the edges, falling away to white as you move in from the edge. Midtones are simulated with dithering of black and white. The Photocopy filter simulates this, substituting the foreground color for black and the background color for white (see Figure 14-12). The amount of detail preserved through dithering is set by the Detail control, as well as the thickness of the dark area edges. The Darkness control sets the darkness (how much of the foreground color is applied to light areas), which also affects the thickness of the dark area edges.

Note Paper   This filter creates an image that appears to have been created from textured paper (see Figure 14-12). The Image Balance control sets the ratio of the foreground color to the background color as with the Torn Edges filter. The Graininess control sets the amount of texture in the paper, while the Relief control sets the depth of the grain.

Halftone Pattern   This filter simulates the effect of applying a halftone screen to the image (see Figure 14-13). A halftone screen overlays the image with a pattern. You can choose the pattern to apply (Dot, Line, or Circle) from the Pattern Type drop-down list. The size of each dot, or the thickness of each circle or line, is controlled by the Size control. Photoshop Elements maintains the overall tonal balance of the image by mixing various shades of the foreground and background colors. Low values of the Contrast control preserve the tonal balance well, while high values increase the contrast, discarding the intermediate tonal values and using just the foreground and background colors.

14

Graphic Pen   This filter uses linear strokes as from a fine pen (see Figure 14-13). The ink is the foreground color, and the paper is the background color. The Stroke Length control sets the length of the pen strokes. Short strokes produce many short foreground-color strokes in the lighter (background) areas and background-color strokes in the dark (foreground) areas. The Light/Dark Balance control determines how dark a light area has to be before it gets the foreground color. The direction of the pen strokes (Right Diagonal, Horizontal, Left Diagonal, and Vertical) is set using the Stroke Direction drop-down list.

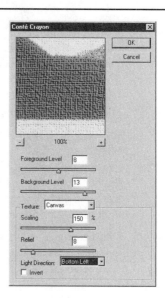

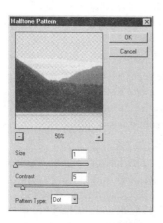

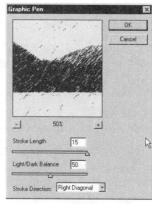

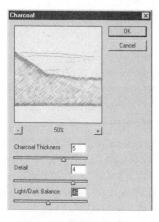

FIGURE 14-13   The second set of Sketch filter dialog boxes (Halftone Pattern, Graphic Pen, Conté Crayon, Charcoal, and Chalk & Charcoal) let you configure these filters.

Conté Crayon   Conté crayons (see Figure 14-13) are those little square crayons artists use, available in black, sepia, or sanguine. This is one of the most flexible of the filters, allowing you to change the following parameters:

Foreground Level   This option controls the mix (balance) of the foreground color to the background color in the dark areas. As you reduce the value of the Foreground Level, lighter shades of the dark areas show more of the background color.

Background Level   This option controls the mix (balance) of the background color to the foreground color in light areas. As you reduce the value of the Background Level, darker shades of the light areas show more of the foreground color.

Texture   You can vary the texture by choosing an option from the Texture drop-down list. Values include Brick, Burlap, Canvas, and Sandstone. As with any other texture, you can also load your own texture by choosing Load Texture from the Texture drop-down list and choosing a texture from the Open dialog box that appears.

Scaling   This option sets the size of the texture pattern. Small values give a fine texture; large values provide a coarse texture.

Relief   This option determines how deep (and visible) the texture is. High values of this control provide deep texture. This does not work well with low values of Scale, as much detail is lost. In addition, since the "bottom" of the texture is rendered in the foreground color, deep texture does not work well in images with a lot of background color.

Light Direction   Since the Texture is a three-dimensional effect, the light direction affects how it looks. Choose the light direction from the Light Direction drop-down list. When light comes from a single direction (Bottom, Left, Top, or Right), you can only see part of the texture pattern. For example, when light comes from the top, you can see only the portion of the texture that runs from left to right. When the light comes from an angle (Bottom Left, Top Left, Top Right, or Bottom Right), you can see both the texture running from left to right and from top to bottom.

Invert   Checking the Invert check box swaps the high and low points of the texture pattern. This effect is subtle and not particularly useful, especially with the finer textures that are more appropriate when using this filter with digital photos.

Charcoal   This filter redraws the image with a charcoal style, using the foreground color for the charcoal and the background color for the paper (see Figure 14-13). Major edges are drawn in bold strokes, while midtones are rendered using finer diagonal strokes. The Charcoal Thickness control determines the size of the charcoal "pen," with smaller values preserving more of the detail of the original image. The Detail control largely sets how carefully the midtones are rendered. Higher values of Detail are quite attractive, with many fine diagonal strokes doing a good job of reproducing the image. The Light/Dark Balance determines how dark a portion of the image must be before it is drawn in charcoal—higher values include lighter areas when rendering in charcoal.

Bas Relief   This filter makes the image appear to have been carved in low relief. The Detail control determines how much texture is added to the image to reproduce the original detail. High levels of Detail are especially effective with detailed cloud patterns and water surfaces. Smoothness determines how smoothly the textured areas blend together. However, values above about 4 blur the texture together so much that the result loses all its detail. The Light Direction drop-down list sets the direction the light comes from. Because Bas Relief simulates a carved surface, the direction of the light makes a *huge* difference in how the image looks. For example, Figure 14-14 is lit from the bottom, while Figure 14-15 is lit from the top left. Quite a difference, isn't there?

Chalk & Charcoal   This filter renders the image in a mixture of chalk and charcoal (see Figure 14-13). Very bright areas are rendered in the background color and show no texture. Light areas and midtones are drawn in gray chalk, showing a mixture of chalk and the background color, depending on the brightness of the area. Dark areas are drawn in charcoal in the foreground color. The Charcoal Area and Chalk Area controls work together to determine how much of the image is rendered in each medium. The Charcoal Area control determines how dark the dark areas must be before they are drawn in charcoal rather than chalk, while the Chalk Area control determines how much of the foreground color shows through the chalk in bright areas. The Stroke Pressure setting determines how much area is drawn in gray chalk. As the Stroke Pressure increases, less of the midtones are drawn in gray chalk.

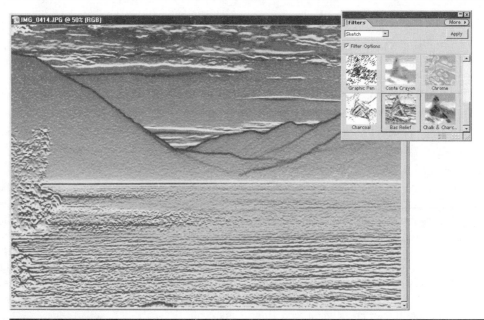

FIGURE 14-14   A Bas Relief filter with the light shining up from below.

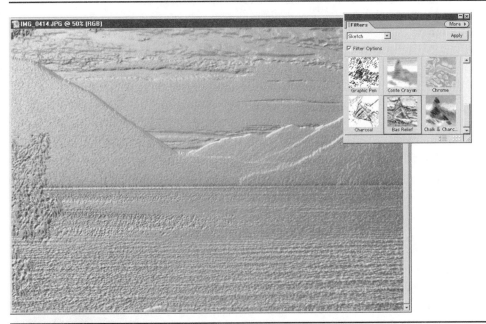

FIGURE 14-15   The same image with the light shining down from the top left.

Use the Stylize Filters

The Stylize filters change an image by displacing pixels and highlighting edges. The image ends up looking quite different from the original (not that unusual with filters), but some of the filters produce results that are nonetheless quite attractive.

Here are the Stylize filters that are useful for working with digital photos:

Trace Contour   This filter is mostly useful for creating stylized backgrounds. It finds transitions of brightness (*not* contrast) and outlines them in false color (see Figure 14-16). The Edge option determines how to outline the areas. Choosing Lower outlines where the brightness falls below the specified value, and choosing Upper outlines where the brightness rises above the specified value. The Level control sets the threshold for evaluating the brightness between 0 and 255. As you vary the Level control, Photoshop Elements finds different contours based both on the specific change (from one level to another) and the amount of brightness change.

14

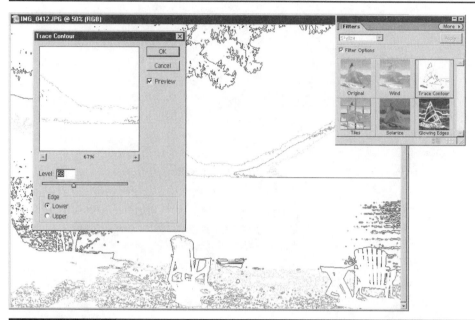

FIGURE 14-16 Trace the contours of edges and apply colors with the Trace Contour filter.

Solarize This filter blends a negative and a positive of the image. In the darkroom, I used to achieve this effect by briefly exposing the paper to light during development. There are no controls available for this filter, but the effect is quite attractive, especially in photos with lots of sunlit areas:

Glowing Edges   This filter identifies the edges of a color and applies a glow to those edges (see Figure 14-17). You can control the Edge Width and Edge Brightness, as well as the Smoothness of the transition between the glowing edge and the adjacent areas. To preserve detail, you should use low values of Smoothness, as high values obliterate some of the thinner edges.

Find Edges   This filter identifies the areas of an image that have significant transitions in color, and outlines those edges with a dark color against a white background. Large blocks of color without any edges are left in their original color. You have no control over this filter. As with the Trace Contour filter, this filter is useful for creating backgrounds.

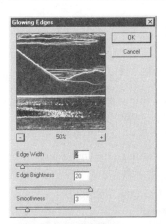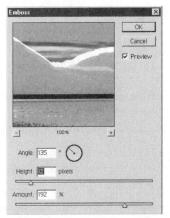

14

FIGURE 14-17   The Stylize filter dialog boxes (shown here for Glowing Edges, Emboss, and Diffuse) let you configure these filters.

Emboss   This filter (see Figure 14-17) makes the image appear to be either raised or lowered (stamped). It takes large blocks of color and converts them to grey, then traces the edges of the colored areas with the original fill color. You can set the following parameters:

Angle   Enter a number or drag the line in the circle to change the embossing angle. Positive values (0 to 360 degrees) raise the surface, while negative values (0 to –360 degrees) lower (stamp) the surface. The value controls the angle at which the edge of the raised or lowered surface is rendered.

Height   This setting controls the amount that the surface is raised (for positive values of Angle) or lowered (for negative values of Angle).

Amount   The Amount control sets the amount of color in the resulting image. Small values of this control leave you with an image that is rendered in a few shades of gray. Large values add more range of colors, effectively increasing the apparent contrast of the edges.

Diffuse   The Diffuse filter makes an image look less focused, especially along sharply defined edges (see Figure 14-17). It does this by mixing pixels. The Mode options set *how* the pixels are mixed:

Normal   This option mixes the pixels randomly.

Darken Only   This option replaces light pixels with darker ones (darkening the overall image).

Lighten Only   This option replaces dark pixels with lighter one (lightening the overall image).

Anistropic   This option softens all pixels.

Adding Texture to Images with the Texture Filters

The set of Texture filters provide various ways of adding texture to an image. Unlike other filters that add texture (such as the Conté Crayon filter), the Texture filters preserve the original colors of the image. The Texture filters are the following:

Texturizer   This filter (see Figure 14-18) enables you to make the image look like it was rendered on a textured surface. You can set the following options in the Texturizer dialog box:

Texture   Vary the texture by choosing an option from the Texture drop-down list. Values include Brick, Burlap, Canvas, and Sandstone.

Scaling   This option sets the size of the texture pattern. Small values give a fine texture; large values provide a coarse texture.

Relief   This option determines how deep (and visible) the texture is. High values of this control provide deep texture.

Light Direction   Since the Texturizer is a three-dimensional effect, the light direction affects how it looks. Choose the light direction from the Light Direction drop-down list. When light comes from a single direction (Bottom, Left, Top, or Right), you can only see part of the texture pattern. For example, when light comes from the top, you can see only the portion of the texture that runs from left to right. When the light comes from an angle (Bottom Left, Top Left, Top Right, or Bottom Right), you can see both the texture running from left to right and from top to bottom.

Invert   Checking the Invert check box swaps the high and low points of the texture pattern. This effect is subtle and not particularly useful, especially with the finer textures that are more appropriate when using this filter with digital photos.

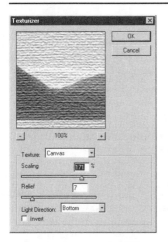
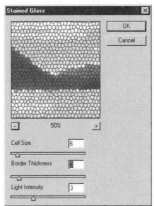
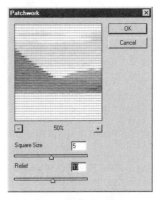
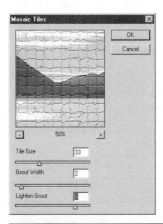
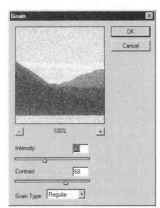
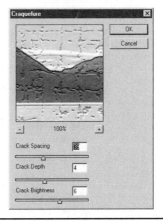

14

FIGURE 14-18   The Texture filter dialog boxes (shown here for Texturizer, Stained Glass, Patchwork, Mosaic Tiles, Grain, and Craquelure) let you configure these filters.

Stained Glass   This filter renders an image that looks like it was created from stained glass (see Figure 14-18). The foreground color is used to outline each piece of glass. A lot of detail can be lost, so you'll want to use an image that doesn't have a lot of detail to start with. The Cell Size sets the size of the stained glass cells—sizes over about 10 leave the image unrecognizable. The Border Thickness sets the width of the lines between the cells. The Light Intensity is a subtle effect that determines whether a cell that renders an area containing both dark and light colors will be dark or light. A higher value of Light Intensity favors the lighter colors.

Patchwork   This filter breaks up the image into small squares, much like sheets of tiles (see Figure 14-18). Each square in the patchwork displays the predominant color for that area. Very light colors result in raised tiles, very dark colors result in recessed tiles. The Square Size control sets the size of the tile. The Relief control determines how much tiles are raised or lowered depending on the brightness.

Mosaic Tiles   This filter makes your image look like it was painted onto tiles, with grout applied between the tiles (see Figure 14-18). The Tile Size control determines the size of the tiles. Large tiles work much better than small ones, because with small tiles the grout breaks up the image in a rather jarring way and a lot of detail is lost. The Grout Width control sets the width of the grout spaces between the tiles—keep this small, especially with the smaller tile sizes. The Lighten Grout control lightens the color of the grout from black (at a setting of 0) to a color that closely matches the colors of the tiles around the grout (at a setting of 10).

Grain   This filter adds a grain pattern to the image (see Figure 14-18). Choose the type of grain you want from the Grain Type drop-down list. The Sprinkles and Stippled grains use the background color for the grain. The Intensity control sets how much grain is added to the image, and the Contrast control sets the overall contrast of the image.

Craquelure   This filter creates the effect of painting an image onto a textured plaster surface, producing a network of cracks that follow the edges of the image (see Figure 14-18). This works especially well with images that feature a wide range of colors, giving an embossed effect. To customize the effect, use the following parameters:

Crack Spacing   A high value of Crack Spacing reduces the number of cracks visible in the image, although there are always cracks along high-contrast edges. A low value provides for many more cracks, giving texture to single-color areas.

Crack Depth   This control sets the depth of the crack. Deeper cracks have a darker color for a given value of Crack Brightness.

Crack Brightness   This control sets the brightness of the bottom of a crack. The color is a shade of the colors around the crack, but low values of Crack Brightness make the cracks more noticeable by making them darker. High values of Crack Brightness set the crack color to be almost identical to the surrounding areas.

Chapter 15

Use Power Filters to Enhance Your Images

How to...

- ■ Use blur to simulate motion
- ■ Precisely control blurring effects
- ■ Liquefy portions of an image
- ■ Create water reflections
- ■ Add light sources to an image
- ■ Build cloud patterns
- ■ Transform portions of an image in three dimensions

In addition to the filters we covered in Chapter 14, Photoshop Elements provides filters to add blur and noise, as well as make your image look like it is being viewed through glass or reflected in water. Some filters enable you to "push" pixels around any way you want, add and remove lighting sources, and even simulate three-dimensional objects like spheres, cubes, and cylinders.

Work with Blur Filters

The Blur filters soften a selection or an image by smoothing sharp edges. These filters are often most useful with selections because you can use blur to soften a "busy" background and leave the subject in sharp focus. We did an example of this in Chapter 8.

Blur and Blur More are very simple filters—they just smooth transitions at sharp edges. I don't tend to use them much because they provide no control at all. As you would expect, Blur More applies more of the effect than does Blur, but you have to apply these filters consecutively to get the amount of blur you want.

Precisely Control Blur with Smart Blur

The Smart Blur filter enables you to control exactly how much blur is applied to the image, as shown in Figure 15-1.

The dialog box lets you set the following parameters:

Radius   This setting determines how far Photoshop Elements searches from an edge to find dissimilar pixels to blur. The larger the radius, the more blurry the image becomes, because Photoshop Elements makes the change over a wider range of pixels. As you make the radius larger, the distance at which some detail is lost (Blurred) from an edge increases.

FIGURE 15-1 Configure the options for the SmartBlur filter with the SmartBlur filter dialog box.

Threshold This control determines how dissimilar pixels have to be before Photoshop Elements blurs them together. A higher value of threshold reduces the number of affected edges.

Quality The Quality drop-down list provides three choices (Low, Medium, and High) that determine the level of calculations that Photoshop Elements does to produce the blur effect. High quality provides smoother transitions, but takes longer to produce the blur effect. I have found little visible difference between the quality levels at most combinations of radius and threshold.

Mode The Normal mode produces results that blur edges without doing anything else. There are two other modes available, however. Edge Only converts the image to black and white; white shows up only at identified edges. Overlay Edge places white lines at the identified edges, as shown in Figure 15-2.

15

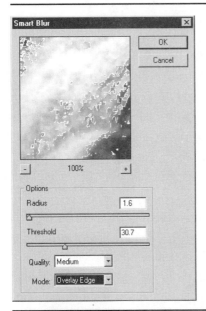

FIGURE 15-2   Choose Overlay Edge to highlight edges in white.

Smart Blur's precise controls enable you to set exactly the amount of blur you want, making it an excellent tool for blurring backgrounds (Gaussian blur is also good for this, as shown in Chapter 8). An unmodified image, with a somewhat distracting background behind it, is shown here on the left. On the right is the same image after I selected the subjects, inverted the selection to select the background, and applied Smart Blur with a radius of 20 and a threshold of 50:

Add Realistic Blur with Gaussian Blur

Gaussian blur is one of the most useful of the blur tools. It can produce a hazy effect and is excellent for blurring backgrounds so they do not distract from the subject of the picture (as we did in Chapter 8). When Photoshop Elements applies a Gaussian blur, it applies a weighted average amount of blur across the radius you specify. This makes Gaussian blur not only a simple (and quick) tool to use, but also makes the blur less intrusive and more like the "slightly out of focus" effect you are usually trying to achieve when blurring a background.

Simulate Motion with Motion Blur

The Motion Blur filter enables you to simulate motion. Provided that you select the "moving" subject before applying the filter, this filter simulates setting up your camera on a tripod, and using a long shutter speed (about one second or so) to shoot a moving subject. The non-moving portions of the image are sharp, but the moving subject is blurred. Now you can achieve that effect even when the subject was *not* moving—as in this image of the Norwegian Sun, which appears to be zipping along like a speedboat, as shown in Figure 15-3.

To achieve this effect, I selected the Motion Blur filter and set the parameters in the dialog box:

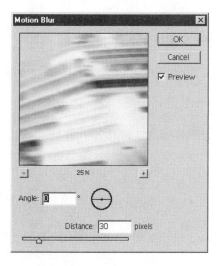

The parameters are:

Angle   This option sets the angle at which the blur occurs. You can either type in a value or click and drag the line in the Angle icon.

Distance   Use the Distance field or slider to control the number of pixels to blur the image. The higher the value, the faster the subject appears to be traveling, but the more distortion you get during the blur.

15

This ship was actually standing still, but I made it appear to be moving with Motion Blur.

Work with Distort Filters

The Distort filters are something of a mixed bag. Some, like the Shear, Twirl, and ZigZag filters, apply severe distortion to an image so that they are of limited usefulness for digital photography. However, even these are kind of fun to experiment with, and can be useful for creating stylized backgrounds. For example, here is a beach scene where I applied ZigZag with amount set to 37%, ridge height of 8, and the style set to Pond Ripples:

Look at Your Image Through Glass

The Glass filter has the effect of overlaying your image with glass. This filter can be useful not only for modifying an image, but to create a background by using the Glass filter on a pattern. You can customize the Glass filter options as follows:

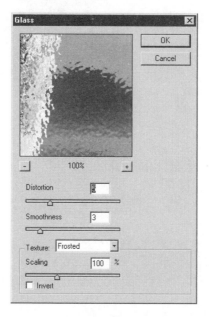

Distortion   As you might expect, increasing the distortion increases the effect of the filter. For example, if you choose a Frosted texture, the amount of frosting increases.

Smoothness   The Smoothness control determines how noticeable the texture is. Low values of smoothness, for example, make the "frosting" in Frosted texture stand out more; high values of smoothness hide the frosting.

Texture   Use the Texture drop-down list to pick from various distortion textures, including Frosted, Canvas, Tiny Lens, and Blocks.

Scaling   The Scaling control determines the size of the applied texture. Smaller values create a finer texture; larger values create a coarser texture.

Create Water Reflections with Ripple and Ocean Ripple

The Ripple filter and the related Ocean Ripple filter are quite useful for simulating an image viewed under water or simulating a water reflection. For example, Figure 15-4a shows an image of a range of hills with water in the foreground.

15

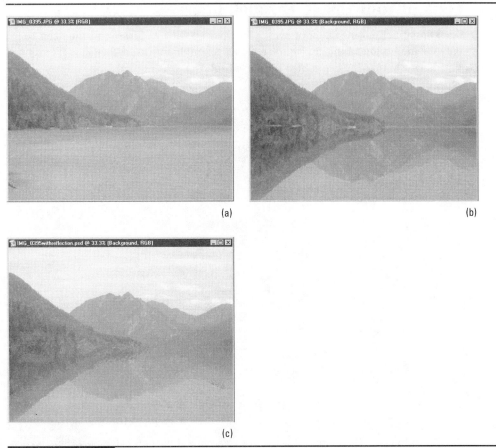

(a)   (b)

(c)

FIGURE 15-4   Applying the Ocean Ripple filter enables you to create a water reflection where there wasn't one.

To make the hills look like they are being reflected in the water, follow these steps:

1. Select the hills down to the waterline with the Magnetic Lasso tool.

2. Copy the selection (Edit | Copy) and paste it back into the image (Edit | Paste) to create a new layer containing the selection.

3. Rotate the layer so it appears upside down in the image. To do so, choose Image | Rotate | Layer 180, then choose Image | Rotate | Flip Layer Horizontal.

4. Pick the Move tool from the toolbox and drag the "reflection" down until the straight edge of the selection (what *was* the bottom) lines up with the waterline of the original image (see Figure 15-4b).

5. To apply the ripple effect so that the reflection looks like it is being reflected in the water, choose the Ripple filter or the Ocean Ripple filter. The Ripple filter enables you to set an amount and size (Small, Medium, Large). The Ocean Ripple allows you more control of the size of the ripples (Ripple Magnitude), so that is what I'll use here:

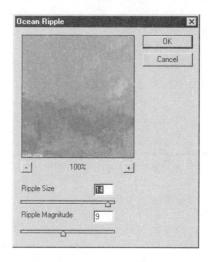

6. I set the both the ripple size and ripple magnitude to 14, because this seemed like a good match to the ripples I could see in the river. I clicked OK to get the result you see in Figure 15-4c.

The Ripple and Ocean Ripple filters distort the edges of the area. Any area that is left blank by this distortion is filled with the background color. Thus, pick a neutral background color that will blend in with the portion of the image to which you are applying the filter. You can also use the Clone Stamp to touch up those areas.

Define Your Own Wave Patterns

If you don't like the Ripple or Ocean Ripple filters, you can build your own ripple-type filter using the Wave filter. This is a very complex filter, as you can tell from the dialog box in which you customize how the filter works, as shown in Figure 15-5.

15

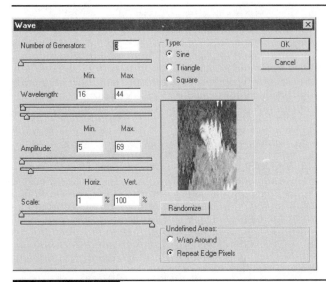

FIGURE 15-5 Configure the options for the Wave filter with the Wave dialog box.

Set the parameters in the Wave filter options dialog box as follows:

Type You can choose one of three types of waves: a square wave, a triangular wave, or a sine wave. A sine wave is an oscillating wave that varies from high to low in a smooth fashion with no sharp points (unlike a triangular wave) and no sharp corners (unlike a square wave). The distortion produced by the filter follows the shape of the wave. For example, the left image shows a sine wave, and the right image shows a triangular wave:

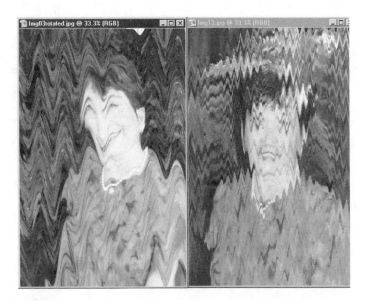

Number of Generators This parameter defines the number of wave generators—the higher the number, the more distortion waves are added to the image. For most effects, more than about 3 or 4 generators produce so much distortion the image is unrecognizable.

Wavelength The wavelength is measured from the top (or crest) of one wave to the next. For example, with a triangular wave, the distance between the points at the top of the wave pattern is the wavelength. Use the Wavelength sliders to set the distance between the crests. You can set the minimum and maximum distance, and the wave pattern will vary between the two. Set the two quantities the same to get a consistent wave pattern.

Amplitude The amplitude is the distance between the highest point and the lowest point in the wave. You can set both the minimum and maximum amplitude, and the wave pattern will vary between the two. Set the two quantities the same to get a consistent wave pattern.

Scale Use Scale to control the percentage of allowed waves that will be drawn in the horizontal and vertical directions. For example, the default setting of 1% for horizontal and 100% for vertical means that there will be very few horizontal waves, and all the allowed vertical waves.

NOTE *A vertical wave is the normal one you think of—you measure the wavelength (distance between the crests) from left to right, just like the ocean. A horizontal wave travels from top to bottom—that is, to measure the wavelength, you'd need a ruler from the top of the image to the bottom.*

Randomize Click the Randomize button to apply random combinations of the parameters. You can click it multiple times until you get a result you like.

Undefined Areas The Wave distortion leaves blank areas at the edges of the image, and you need to tell Photoshop Elements how to fill in these area. You have two options: to wrap pixels around and to repeat the nearest edge pixels.

Simulate a Diffusion Filter

The Diffuse Glow filter lets you add both grain and a glow that fades from the center of an image, as shown in Figure 15-6. Use the Diffuse Glow dialog box to set the following three options:

Graininess This option adds grain (Noise), most noticeably in lighter areas of the image.

Glow Amount Use this option to add the glow color to the image. The glow color is the background color, so be sure to set the background color to the glow color you want before invoking the filter. Also, high values of this quantity drown out most of the detail in the image, so go easy—a good value is 2 or 3.

Clear Amount Think of the Clear Amount control as a color layer over the image (the color of this layer is the glow color). As you decrease the clear amount, you can see less and less of the image underneath. At a clear amount of 0, the layer is completely opaque and you can't see the image at all.

15

FIGURE 15-6   Configure the options for the Diffuse Glow filter with the Diffuse Glow dialog box.

Melt Your Image with the Liquefy Filter

Using the Liquefy filter, you can expand, contract, twist, warp, shift, and reflect areas of an image. Many of these effects might seem to be of limited usefulness in digital photography, but you never know. For example, the Bloat tool turns out to be great for increasing the size of someone's eyes, lips, or other features. Subtle adjustments can make a portrait much more attractive, as we'll see.

To fire up the Liquefy filter, double-click the Liquefy entry in the Filters palette (make sure to choose the Distort category first). Or choose Filter | Distort | Liquefy. Either way, Photoshop Elements opens a large preview of the selected image in the Liquefy dialog box, as shown in Figure 15-7.

The liquefy tools are in a vertical row in the upper-left corner of the dialog box. There are also some basic tools you'll need to use for almost any liquefy effect. They are:

Hand tool   The Hand tool enables you to reposition the picture in the preview area. Click the Hand tool and move it over the image in the preview area. Click and drag the image to reposition it.

Zoom tool   The Zoom tool is located just above the Hand tool. Click the image to increase the magnification, or ALT-click to reduce the magnification. You can also adjust the magnification by using the drop-down list in the lower-left corner of the dialog box. Pick the magnification percent you want from this list. This list reflects the current magnification when you use the Zoom tool.

Reconstruction tool   If you overdo it with a liquefy tool, you can back out of part of the change using the Reconstruction tool. Simply choose the Reconstruction tool (the brush icon just above the Zoom tool) and begin painting over an area where you used a Liquefy effect. Each stroke backs out part of the change, until the area is back to its original state.

To revert the preview back to the state of the original image, click the Revert button.

Brush Size   The Brush Size is on the right side of the dialog box. All of the liquefy tools use a brush; type in a value for the brush size in pixels or click the arrow and use the Brush Size slider to set the brush size.

Brush Pressure   Type in a value or use the Brush Pressure slider to control the pressure. Higher brush pressures create more distortion with each stroke. I recommend you use a low value for Brush Pressure to avoid overdoing it.

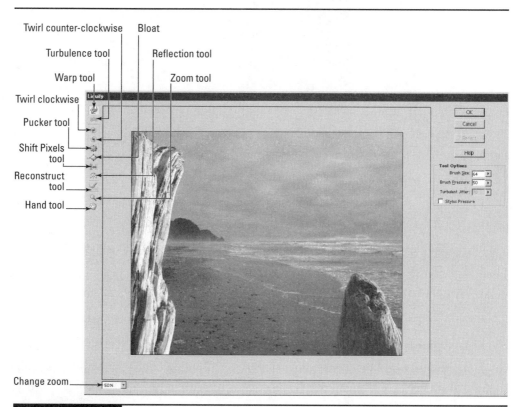

15

FIGURE 15-7   Make changes to a preview of your image, then click OK to apply the changes to the original image.

The liquefy tools include Warp, Jitter, Twirl (clockwise and counter-clockwise), Pucker, Bloat, Shift Pixels, Turbulence, and Reflection. Each tool has its own uses and idiosyncrasies.

Use the Warp Tool to Push Pixels

The Warp tool pushes pixels forward as you drag the brush. The effect is somewhat akin to smearing your finger in wet paint, as you can see here:

With some care and even strokes, you can simulate the reflection of bright colors in a wet surface. It is also handy for turning a distracting background into a surreal montage.

To apply the Warp tool in a straight line, click in the preview area where you want the line to begin. Move the mouse pointer to the location at the end of the line, and SHIFT-*click. Photoshop Elements applies the distortion in a straight line between the two points.*

Mix Pixels with the Turbulence Tool

The Turbulence tool smoothly mixes the pixels it encounters. As you continue to apply this tool, it mixes in pixels from farther and farther away from the brush. This tool can be handy to create waves, spread the effect of water reflection, create a large fire from a small one, and expand sunlit holes in a dark, cloudy sky. It is also especially good at creating ripples in a watery surface, as shown in Figure 15-8. The Turbulent Jitter option controls the smoothness—higher values increase the smoothness of the mixture.

Expand and Contract a Shape with Pucker and Bloat

The Pucker and Bloat tools are effectively opposites of one another. The Pucker tool "sucks" everything inside the brush toward the center, while the Bloat tool expands everything out from the center. When applied with care, you can use the Bloat tool to enlarge eyes in a photo. This is especially effective with infants and puppies, as larger eyes make them more adorable. To use the Bloat tool to increase the size of eyes, follow these steps:

1. Open the image you want to modify and choose Filters | Distort | Liquefy. Choose the Bloat tool.

2. Select a brush size that matches the size of the eye you want to expand, and set the brush pressure to a low value (about 30) to avoid making the change too fast.

Ripples added with the Turbulence tool

FIGURE 15-8   The ripples to the left of the image were added using the Turbulence tool.

15

3. Move the brush so that it is centered over the eye:

4. Click to enlarge each eye.

You can correct a partial squint using this technique as well. Depending on how much correction you wish to do, you may need to enlarge the brush part way through the correction.

Move Pixels Perpendicular with Shift Pixels

The Shift Pixels tool moves pixels in a direction perpendicular to the direction in which you drag the brush. Table 15-1 summarizes the direction in which pixels move when you drag the brush in a given direction.

Drag the Mouse in this Direction	Pixels Shift in this Direction
Left	Down
Right	Up
Up	Left
Down	Right

TABLE 15-1   Pixel Movement Caused by the Shift Pixels Tool

TIP *You can reverse the direction in which pixels shift by pressing the ALT key. Thus, if you hold down the ALT key and drag the mouse left, the pixels will shift up.*

Create Reflections with the Reflection Tool

The Reflection tool is one of the most useful in the Liquefy arsenal. It copies pixels into the brush area in a direction perpendicular to the direction in which you drag the brush. For example, if you drag the brush left, Photoshop Elements populates the brush area with the pixels above the brush. Here is an example showing the results of dragging the brush to the left below one of our floats:

As you can see, by making the brush about the same size as the float, I was able to get a fair simulation of a water reflection. Table 15-2 summarizes where the pixels come from when you drag the Reflection tool across an image.

Drag Reflection Tool in this Direction	Reflected Pixels Come From
Left	Above
Right	Below
Up	Right
Down	Left

TABLE 15-2   Pixel Movement Caused by Dragging the Reflection Tool

15

The Reflection tool behaves quite a bit differently if you hold down the ALT key when dragging. In this case, it reflects the area in the direction opposite to the direction of the stroke. For example, if you drag the Reflection tool downward, the reflection comes from the area above the starting point of the stroke. As you drag away from the starting point, the pixels come from farther away in the opposite direction. Thus, when the tool reaches a point 1 inch *below* the starting point, the pixels come from a point 1 inch *above* the starting point. This enables you to create a reflected image, such as I did here:

Table 15-3 summarizes where the pixels come from when you drag the Reflection tool with the ALT key held down.

Drag Reflection Tool with ALT in this Direction	Reflected Pixels Come From
Right	Left and moving left
Left	Right and moving right
Up	Below and moving down
Down	Above and moving up

TABLE 15-3   Pixel Movement Caused by Dragging the Reflection Tool and Using the ALT Key

Work with the Noise Filters

Back in Chapter 7, I used the Dust & Scratches filter (one of the noise filters) to remove small scratches and dust spots from a photo. There are some other noise filters that are also useful.

Use Median to Reduce Motion Blur

The Median filter blends the brightness of pixels within a selection together to reduce motion blur. You don't want to apply this to a whole image because it reduces detail considerably—for example, our floats picture becomes a set of orange blobs. The radius parameter sets the distance for which the filter searches for pixels of similar brightness. Pixels that differ too much from their adjacent pixels are discarded, and the center pixel is replaced with a pixel that has the median brightness of the sampled pixels:

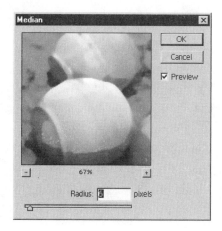

Accentuate Edges with Despeckle

The Despeckle Noise filter detects the edges in an image and blurs everything except for those edges. This accentuates the edges, but can also accentuate noise (despite what the manual says).

Add Noise to an Image with the Add Noise Filter

The Add Noise filter enables you to add "grain" to an image. It can also be used to reduce the banding effect in feathered selections and graduated fills. For example, here is an image in which an object has been copied with a wide feathering, then pasted back into the image. By adding some light noise, the edges of the pasted object becomes easier to see.

You can also apply noise to the entire image to get the effect of an extreme enlargement or of "push processing" film. "Push processing" refers to chemically treating the film after it is exposed to try and increase the speed. For example, in the past many people would push process 400-speed film to get an effective speed of 800 or even 1200 under low-light conditions. This technique introduces graininess to the result, as I simulate with the Add Noise filter in Figure 15-9.

When you select the Add Noise filter, Photoshop Elements displays the dialog box for you to customize the filter, as shown in Figure 15-10.

The parameters are as follows:

Amount   This parameter sets the amount of grain present. Use this control in moderation, as values over about 20 produce a rather jarring result.

15

FIGURE 15-9   Add grain to an image with the Add Noise filter.

FIGURE 15-10   Applying noise to a feathered selection makes the edges easier to see.

Distribution   You have two options for the Distribution parameter: Uniform and Gaussian. Choosing Uniform distributes the color values of the grain (Noise) randomly between 0 and the value specified in the Amount field. Gaussian uses a different distribution—a bell-shaped curve that varies between 0 and the value specified in the Amount field. You tend to get a more noticeable grain pattern with a Gaussian distribution.

Monochromatic   Checking the Monochromatic check box applies the grain pattern only to the tonal values (Brightness) and does not modify the colors.

Work with the Render Filters

The Render filters enable you to apply 3-D shapes, create cloud patterns, simulate lens flare, and specify a wide variety of lighting effects.

Build Your Own Cloud Patterns

It can be very handy to create a quick cloud pattern to use for a background. For example, you can take a studio portrait with a single-color background, remove the background easily with the Magic Eraser, convert the background to a layer, and create a new background with a cloud pattern.

The Cloud filter generates a cloud pattern using random mixtures of the foreground and background color. Here is an example of a cloud pattern with the foreground color set to a deep blue, while the background color is a light yellow:

If you want a dark, threatening cloud formation instead, set the foreground color to gray or blue-gray. An effective set of parameters is to set the colors to R=33, G=88, and B=95.

Tint Your Image with Difference Clouds

The Difference Clouds filter works initially like the Cloud filter—it generates a cloud pattern using random mixtures of the foreground and background color. However, instead of then simply creating an opaque cloud pattern, it overlays the result onto the original image in Difference mode. That is, if the cloud color has a greater brightness than the image color, the filter subtracts the image color from the cloud cover. If the image color has a greater brightness than the cloud color, the filter subtracts the cloud color from the image color. When working with digital photos, I have found that the effects are more stunning (and somewhat more subtle as well) if you apply the Difference Clouds filter twice, and set both the foreground and background colors to light pastels (like pink and yellow). For example, on the left is the original image and on the right is the same image after applying Difference Clouds twice with light colors:

Add Lens Flare to a Bright Picture

Lens flare is an effect that occurs when a bright light (such as the sun) interacts with the camera lens to create a bright spot that obliterates part of the picture. This is rare in high-quality lenses, and it is normally something you want to try and avoid! But the lens flare can give a very realistic effect to a photo. For example, the images shown on the following page illustrate the before and after results of this effect. The photo on the left, with the bright sun peeking out from behind a cloud, is exactly the sort of photo that can lead to lens flare (in fact there *is* a little lens flare visible). If I add some noticeable lens flare, I could achieve a result like the one shown on the right.

To configure the Lens Flare filter, use the Lens Flare dialog box:

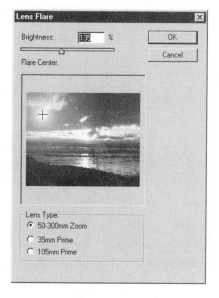

You can set the location of the lens flare by clicking in the preview area or by dragging the crosshair of the lens flare. You can also adjust the shape of the lens flare by picking a Lens Type option. The 105mm (Portrait) lens has the most intense lens flare effect, while the 35mm (Wide Angle) has additional reflections off to the side of the flare and a distinct ring around the flare. The 50–300mm Zoom lens has about the same intensity as the 35mm lens and the same ring, but with a different reflection pattern. Use the Brightness field or slider to set the intensity of the lens flare.

15

Add Lights to Your Image with Lighting Effects

You can vary the lighting in a picture even after it is taken, adding multiple lights chosen from three different kinds of light sources, changing the color of the lights, the distance and focus, the reflectivity of the scene, and many other parameters to get just the effect you want. You can also select lighting styles from a predefined menu, and save your own styles for later use.

The Lighting Effects dialog box can be somewhat overwhelming, but it is logically arranged, as shown in Figure 15-11.

To ease the learning curve for understanding and using the Lighting Effect filter, you should set up the lights in a certain order. Of course, you can go back and tweak the settings later, but I recommend you do things in the following order:

1. Pick a style from the Style drop-down list that most closely matches what you are trying to achieve. If none of the styles match, you can skip this step.

2. Set the properties of the photo and the ambient light in the bottom section of the dialog box. This sets the baseline you'll work with, so it is best to do this first.

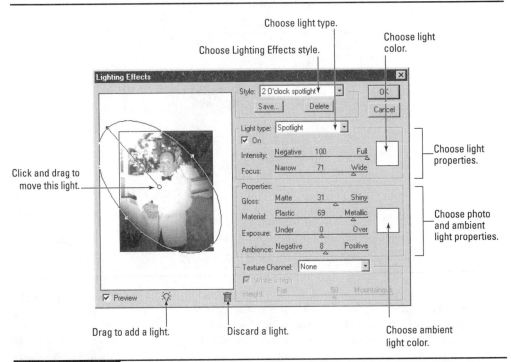

FIGURE 15-11   Use the Lighting Effects dialog box to set the lighting the way you want and fine-tune the result.

Turn off the default lights (clear the On check box in the upper section of the dialog box) before setting the properties of the photo and the ambient light.

3. Choose a style of light and position the light in the preview area.

4. Set the properties of the light, including intensity, focus, color, angle, and distance.

Select a Pre-existing Light Style

You can select from a wide range of predefined light styles in the Style drop-down list. Each style defines all the parameters you can view and set in the Lighting Effects dialog box. These lighting styles are an excellent place to begin customizing. Here is a sample of the preview you see when you pick the light style Five Lights Up:

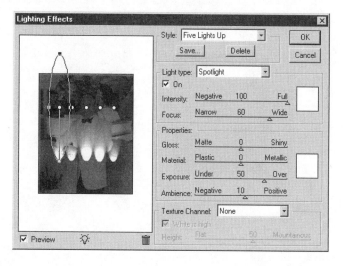

As you modify the settings in the Lighting Effects dialog box, you may find that you want to save your settings as a new style. To do so, click the Save button, provide a name in the Save As dialog box, and click OK. The new style then appears in the drop-down list.

Set the Photo and Ambient Light Properties of the Image

Since you'll be adding your lighting effects to the existing photo, the next step is to set the properties of the photo and the ambient light source. This is done in the bottom portion of the Lighting Effects dialog box. The parameters you can set are:

Gloss   Gloss determines how much light the photo reflects. A matte finish reflects very little light, whereas a shiny finish reflects a lot of light, creating a glare effect from a powerful light.

15

Material   Material determines whether the photo reflects the light's color or its own color. Plastic reflects the color of the light, while metallic reflects the color of the photo. This effect is fairly subtle and is most noticeable with a spotlight using a color other than white.

Exposure   Exposure determines whether the image appears overexposed (with highlights washed out) or underexposed (loss of contrast and muddy dark areas). I am not sure why anyone would want to deliberately set the exposure wrong, but you can if you want.

Ambience   Ambience sets whether your alternate light source is diffused (Mixes) with other (Ambient) light. A value of 100 provides the full strength of the ambient light in addition to the alternate light source. A value of –100 turns off the ambient light source altogether. For example, here is a preview of an image with very little ambient light and a strong spotlight:

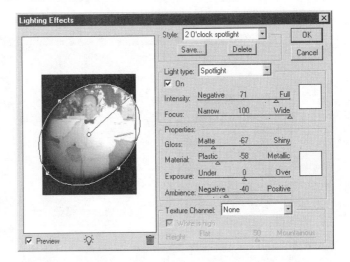

Ambient Light Color   You can change the color of the ambient light, which tints the image in the areas where the ambient light is the primary light source. To set the color of the ambient light, click the square in the Properties section of the dialog box. Pick the color of the light from the Color Picker, and click OK.

Apply a Texture to the Image

You can use the Lighting Effects dialog box to apply texture to an image as well. In effect, you can attach a "height" to the brightness of the image, and set the height individually for all three colors (Red, Green, and Blue). To set up a texture for an image, follow these steps:

1. Pick the color (Red, Green, or Blue) from the Texture Channel drop-down list.

2. Specify the height to apply to this texture channel, from 0 (Flat) to 100 (Mountainous).

3. To raise the light parts of the channel, check the White Is High check box. To raise the dark parts of the channel, clear the White Is High check box.

4. Repeat steps 2 and 3 for the other two channels.

Here is an example of applying substantial texture to an image:

Add and Edit Lights

The whole reason for having the Lighting Effects filter is so you can add light sources to the image, and customize how the light sources work. To add a light to the image, click the light bulb icon at the bottom of the dialog box and drag the light into the preview area. To move a light, click the hollow circle and drag the light to a new location. This hollow circle is visible at the end of a line (Directional Light), in the center of a circle (Omni Light), or in the center of an oval (Spotlight).

To discard a light you no longer need, click the hollow circle and drag it to the trashcan icon at the bottom of the dialog box.

15

There are three types of lights available for you to use:

Spotlight   The Spotlight is a highly directional floodlight that casts an elliptical beam. The intensity of the beam is higher at the source end of the beam, and you can control the focus and shape (Angle) of the beam.

Omni The Omni light shines in all directions from above the image, like a light bulb hanging over the picture. Of course, since you are looking at the image from the front, you are looking "through" the light bulb. You can adjust the size of the lighted area, as well as the intensity of the light bulb.

Directional A Directional light shines from one angle, like the sun shining down on the image. You can adjust the angle and distance of the light. As the light gets closer to the image, it gets more intense, but you can also adjust the intensity.

Adjusting each of the lights works slightly differently, although there are certain similarities. You can change the intensity of all the lights using the Intensity slider. You can also change the light color by clicking the square in the upper portion of the dialog box and picking the light color from the Color Picker.

Adjust the Omni Light The Omni light is represented by a circle with the hollow dot in the middle:

The only other adjustment you can make for the Omni light is to move it closer to the image or farther away. To simulate moving it farther away (and thus increasing the radius of the light), drag the sizing handles to expand the circle. To simulate moving the light closer to the image, drag the sizing handles to make the circle smaller.

 *You would expect that as you move the light farther from the image, the intensity would decrease, but that is not what happens with this filter. To reduce the intensity, you'll need to reduce the value of the Intensity field.*

Adjust the Directional Light A Directional light is represented by a straight line. The line has the hollow dot (for moving the light) at one end and a solid square at the other end. This square represents the position of the light:

For a Directional light, you can vary both the angle and distance of the light from the image by clicking and dragging the square dot. If you drag the square dot to shorten the line, the light moves closer to the image, and the intensity of the light increases. The angle of the light is represented by the angle of the line.

To change the direction of the line but not the length of the line (distance from the image), hold down the CTRL key while dragging the square dot. To change the length of the line but not the angle, hold down the SHIFT key while dragging the square dot.

Adjust the Spotlight   Understanding how the Spotlight works is a little tricky because there are so many options you can adjust. The Spotlight is represented in the preview area by an oval. The oval represents the position of the light relative to the image, the distance of the light from the image, and the angle at which the light is shining on the image:

Imagine a flashlight shining on a photograph. If the flashlight were positioned above and to the left of the image, and the light were shining down back down on the image at a steep angle, you might see something similar to the last illustration. Under these circumstances, the light would form an oval pattern on the image. There are three things you can do to change how the light shines on the image. They are:

Reposition the light   You can move the light while maintaining both the distance from the image and the angle of the light. In this case, neither the shape of the light nor its intensity would change. However, the "hot spot" (most intense point) and the light pattern around the hot spot would move. This is exactly what happens when you click and drag the hollow spot.

Rotate the light over the image   You can rotate the angle at which the light falls on the image. Think of taking your flashlight and rotating it from its position above the upper-left corner to a position directly over the image, shining straight down on the image. During this rotation, the shape of the light will change from the oval you saw before to a circle when the light is directly over the image, as shown in Figure 15-12a. To accomplish this, you need to change the shape of the oval. You can do that by either clicking and dragging the square at the end of the line (the light position), or by clicking and dragging the sizing handles on the oval to change its shape. Clicking and dragging the square at the end of the line also has the effect of moving the light either closer or farther away from the image. As you would expect (and can see in Figure 15-12b), if you move the light very close to the image, only a portion of the image is lit. If you hold down the SHIFT key while dragging the square or the other sizing handles, the angle of the line remains constant.

15

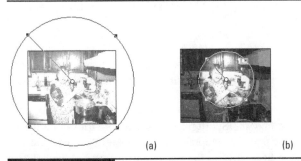

(a)   (b)

FIGURE 15-12   Moving the light directly over the image lights the whole image in a circular pattern (a) and bringing the light very close to the image lights only a small portion of the image (b).

Rotate the light around the image   You can rotate the light around the edge of the image. For example, you can take your flashlight and move it from its position above the upper-left corner to a position above the lower-left corner. The distance from the image doesn't change nor does the shape of the light (angle at which the light shines *down* on the image). To rotate the light around the image, click and drag the square sizing handle and the end of the line to change the angle of the line. To ensure that only the angle of the line changes and the oval dimensions remain unchanged, hold down the CTRL key while dragging the sizing handles.

The Spotlight has one more control: the Focus slider. This controls the focus of the light—how much of the oval is filled with light. Setting the focus to wide disperses the beam widely, filling the oval. Setting the focus to narrow keeps the beam narrowly focused and leaves much of the oval unlit:

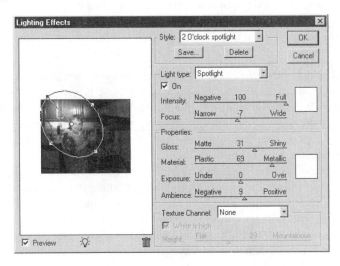

Add Three-Dimensional Effects with the 3D Transform

One of the more interesting filters is the 3D Transform filter. It enables you to specify a portion of an image as a three-dimensional shape (Sphere, Cube, or Cylinder) and manipulate that portion of the image in three-dimensions. For example, Figure 15-13 shows two views of a bottle. The view on the left is the original; the view on the right is how it looked after I rotated the bottle in three dimensions.

The first step in using the 3D Transform filter is to open the image and choose the 3D Transform filter. This displays the 3D Transform dialog box, as shown in Figure 15-14.

The Zoom control (magnifying glass) works just like the Zoom tool in the toolbox: click the image to zoom in, ALT-click to zoom out. If the entire image isn't visible in the preview area, you can pan the image around to see different parts of it by clicking and dragging with the Hand tool.

The 3D Transform dialog box only previews the active layer. Thus, you can't see any layers below the object layer to preview how the result will look against those layers.

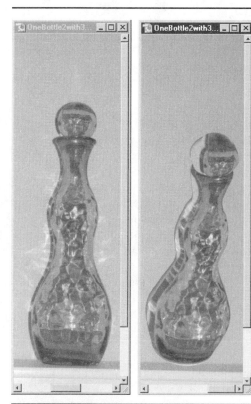

FIGURE 15-13   A bottle before and after a three-dimensional rotation.

15

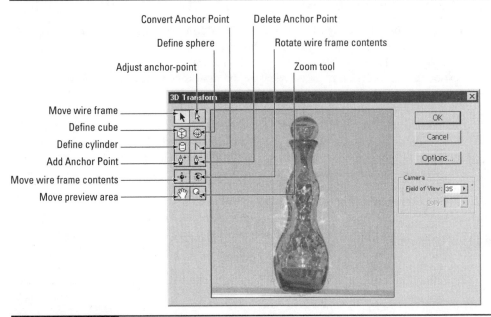

Convert Anchor Point   Delete Anchor Point

Define sphere   Rotate wire frame contents

Adjust anchor-point   Zoom tool

Move wire frame

Define cube

Define cylinder

Add Anchor Point

Move wire frame contents

Move preview area

FIGURE 15-14   The 3D Transform dialog box provides all the tools necessary to define and manipulate objects in three dimensions.

Did you know?

The best use of the 3D Transform is to manipulate objects such as globes, bottles, and boxes against a blank background, then copy and paste the result into another image. Or you can use the option (in the Options dialog box) to keep only the manipulated shape, separating it from the original background. If you manipulate these shapes against a detailed background, a certain amount of distortion is unavoidable because the shape definition will invariably include small portions of the background you didn't want. With shapes shot against a single-color background or separated from the background, on the other hand, you can get exactly the effect you want, then select just the shape and add it to another image.

Set the 3D Transform Options

The 3D Transform dialog box has some options you can set. To set the options, click the Options button to display the Options dialog box:

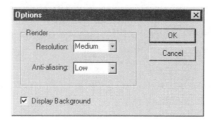

The options are:

Resolution   Pick High, Medium, or Low from the Resolution drop-down list. This option determines the quality of the rendered image. It has the most effect with complex images with curved surfaces, such as cylinders and spheres.

Anti-aliasing   Pick None, Low, Medium, or High from the Anti-aliasing drop-down list. This option determines how much anti-aliasing will be applied to the rendered image to help it blend with the background.

Display Background   The Display Background check box determines whether the preview area *and the rendered image* include the background outside the wire frame shape once you choose either the Pan Camera or the Trackball tool. By clearing this check box, you can separate the shape from its original background. This makes it easy to "touch up" the edges and paste the shape into another image after completing the 3D Transform.

Understand the 3D Transform Shapes

There are a trio of three-dimensional tools to work with: a sphere, a cube, and a cylinder:

Sphere   Use the Sphere to map to a spherical surface, such as a ball or a globe.

Cube   Use the Cube to map to a cubic surface, such as a box, cabinet, or even a house.

Cylinder   Use the Cylinder to map to a cylindrical surface, such as a can, coffee cup, or a pole. Because you can modify the shape of a cylinder, you can also map the cylinder shape to lathed shapes such as a bottle or a wine glass.

15

Each of the three-dimensional shapes has a Wire Frame tool you can use to define the shape in the image.

Create and Manipulate a 3-D Shape

You use the same techniques to define the wire frame regardless of the shape you choose. To define the wire frame, follow these steps:

1. Click the tool you want to use in the 3D Transform dialog box.

2. Move the mouse pointer over the preview image, and click and drag to define the initial wire frame (see Figure 15-15a).

To remove a wire frame, choose the Selection tool, click the wire frame, and press the DELETE key.

3. If necessary, reposition the wire frame to better match the image by choosing the Selection tool and clicking and dragging any edge of the wire frame. The Selection tool is the solid arrow in the upper-left corner of the tool palette.

4. If necessary, resize the wire frame by choosing the Direct Selection tool and clicking and dragging an anchor point on the edge of the wire frame. The Direct Selection tool is the hollow arrow in the upper-right corner of the tool palette.

(a)

(b)

(c)

FIGURE 15-15   Select, copy, and rotate a three-dimensional shape in 3D Transform.

5.   If you are using a cylindrical shape, you can modify the shape using the Add Anchor Point, Subtract Anchor Point, and Convert Anchor Point tools, as described in "Work with a Cylindrical Shape," later in this chapter.

6.   Use the Field Of View control to fine-tune the viewing angle for cylinders and cubes, as described in the next few sections. For spheres, this control has no effect while the wire frame is still visible.

7.   Use the Pan Camera control to click and drag the contents of the wire frame to another location in the preview area (see Figure 15-15b).

8.   Use the Trackball tool to rotate the shape (see Figure 15-15c).

9.   Use the Field Of View control in the Camera section of the dialog box to adjust the field of view. As the field of view decreases, the 3-D object gets larger, and if it is not centered in the image, it moves toward the closest edge.

The easiest way to understand field of view is to think of a set of zoom binoculars. As you zoom in with the binoculars, everything gets bigger, but you can see less of the overall picture, and objects that are not in the center of the image (assuming you are focused on the center of the image) seem to move off the edges of your field of view. Effectively, as you zoom in, you are decreasing the field of view; as you zoom out, you are increasing the field of view.

10.   Use the Dolly control to simulate moving the camera closer (decreasing values) or farther away (increasing values).

11.   Click OK to render the image.

Work with a Spherical Shape

To create and render a spherical surface, choose the Sphere tool and drag in the preview area to define the circular wire frame. Adjust the position and size following the instructions in the last section. In Figure 15-16a, I used a single ball shot against a fairly featureless background.

Once I had defined the sphere, I moved the shape off to the side using the Pan Camera tool, rotated the ball using the Trackball tool, and adjusted the field of view down a bit to increase the size of the ball. I got the result shown in Figure 15-16b.

Notice the left edge of the rendered image. I deliberately rotated the ball so far that it left a hole because Photoshop Elements doesn't *really* know what is behind the ball, and so it simply leaves that area blank. However, it was pretty easy for me to clean this area up with the Clone tool. It is even easier to turn off the background (in the Options dialog box) and then render, leaving me with just the rendered object on a black background. Then I can do the following:

1.   Select the object with the Magnetic Lasso.

2.   Copy the object to the clipboard (Edit | Copy).

15

3. Use the Undo History palette to undo the 3D Transform, leaving me with the unmodified original image.

4. Paste the transformed 3-D object back into the image (see Figure 15-16c). Voilà!

Work with a Cube Shape

To create and render a cube, choose the Cube tool and drag in the preview area to define a cube-shaped wire frame. Adjust the position and size to match the shape, as I did here:

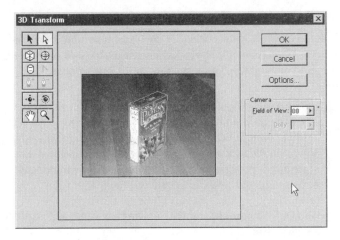

If the Cube tool doesn't fit the shape well, you can try adjusting the field of view. As you increase the field of view while the wire frame is visible, the angle of the top of the cube changes and the top appears to rotate down. Thus, in this case, I got a good fit by using a field of view of 88 degrees.

If you do change the field of view while the wire frame is visible, be prepared for a surprise when you switch to the Pan Camera or Trackball tool. When you switch to one of these tools, Photoshop Elements returns to the default field of view (35 degrees), which may mean that the object changes size drastically in the preview—or may disappear completely because it is outside of your field of view at the default setting. What you need to do is make a note of the field of view setting before switching to the Pan Camera or Trackball tool, then manually change the field of view back to the value you had set previously after picking one of these tools.

Manipulating a cube shape can be fun. For example, here I rotated the box of cereal into several different orientations. You'd never know I only had one box! Something else to notice is that Photoshop Elements does a good job with sides it doesn't have data for (like the bottom of the box). And, of course, it is easy to use the eye dropper to pick up the color of the side panel, and use the Paint Bucket to recolor the bottom of the box (which is what I did in Figure 5-17).

(a)   (b)

(c)

FIGURE 15-16   Use the Sphere tool to define a three-dimensional globe both with (b) and without (c) a problem rotation area.

FIGURE 15-17   Use the cube shape in the 3D Transform filter to rotate cubes to different angles.

Drag up and down to change cylinder length;
left and right to adjust cylinder top diameter.

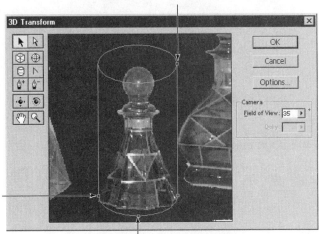

Drag left and right to adjust
cylinder bottom diameter, up
and down to tilt side of cylinder.

Drag up and down to roll cylinder front to back.

FIGURE 15-18   Use the Cylinder sizing handles to adjust the shape of the cylinder as well as the size.

Work with a Cylindrical Shape

To create and render a cylinder, choose the Cylinder tool and drag in the preview area to define a cylindrical wire frame. Adjust the position and size to roughly match the shape.

It's definitely worth experimenting with the sizing handles on the cylinder. You can use the sizing handles to not only adjust the overall size of the cylinder, but also to roll the cylinder front to back, adjust the size of the top and bottom independently, and even tilt the cylinder left or right. These sizing handles are shown in Figure 15-18.

As with the Cube, you can adjust the field of view to get a better fit to the object.

Despite all our efforts, the cylinder doesn't fit the shape of the bottle very well. However, you can add anchor points to get a better fit. Here is how you do that:

1. Click the Add Anchor Point tool in the tool palette (the fourth tool down from the top on the left side).

2. Move the mouse pointer to where you want to add the anchor point and click. You can only click the right side of the cylinder.

(a)   (b)

FIGURE 15-19   Add and drag anchor points to fit the Cylinder to a complex shape.

NOTE
To remove an anchor point you've added, click the anchor point with the Remove Anchor Point tool (located right next to the Add Anchor Point tool).

3. Switch to the Direct Selection tool and drag the anchor point to fit the side of the cylinder to the shape. As you drag the new anchor point on the right side, *both* sides move. Thus, the shape must be symmetrical (see Figure 15-19a).

TIP
Click and drag with the Add Anchor Point tool to both add an anchor point and move that anchor point to its new location.

4. Continue adding anchor points and adjusting the shape until you have a good fit to the object (see Figure 15-19b).

5. If you wish, switch to the Pan Camera tool to move the shape to another portion of the image, then use the Trackball tool to rotate the shape to its new orientation.

6. Click OK to render the 3-D object:

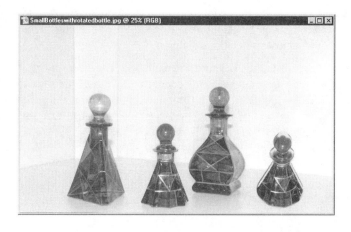

15

There are two kinds of anchor points. A smooth anchor point creates a gentle curve when you adjust it; a corner anchor point creates a sharp corner. To switch an anchor point from one type to the other, click the anchor point with the Convert Anchor Point tool (just below the Sphere tool).

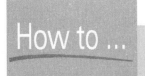

Align a 3-D Shape with an Underlying Layer

One common technique when building 3-D objects is to copy the object from the background or another layer and paste it into its own layer. This way, your modification doesn't change the background or original layer, and you can always discard the object layer and start over if you wish. However, the problem with this approach is that if the object is on its own layer, you can't see the layer underneath (the one you want to align with) in the 3D Transform preview. To get around this limitation, follow these steps:

1. Copy and paste the object you want to transform into its own layer.

2. Duplicate the layer with which you want to align. The easiest way to do that is to right-click on the layer in the Layers palette, and choose Duplicate Layer from the context menu. Give the layer a name in the Duplicate Layer dialog box, and click OK.

3. Set up the stacking order of the layers so that the object you want to transform is directly above the duplicated layer.

4. Choose Layer | Merge Down to merge the object layer into the duplicated layer you want to align with.

5. Add the appropriately shaped wire frame and transform the object, making sure that the Display Background check box is checked in the Options dialog box.

6. Open the Options dialog box, clear the Display Background check box to hide everything on the duplicated layer except the contents of the wire frame, and click OK to close the Options dialog box.

7. Click OK in the 3D Transform dialog box to render the transform. When it is done, the only thing left visible on the object layer is the transformed object, now aligned with the original of the layer you duplicated. You can see the layer with which you want to align *through* the object layer because everything on the object layer (except the object itself) is transparent.

Sharpen Photos with the Sharpen Filters

The set of Sharpen filters increases the contrast of adjacent pixels, sharpening the apparent focus. The Sharpen and Sharpen More filters do not provide any options; they simply make this change on the entire image. As the name would imply, Sharpen More applies a more intense effect than Sharpen. You can apply either of these filters multiple times to increase the sharpening effect.

The Sharpen Edges filter sharpens only "edges"—areas where there is a significant difference in contrast between adjacent pixels. As with Sharpen and Sharpen More, you don't have any control over this filter, although you can apply it multiple times to achieve more sharpening.

The most sophisticated sharpening filter is the Unsharp Mask. As described in Chapter 4, this filter enables you to set the amount of contrast you consider to define an edge (Threshold), how much additional contrast to apply (Amount), and how far from the edge the filter should apply the change (Radius).

Combine Filters with Effects

Photoshop Elements offers you the ability to combine filters and layers to create some specialized effects, such as frames, textures, Text Effects, and Image Effects. You can select an effect from the Effects palette:

Build a Custom Filter

If all the filters included still don't provide the effect you need, you can build your own filter using the Custom filter in the Others category (or choose Filter | Other | Custom). This opens the Custom dialog box:

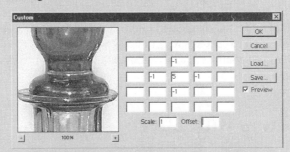

The Custom dialog box contains a matrix that represents a 5 × 5 collection of the pixels. The field (Pixel) at the very center is the current pixel being evaluated, the fields around that center field represent the pixels surrounding it. To create a custom filter, follow these steps:

1. Type a number into the center field. This is the value by which you want to multiply the pixel's brightness value. The range of values can vary from –999 to +999. Negative values decrease the brightness of the pixel, and positive values increase the brightness of the pixel.

2. Select one of the adjacent fields, and enter the value by which you want to multiply that pixel's brightness. For example, if you want to triple the brightness of the pixel immediately to the right of the center pixel, type **3** into the field immediately to the right of the center field.

3. Continue adding values to the adjacent fields. You don't have to enter values in all the fields.

4. Type a number into the Scale field. The Scale field is the value to divide the sum of the brightness values of the pixels included in the matrix. Larger values of Scale darken the overall image.

5. Type a number into the Offset field. The Offset field is the value to add to the result of the Scale calculation. A larger value of Offset increases the brightness of the image.

To save a custom filter, click the Save button, enter the name of the filter in the Save dialog box, and click OK. To load a filter you saved, click the Load button, choose the filter from the Load dialog box, and click Load to retrieve the filter definition.

 *The sum of the values in the fields should equal 1. A sum equal to 3 or more basically turns the entire image white; a sum equal or less than –3 turns the whole image black.*

Using effects is very simple: choose the category of effect you want to use from the drop-down list in the upper-left corner of the Effects palette, then either double-click the effect you want in the Effects palette, drag and drop the effect onto the image, or click the effect and then click the Apply button or choose Apply in the palette menu. There are no controls for customizing the effects.

Undoing the application of an effect is somewhat more complex than undoing a filter or other action. Many effects use multiple filters and may create layers as well. For example, the Lizard Skin effect (in the Image Effects category) utilizes Pointillize, Gaussian Blur, and Stained Glass.

The Effects categories are the following:

Frames   These effects apply frames, including Drop Shadow, Photo Corners, Vignettes, Wood, Brushed Aluminum, and Foreground Color frames. Effects are available that replace the edges of the image with a variety of frame patterns, such as Waves and Spatters. In addition, you can specify an effect that cuts out the selection, turning the initial photo into a frame and leaving you with a space where you can place another photo. Here is the Effects palette for Frames:

15

Textures   These effects provide an opaque texture on a layer. Textures include Sandpaper, Wood, Asphalt, Rusted Metal, Cold Lava, and many others.

Text Effects   These effects are applied on type (Text) layers (see Chapter 16 for information on creating text and type layers). They modify the text with effects such as Outlining, Wood Paneling, Water Reflection, and Shadows. The type layer is simplified when you apply a Text Effect, meaning that you can no longer change either the text or the text attributes (Font, Size, and so on) after you apply a Text Effect.

Image Effects   The Image Effects apply to entire images. Some are familiar, such as the Blizzard effect, others combine a variety of filters to produce a combination effect, such as the Fluorescent Chalk, Neon Lights, and Oil Pastel effects. There are also color-based effects, such as Horizontal Color Fade, Quadrant Color, Vertical Color Fade, Soft Flat Color, and Colorful Center.

Chapter 16

Add Type to
Your Images

How to...

- Add text to an image
- Modify the properties of the text
- Fill the text with color, patterns, and gradients
- Warp the text to create custom effects
- Apply text effects to the text
- Create a text-shaped mask

Adding text to an image can be useful. Not only can you label the image to point out important parts (as we did in Chapter 13), but you can also:

Add titles　How often have you put together a photo album and wished you had a picture to put on the cover or the first page that stated the subject of the album? Now you can add titles, choosing the font, size, style, and color of the text. You can also customize the text with text effects (from the Effects palette), as well as warp the shape to make it more interesting.

Add "text-shaped" holes　You can mask an image using the shape of your text. This way, you can see your image "through" a short descriptive phrase (like "Aruba").

Fill text with patterns or images　Another alternative is to create your text and fill it with a pattern or picture. This technique can produce a result similar to creating a text-shaped hole.

　*Photoshop Elements terminology is confusing when referring to text. The toolbar tools are called type tools, but options in the options bar refer to text. For example, various options allow you to change the text alignment, text color, warp text, and change the text orientation. The applicable effects in the Effects palette are also categorized as "text effects."*

Create Your Text

To create text in an image, choose one of the type tools from the toolbox:

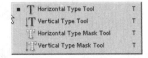

The two top selections enable you to create text in the image. The two bottom selections create a text-shaped mask. The four available tools fulfill the following purposes:

Horizontal Type tool   Enables you to type horizontal text. The first time you create text with the Horizontal Type tool, Photoshop Elements creates a separate layer (called a *type layer*) for the text.

Vertical Type tool   Enables you to type vertical text. The first time you create text with the Vertical Type tool, Photoshop Elements creates a separate type layer for the text.

Horizontal Type Mask tool   Creates a selection in the shape of horizontal text. This selection behaves much like a selection created with the Lasso or Marquee tool.

Vertical Type Mask tool   Creates a selection in the shape of vertical text.

> NOTE   *A text layer behaves very much like other layers I have discussed. For example, you can apply a blending mode, change the opacity, and apply layer styles to a text layer.*

Once you choose either the Horizontal Type tool or the Vertical Type tool, the mouse cursor turns into an insertion point text cursor, which looks like an "I," and the options bar displays the text options, as shown in Figure 16-1.

To type text into the image, click in the image to set the starting point for the text, and start typing. As you type, Photoshop Elements draws the text using the properties (style, typeface, size, alignment, anti-alias, and color) as specified in the options bar. To begin a new line, press ENTER.

> NOTE   *If you wish, you can set the options prior to clicking in the image and starting to type—it is up to you. As you'll see shortly, it is easy to change the options for existing text any time you want.*

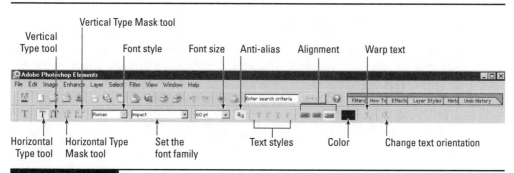

FIGURE 16-1   Use the text options in the options bar to specify the text properties.

16

You can move the insertion point around much like you would with a word processor. You can use the LEFT ARROW and RIGHT ARROW keys to move the insertion point back and forth in the current line of text, and use the UP ARROW and DOWN ARROW keys to move the insertion point to other lines of text. Pressing the BACKSPACE key erases the previous character, and pressing the DELETE key deletes the current character.

While you are typing the text, you are in Edit mode. The two controls at the right end of the options bar enable you to exit Edit mode and either keep your changes (click the check mark labeled Commit Any Current Edits) or cancel your changes (click the "not" symbol labeled Cancel Any Current Edits). You can also exit Edit mode and keep your changes by pressing CTRL-ENTER.

While you are in Edit mode, you can make any changes to the text that you want, including changing text properties, typing in new text, editing, and so on. However, if you try to execute non–text-related commands (such as changing the opacity of the layer or blending mode, clicking in the image, or making a selection from a palette), Photoshop Elements exits Edit mode and applies your changes. To reenter Edit mode (so you can make more changes to your text), choose one of the type tools again, and click in the existing text.

If you click outside the existing text area, Photoshop Elements creates another text layer. If this isn't what you wanted, click Cancel Any Current Edits in the options bar.

Edit and Modify the Text Properties

Once you have typed in your text, you can select all or a portion of the text, edit it, and change how the text looks. You have quite a bit of flexibility in performing these actions. For example, you can (if you wish) make each text letter a different color, font, and size.

Select Text for Editing

To make changes to your text, you must select the portion of the text you want to modify. Photoshop Elements lets you know which text is selected by highlighting the text:

There are a variety of ways to select the text:

Select all the text on the layer   To select all the text on a layer, double-click the Text layer in the Layers palette to highlight the text. You can also click the Text layer in the Layers palette and then choose a type tool. In either case, any changes you apply (such as changing the text size) apply to all the text.

Select with the text cursor (mouse)   To select a portion of the text on a layer, choose a type tool, then click with the mouse cursor and drag to highlight the text you want. In addition, you can:

- Double-click a word to select the whole word.
- Triple-click anywhere on a line to select the entire line.
- Quadruple-click anywhere in the text to select all the text.
- Click to set the insertion point at the beginning of the selection, then SHIFT-click at the ending point to select everything between the two points.

Select using the arrow keys   Once you select a type tool and click in the active text, you can select text using the arrow and SHIFT keys, just as you would with a word processor. Simply hold down the SHIFT key and press the arrow key to move the insertion point in the direction you want, selecting text as it moves. For example, to select the three characters to the left of the insertion point, hold down the SHIFT key and press the LEFT ARROW key three times. You can also make quick selections by doing the following:

- Select from the insertion point to the beginning of the current word by pressing the LEFT ARROW key while holding down the SHIFT and CTRL keys.
- Select from the insertion point to the end of the current word by pressing the RIGHT ARROW key while holding down the SHIFT and CTRL keys.
- Select from the insertion point to the beginning of the current line by pressing the SHIFT and HOME keys.
- Select from the insertion point to the end of the current line by pressing the SHIFT and END keys.

Modify the Text Properties

Photoshop Elements enables you to change all the text properties after you type the text. The easiest way to change the properties is to use the tools in the options bar, but some of the properties are available in the context menu as well. Some of the property changes (such as font, size, and color) apply just to the selected text, while others (such as anti-alias and alignment) apply to all the text.

16

Change the Font and Style

To change the font (Typeface) of the selected text, choose the font you want from the Set The Font Family drop-down list (second from the left in the options bar):

This list displays all the fonts you have available on your computer, and so will look different on your computer than it does on mine. Pick the font you want to use from the list.

 *If you want a very square (blocky) font to use when creating text "holes" for your images, either Arial Black or Impact works well.*

Depending on the font you pick, you can choose a style from the Font Style drop-down list (at the left end of the options bar). For example, if you pick Arial as your font, you can choose Regular, Italic, Bold, or Bold Italic for the font style. Some fonts (such as Impact) don't have any selectable styles (Impact has only the default *Roman* style). To choose a style, pick it from the list.

The four Text Style buttons near the center of the options bar provide additional options for customizing the text:

Faux Bold   If the font you choose (such as Impact) does not have a Bold style available in the Style drop-down list, you can click the Faux Bold button to simulate a bold style. Since this "fake bold" doesn't do as good a job as the Bold style, you should choose Faux Bold only if the "real bold" is not available for the chosen font. You can also choose the Faux Bold from the context menu.

Faux Italic   As with Faux Bold, if the font you choose does not have an Italic style available in the Style drop-down list, you can click the Faux Italic button to simulate an italic style. You should choose Faux Italic only if the "real italic" is not available for the chosen font. You can also choose the Faux Italic from the context menu.

Underline   Click the Underline button to underline the selected text.

Strikethrough   Click the Strikethrough button to create a line that runs through the selected text:

Change the Text Size

To change the size of the selected text, choose the size you want from the Set The Font Size drop-down list (third from the left in the options bar):

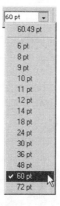

You set the size in *points* (72 points to the inch), and the maximum size you can set is 72 points using the drop-down list. However, as you'll see later, you can scale the text to increase the size. You can also type in a size. To do so, click anywhere in the font size field to display a text cursor. Then type in the size you want. The size of the text adjusts instantly as you type in the new size.

If you wish, you can change the unit of measure for the font size to either pixels or mm from the Type drop-down list in the Preferences dialog box (Edit | Preferences | Units & Rulers).

Change the Text Color

To change the color of the selected text, click the colored rectangle in the options bar (Set The Text Color). This action opens the Color Picker so you can choose any color you want. The Text Color rectangle normally shows the color of the selected text. However, if your text selection includes characters of more than one color, the Text Color rectangle is displayed in white with a small question mark in the center.

16

Use Anti-Aliasing to Smooth Text

Photoshop Elements can apply anti-aliasing to your text to make it blend more smoothly with the background. This effect applies to all the text on a layer, regardless of whether the text is selected or not. Anti-aliasing works by adding pixels along the edges of the text that blend the colors of the text with the colors of the background. For example, the following graphic on the left is a high magnification image of text against a background with anti-aliasing turned on. If we turn off anti-aliasing, the text shows jagged edges, especially along diagonal surfaces (such as the "w"), as shown on the right:

To turn anti-aliasing on and off, click the Anti-aliased button in the options bar (just to the right of the text size drop-down list). You can also choose either Anti-Alias Off or Anti-Alias On from the context menu. Whichever option is selected displays a check mark next to it:

Change the Text Alignment

Photoshop Elements provides three alignment controls in the options bar, just to the left of the Text Color rectangle control. These controls change depending on whether you are using horizontal text or vertical text orientation (see the next section for more about orientation) and apply to all the text on a layer. However, regardless of the alignment control you choose, the text always starts at the position where you click to create the initial insertion point.

For horizontal text, the three alignment controls are:

Left align text   All text is placed to the right of the starting point. That is, the original insertion point defines the left margin of the text.

Center text   The text is horizontally centered on the starting point. That is, half the text is placed to the left of the original insertion point, and half of the text is placed to the right.

Right align text   All text is placed to the left of the starting point. That is, the original insertion point defines the right margin of the text.

For vertical text, the three alignment controls are:

Top align text   All text is placed below the starting point. That is, the original insertion point defines the top margin of the vertical text.

Center text   The text is vertically centered on the starting point. That is, half the text is placed above the original insertion point, and half of the text is placed below.

Bottom align text   All text is placed above the starting point. That is, the original insertion point defines the bottom margin of the vertical text.

Change Text Orientation

As mentioned earlier, you can create text that runs horizontally (left to right) or vertically (top to bottom). You've seen a few examples of horizontal text. Here is some vertical text:

You can switch between horizontal and vertical orientation for all text on a layer (regardless of whether it is selected or not) by clicking the Change The Text Orientation button at the right end of the options bar. In addition to switching the orientation, the alignment of the text changes to the alignment that occupies the same position on the options bar. For example, if your horizontal text was left-aligned (the left-most alignment control for horizontal text), the vertical text will be top-aligned (the left-most alignment control for vertical text). You can, of course, change alignment after you adjust the text orientation.

Warp Text into Strange Shapes

You can change the overall shape of the text, forming it into an arc, bulge, flag, fish, and a whole host of other shapes. To do so, choose a type tool and click the Create Warped Text button in the options bar. Alternatively, you can right-click in the active text area and choose Warp Text from the context menu. Either way, the Warp Text dialog box appears:

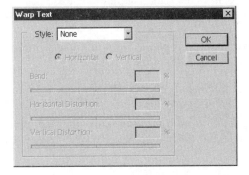

The first step in warping text is to choose the style from the Style drop-down list. A variety of basic shapes are available:

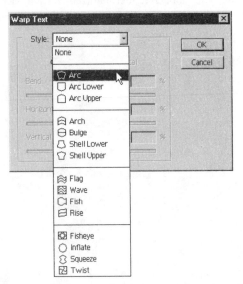

The next step is to decide whether you want the style to apply horizontally (click the Horizontal option) or vertically (click the Vertical option). The Horizontal option applies the deformation to the shape similar to how the shape is shown in the Style drop-down list. The Vertical option applies the deformation to the text as if the shape was rotated 90 degrees. Figure 16-2a shows an example of using both the Horizontal wave (on the left) and the Vertical wave (on the right). The same effect is applied to vertical text in Figure 16-2b.

To control the magnitude of the effect, using the Bend control. You can use the slider or you can type in a number between –100 and 100. A positive value for Bend increases the amount of the effect. A negative value for Bend reverses the effect and then increases the amount of the reverse effect. For example, Figure 16-3 displays the Squeeze effect with the horizontal option. The text on the left uses a large positive value of Bend. Notice that the text has taken on the shape of the Squeeze style. The text on the right uses a large negative value of Bend. Notice that the shape bulges out, rather than squeezing in.

The last two warp controls are the Horizontal Distortion and Vertical Distortion. The Horizontal Distortion controls the amount of distortion that occurs between the left and right end of the text. A positive value of Horizontal Distortion squeezes the left side and expands the right side of the text:

The Vertical Distortion controls the amount of distortion that occurs between the top and bottom of the text. A positive value of Vertical Distortion squeezes the top of the text and expands the bottom:

A negative value of Vertical Distortion reverses this effect, expanding the top of the text and squeezing the bottom.

A negative value of Horizontal Distortion reverses the effect, expanding the left side and squeezing the right side.

16

(a)

(b)

| FIGURE 16-2 | Warp both horizontal and vertical text using a variety of styles. |

Squeeze with large
positive value of Bend.

Squeeze with large
negative value of Bend.

| FIGURE 16-3 | The value of Bend controls not only how much of the effect to apply but in which direction. |

Reposition and Transform Text

Once you exit Edit mode (by clicking either the Cancel Any Current Edits button or the Commit Any Current Edits button), you are free to move your text or apply transformations.

To move the text, choose the Move tool from the toolbox. If you have the Select Bounding Box check box checked, you'll see the bounding box around the text, complete with the sizing handles and reference point (initially located in the middle of the bounding box). Simply click inside the bounding box and drag the text to a new location.

Moving the text can be very handy when you change the text orientation or alignment, since performing these operations usually leaves your text in a non-ideal position—often portions of the text are completely outside the image.

To apply a transformation to the text (and its bounding box), either click a sizing handle or make a selection from the Image | Rotate menu or the Image | Transform menu. Once you do, the options bar for transforms appears, and you can apply rotation, scale, or skew transforms as described in Chapter 11. For example, to resize the text, follow these steps:

1. Choose the Scale transform in the options bar.

2. Click a corner sizing handle and hold down the left mouse button.

3. Hold down the SHIFT key and drag the mouse cursor. This ensures that the aspect ratio remains unchanged.

If you scale the text as described above, then switch back to Edit mode (click a type tool, then click in the active text), you'll find that the new size is now displayed in the Font Size drop-down list.

When working with a text layer, you can't apply a Distort or a Perspective transform. Both of these choices are unavailable in the Image | Transform submenu. To perform one of these transforms, you must simplify the text layer first. To do so, select the layer in the Layers palette and choose Layer | Simplify Layer.

CAUTION   *Once you simplify a text layer, you can no longer edit the text on that layer, including changing the size, font, style, orientation, alignment, or color. As with other layers, a simplified text layer is just a set of pixels (which happen to look like text) that you can modify with brushes, the Paint Bucket, Gradient, Smudge, and other toolbar tools.*

Change the Text Layer

Since the text layer is indeed a layer, you can perform many of the same operations on it as you can with other layers. Some of these operations require that you simplify the text layer; others can be applied while leaving the text still editable.

16

Apply Layer Styles

As you'll recall from Chapter 10, *layer styles* are styles that you can apply to the entire contents of a layer. If you apply a layer style to a text layer, it applies to all the text, regardless of whether you have selected any text or not. There is really nothing special about layer styles when applied to a text layer, except that some styles are useful for text that were *not* useful for images. For example, here is our text with an applied drop shadow (very useful against a light background) and Wow-Neon Green Off. Pretty eye-catching, yes?

Apply Filters to Type

Filters are also very useful when applied to text, although you'll have to simplify the text layer before applying filters. For example, you can apply texture to the text with Underpainting (in the Artistic category), as shown in Figure 16-4a, or the Texturizer filter (in the Texture category).

(a)

(b)

| FIGURE 16-4 | Change the "look" of your text by applying filters, such as the Underpainting and Pointillize filters. |

Other useful filters are those that add colors to the text, such as the Pointillize filter (in the Pixelate category), which uses the background color in addition to the text color to generate this result, as shown in Figure 16-4b.

Apply Effects to Jazz Up Your Text

The Effects palette includes a whole set of effects designed specifically to work on text. To gain access to these effects, open the Effects palette and choose Text Effects from the drop-down list in the upper-left corner of the palette. Photoshop Elements displays the available text effects in the palette:

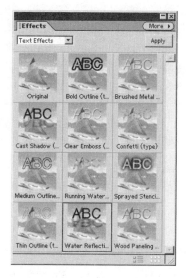

Applying an effect is simple. Select the Text layer in the Layers palette, then do one of the following:

- Double-click the effect you want.

- Click the effect and click the Apply button in the Effects palette or in the palette menu.

- Drag and drop the effect from the Effects palette onto the text.

As with the other effects, discussed in Chapter 15, you have no control over applying text effects. However, they do provide easy access to some complex results. For example, the Cast Shadow effect is shown in Figure 16-5a. The same figure shows the Water Reflection effect, which is handy when (as is in Figure 16-5b) the area under the text happens to be over a body of water.

Make sure you are done editing your text before applying an effect. This is because the text layer is automatically simplified when you use an effect. Photoshop Elements does not ask you for confirmation before making this change.

(a)

(b)

FIGURE 16-5 Applying effects (such as Cast Shadow or Water Reflection) customizes a text layer.

Apply a Fancy Fill to Text

Once you simplify your text layer, you can fill the text with a gradient, pattern, or picture. This can be a *lot* more interesting than the single color fill you can use with editable text. To change the text fill, follow these steps:

1. Simplify the text layer by choosing Layer | Simplify Layer or by right-clicking the Text layer in the Layers palette and picking Simplify Layer from the context menu.

2. Select just the text contents of the simplified layer by CTRL-clicking the simplified text layer:

3. Pick the fill tool you want to use (as described below) and apply the tool to the simplified text layer. Since only the text is selected, only the text will be affected by the results of your actions.

Add a Gradient Fill to Your Text

To apply a gradient fill, pick the Gradient tool from the toolbox. In the options bar, pick the gradient you want to use, as well as the gradient type (linear, radial, angle, reflected, or diamond). Drag the gradient line through the selected text, and the text is filled with the gradient:

Fill Text with a Pattern

To fill the selected text with a pattern, choose the Paint Bucket tool from the toolbox. In the options bar, choose Pattern from the Fill drop-down list, and pick the pattern from the Pattern drop-down list. If you want to fill all the letters with the same pattern, make sure the Contiguous check box is not checked, then move the Paint Bucket over one of the characters and click:

If you want to fill each letter with a different pattern, clear the Contiguous check box and repeat the cycle of picking a pattern and clicking a letter for each letter.

16

Fill Text with a Picture

To fill the selected text with a picture, follow these steps:

1. Open the file containing the image you want to use.

2. Select the portion you want using one of the selection tools (Marquee, Lasso, Magic Wand, or Selection Brush).

3. Copy the selection to the clipboard (Edit | Copy).

4. Switch back to the image containing the selected text.

5. Select the text on the simplified text layer by CTRL-clicking the Text layer in the Layers palette.

Make sure that the two images have the same resolution, or the results may not be what you expect. If the source image is much higher resolution than the text image, the text will be filled with only a small portion of the image you intended. If the source is much lower resolution than the text image, the text will only be partially filled with the image.

6. Paste the contents of the clipboard into the selected text (Edit | Paste Into):

Group an Image Layer with a Text Layer

One of the more interesting effects you can achieve with text is to use it as a *mask*—that is, a shape through which you can view an image. If you make the text descriptive of the image, the result not only displays the picture, but tells people what the image represents.

Creating a text mask combines several of the things you've learned about layers, including (most importantly) the fact that you can group layers together to use one layer as a mask for another. You can do this with any layer, including text layers, and since you don't have to simplify the layer first, you can go back and adjust the text layer to modify the results.

To use a text layer as a mask for an image, follow these steps:

1. Open the image that you want to view through the text layer mask.

2. Select the type tool from the toolbox.

3.   Click in the image where you want the text to reside, and type in the text. This action creates the new text layer. In the example shown in Figure 16-6a, I typed the "A" in "Aruba" on its own text layer so I could resize it independently of the other letters. I then placed the rest of the letters on their own layer.

4.   If necessary, adjust the font, size, style, alignment, and position of the text to get it looking just like you want. In the same example, I stretched the "A" across the entire width of the image and down to the point where it just left enough room for the rest of the island's name, as shown in Figure 16-6b.

> **TIP**   *If you find it difficult to select one of the text layers without selecting the other one, turn off the visibility of the text layer you don't want to select before selecting the other text layer.*

5.   Convert the background layer to a regular layer so you can move a layer underneath it (remember you can't move layers underneath a background layer). To convert the background layer to a regular layer, select the Background layer in the Layers palette, choose Layer | New | Layer From Background. Give the layer a name in the New Layer dialog box (I called mine "Image"), and click OK.

6.   Drag the text layer to a position below the image layer (the one we converted from the background layer in step 5). The text disappears because it is now behind the image layer.

7.   Click the image layer and choose Layer | Group With Previous. This causes the text layer to be used as a mask—the image layer is now only visible "through" the text in the text layer, as shown in Figure 16-6c.

The only problem with the final result is that the picture is blank outside the text mask. There are a couple of ways to fix this. The first way is to insert a pattern layer to fill in the blanks. To do so, choose Layer | New Fill Layer | Pattern. Give the layer a name in the New Layer dialog box, click OK, choose the fill from the Pattern Fill dialog box, and click OK. Make sure that the new pattern layer is positioned at the bottom of the stack. Here is what the image and Layers palette look like:

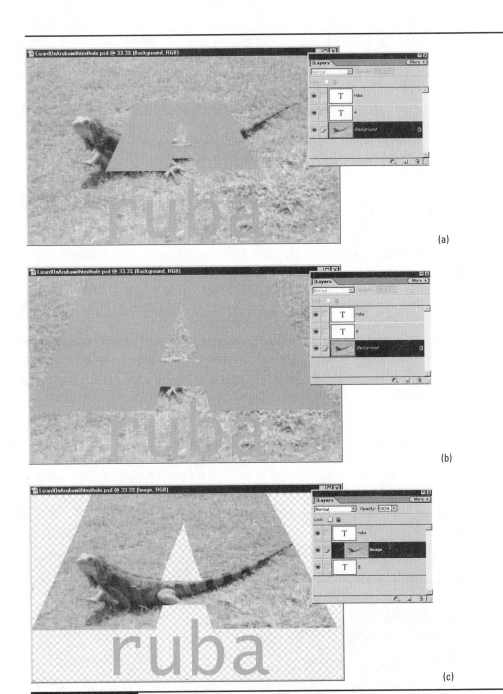

FIGURE 16-6   Group an image layer with a text layer to view the image through a text mask.

Another way to achieve the same effect with a pattern fill layer is to follow these steps:

1. CTRL-click the layer containing the text mask (the bottom layer containing the "A" in our example). This creates a selection in the shape of the text mask.

2. Invert the selection (choose Select | Inverse) so that everything *except* the text mask is selected.

3. Add a new pattern fill layer to the composition. To do so, choose Layer | New Fill Layer | Pattern. Give it a name in the New Layer dialog box, click OK, choose the fill from the Pattern Fill dialog box, and click OK. The pattern fill layer is only filled in the selected area. The result is identical to the previous illustration.

4. Make sure that the pattern fill layer is above the image layer but below the text layer containing any text that is not part of the mask ("ruba," in our case).

Another option is to paste in a picture to fill in the area outside the text mask. To do so, follow these steps:

1. Open the file containing the image you want to paste into the blank area.

2. Add the contents of this image to the original picture. The easiest way to do that is to click and drag the background layer for the new image from the Layers palette into the picture containing the text mask. This adds a new layer to the original picture that contains the new image. We'll call this new layer the *image fill layer*.

> **TIP** *You can also select a rectangular portion of the image to copy and paste into the image with the text mask.*

3. Position the image fill layer so that it is above the original picture layer and not grouped with any other layer. In our example, the image fill layer is above the original picture layer but below the text layer containing any text that is not part of the mask. Figure 16-7a shows what the picture looks like at this point.

4. Make sure the image fill layer is selected, then CTRL-click the layer containing the text mask (the bottom layer containing the "A" in our example). This creates a selection on the image fill layer in the shape of the text mask.

5. Choose Edit | Cut to punch the hole in the image fill layer, giving you the result shown in Figure 16-7b.

FIGURE 16-7   Fill in the edges of a text-masked image with the contents of another image.

Create a Text-Shaped Selection

Besides the two type tools, Photoshop Elements provides two *type mask* tools: the Horizontal Type Mask tool and the Vertical Type Mask tool. You use these tools pretty much the same way you use the type tools: choose the tool, click in the image, and begin typing. However, instead of creating text on a separate layer, the type mask tools create a selection in the shape of the text on the chosen layer.

When you first begin typing, Photoshop Elements provides a mask to show you the shape of the selection, as shown in the following graphic on the left. After you choose the Commit Any Current Edits button in the options bar, you can see the selection you created, as shown in the graphic on the right:

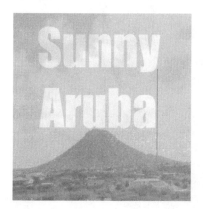 

TIP   *To remove the text selection, choose Select | Deselect.*

Unlike the type tools, you cannot reselect the text and change the properties after you commit the edit. The font, size, style, alignment, orientation, and warp are fixed. Any adjustments you make after committing the edit are used the next time you use the type mask tools. However, you *can* adjust the properties while the mask is still visible and before committing the edit.

Another limitation of the type mask tools is that you can't add more text to the selection once you commit the edit. Thus, if you click a layer with a type mask tool and begin typing more text, the new text selection will remain and the previous text selection will disappear once you commit the edit. You can, however, use the selection tools (Marquees, Lassos, and Brush Selection tool) to add selected areas to the text or subtract areas from the text. For example, if I use the Horizontal Type Mask tool to create a text selection that says "Aruba," then use the Rectangular Marquee tool to add to the selection, I get the result shown in Figure 16-8.

As with other selections, you can apply transforms such as scale, rotate, skew, distort, and perspective. You can also use the Move tool to move the selection on either a background layer or regular layer. As with transforms on any other selection, you must commit the transform (click the check mark on the options bar) to accept the change.

16

FIGURE 16-8 Using the selection tools to add selected areas to text.

NOTE   *The first time you want to move a text selection, you must click inside one of the letters to drag the selection to a new location. If you click between the letters (including on the reference point in the middle of the bounding box), you are actually clicking the layer immediately behind the text selection. This ends up either moving that layer if it is not the background layer, or presenting you with a warning that the layer is locked (if it is the background layer). After you have clicked inside one of the letters, you can then click anywhere inside the bounding box to move the text selection.*

Create a Mask with the Type Mask Tools

Another way to create a text mask is to use the type mask tools. Since these tools are designed specifically for creating selections, they can be less complex to use for creating masks as long as you do things in the right order. Here is how to proceed to create a text-shaped hole in a fill layer:

1. Open the picture you want to view through the mask.

2. Create a new pattern fill layer with the pattern you want.

3. Select one of the type mask tools and add the text selection to the fill layer.

4. Move or transform the text selection to adjust the size of the mask.

Reduce the opacity of the fill layer so you can see the image underneath while sizing the text selection. Do not turn off the visibility of the fill layer, because then the text selection is residing on the background layer.

5. Simplify the pattern fill layer by choosing Layer | Simplify Layer.

6. Cut out the text-shaped hole in the simplified fill layer by choosing Edit | Cut. Figure 16-9 shows you what you might get as a result.

If you'd like to use a picture rather than a fill layer, follow the instructions above, then follow these steps:

1. CTRL-click the simplified pattern fill layer to select all the opaque portions of the layer. This selects everything *except* the holes left by cutting out the text.

2. Open the file containing the picture you'd like to paste into the image.

3. In the newly opened image, choose Select | All to select the entire image, or use a marquee (or other selection) tool to select the portion you want.

4. Copy the selected portion to the clipboard (Edit | Copy).

5. Switch to the original image and paste the contents of the clipboard into the selected layer (Edit | Paste Into), as shown in Figure 16-10. Voilà!

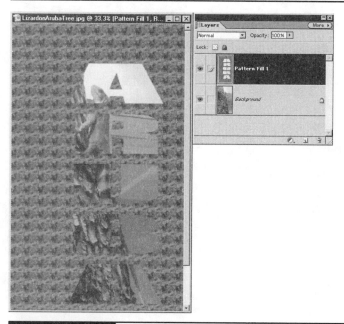

FIGURE 16-9   Cut a text-shaped hole in a pattern fill layer.

16

FIGURE 16-10   Cut a text-shaped hole in an image to allow another image to show through.

Chapter 17

Build Panoramics from Your Images

How to...

- Create images suitable for building a panoramic
- Align pictures and create the panoramic
- Adjust perspective and vanishing point
- Remove perspective distortion
- Generate the panoramic

Sometimes, no matter how hard you try, you just can't fit an entire scene into a single photograph. Wide-angle lenses can help, but if you want to take a picture of an entire city skyline, you are going to have to take multiple pictures and patch them together to form a *panoramic view*, or *panoramic* (for short). You may also find it useful to take a vertical panoramic of a tall building or landmark.

Understand the Photomerge Tool

Photoshop Elements provides the Photomerge tool to help you "patch together" (or merge) multiple photos into a panoramic, as shown in Figure 17-1. The tool is split into two main areas: the *light box* that holds images you want to add to the panoramic, and the *work area*, in which you build the panoramic itself. If you follow the rules for creating images, the Photomerge tool does a pretty good job of automatically matching the images to create the panoramic with little effort on your part.

Build a Panoramic Image

To build a panoramic image, follow these steps:

1. Choose File | Create Photomerge. This opens the Photomerge dialog box:

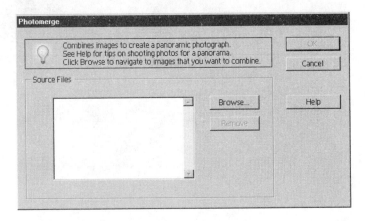

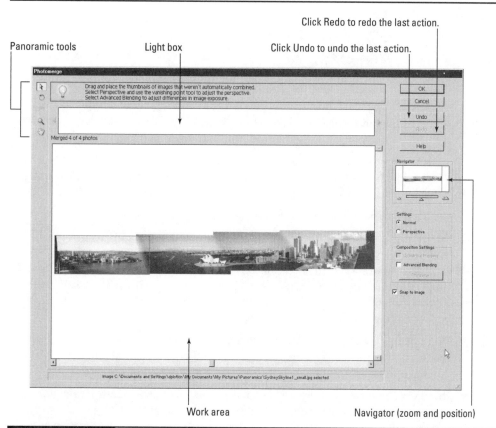

Click Redo to redo the last action.

Panoramic tools   Light box   Click Undo to undo the last action.

Work area   Navigator (zoom and position)

FIGURE 17-1   Use the Photomerge tool to join images together into a panoramic.

You can actually see the effect of different exposures (which I deliberately did incorrectly) in Figure 17-1. The two center images are darker than the two end images—courtesy of the film developer. In addition, the staggering of the images was necessary to get them to line up because I didn't have a tripod with me and had to hold the camera in my hands as I rotated it. Of course, it didn't help that I had just climbed over 500 stairs up to the observation deck of the Sydney (Australia) Harbor Bridge!

2. Click the Browse button to display the Open dialog box. Navigate to the folder containing the images you want to use, and choose them. To pick multiple files, click the first file, hold down the CTRL key, and click the other files. If you accidentally include a file you didn't need, click it again (with the CTRL key still held down).

17

Take Panoramic Pictures Correctly

If you know ahead of time that you are going to try and merge multiple images into a panoramic, following certain rules will increase the probability of being successful:

Overlap your images   Overlap your images by about 30%. The Photomerge tool uses the edges to detect similarities between the images and match them up. If there is insufficient overlap, Photoshop Elements will be unable to perform this function. Of course, you can manually order and align the images if the Photomerge tool can't do it for you.

Keep a constant focal length   As you take your pictures, you should not change the zoom setting (focal length) between the images. If you do, you won't be able to line up the multiple images.

Keep the camera level   It is very important to keep the camera level as you rotate it to snap the photos. Ideally, you should use a tripod with a pan head. If you don't have one with you, set your camera on a flat, hard surface and keep it stable as you rotate it (for horizontal pans). For vertical pans, you *really* need a tripod to make this work.

Don't change your viewpoint   Don't change your position between photographs. Pick a spot from which you can see everything you want to take a picture of, and shoot all your images from that point.

Don't change your exposure   This can be a tricky one, especially with automatic cameras. The problem is that if the exposure is different for each photo, the tone and brightness will vary from one image to another. Most cameras have a way to lock the exposure and take each picture with the same settings. And of course, you *can* fix the tone and brightness using Photoshop Elements (you do remember how, right?). You may have to do this with film-based images anyway, because many commercial processors exercise little care when printing your negatives.

Don't use fisheye lenses   Lenses that provide extreme wide-angle perspective introduce distortion, especially at the edges—right where the Photomerge tools need undistorted data to match the images.

NOTE   *Creating a panoramic is a very memory-intensive operation. Photoshop Elements must open each of the images, and create various copies of them as it attempts to merge them into a panoramic. Thus, it is best to keep the images small to avoid getting memory errors or spooling huge quantities of data to the hard drive. To keep the images small, reduce them to their viewable or printed size using Image | Resize | Image Size. Set the Resolution to a maximum of 72 dpi for viewing or 300 dpi for printing.*

3. Click OK to return to the Photomerge dialog box.

   *If the list of files in the Photomerge dialog box includes any files you don't need, click the file and click Remove.*

4. Click OK to start the process of creating the panoramic. You'll see Photoshop Elements open each file and then attempt to create the panoramic.

Once the process of creating the panoramic is completed, you'll see a larger version of the Photomerge dialog box. One of three results is possible:

All photos matched successfully   If Photoshop Elements is able to merge all the photos into a single panoramic, the image is visible in the work area of the Photomerge dialog box, and the light box is empty. This condition is shown in Figure 17-2.

No photos matched successfully   If Photoshop Elements is unable to merge any of the photos into a panoramic, it warns you with a small dialog box (click OK), and then presents the Photomerge dialog box with an empty work area and all the photos loaded into the light box. You'll need to manually merge the photos, as described next.

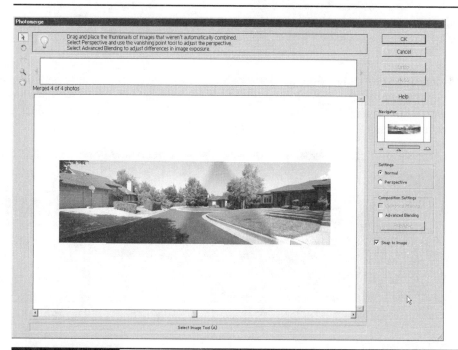

FIGURE 17-2   If Photoshop Elements is able to merge all the photos, you're pretty close to done!

17

Some photos matched successfully If Photoshop Elements is able to merge some photos and not others, it will warn you of this fact. Once you click OK, the Photomerge dialog box is presented with the merged photos in the work area and the unmatched photos in the light box. You'll need to manually merge the unmatched photos, as described next.

To create a panoramic manually—or add images to an automatically generated panoramic—you must click and drag an image from the light box and into the work area. As you pull the thumbnail of the unmerged image into the work area, it is presented as a full-size image.

If the work area is empty, simply drag the image to a location in the work area that is reasonable. For example, if the image is near the left side of the panoramic, drag it to the left edge of the work area.

If the work area is *not* empty, drag the image to edge where it should line up. As you drag one image on top of another, the image you are dragging becomes partially transparent so you can line it up with the existing image (shown below on the left). Line up the dragged image with the existing image and release the mouse button (shown here on the right).

Continue adding photos from the light box to the work area until you have built the entire panoramic. You can use the various tools in the Photomerge dialog box to view and adjust the properties of the panoramic, as I'll discuss in the next section. When you're done, click OK to create the panoramic and view it in Photoshop Elements:

If you check the Snap To Image check box, you don't need to get very close in lining up the two images—Photoshop Elements will line up the two images once you release the mouse button. If you don't check the Snap To Image check box, Photoshop Elements will leave the image right where you dropped it, and make no attempt to line the two images up.

CAUTION *Make sure your Photomerge file is exactly the way you want it before clicking OK to render the panoramic. Unlike version 1 of Photoshop Elements, you cannot reopen a panoramic in the Photomerge dialog box and modify how the images are merged or apply any other Photomerge tool modification (such as rotating one of the images, applying perspective, and so on).*

The last step in creating the panoramic is to save the Photomerge file. You can save it as a JPEG or other file type if you wish, but until you save it as a PSD file, Photoshop Elements will warn you that you haven't saved it if you try to close the file.

Modify the Photomerge Composition

You can adjust the images in your composition by moving or rotating them. To move an image, follow these steps:

1. Choose the Select Image tool in the upper-left corner of the Photomerge dialog box.

2. Choose the image to move by clicking the image. The selected image is displayed with a red border.

3. Drag the image to its new location. As you drag the image, the portions that overlap other images become partially transparent. To limit the drag to 45-degree increments, hold down the SHIFT key while dragging.

You may find that you need to rotate an image slightly if you were unable to keep the camera level while taking the photo. You *can* correct minor orientation differences. You may also find it useful to rotate an image if the perspective is particularly noticeable. To rotate an image, choose the image using the Select Image tool, then choose the Rotate Image tool (just below the Select Image tool). Click and drag to rotate the image. For example, the rightmost photo in this composition must be tilted (because of the perspective) in order to merge it properly into the panoramic:

17

Change the View Options of the Photomerge Dialog Box

The Photomerge dialog box provides a number of tools that enable you to control the zoom and positioning of your composition. The Zoom tool (magnifying glass) on the left side of the Photomerge dialog box works just like the Zoom tool in the toolbox: click to increase the magnification of the image; ALT-click to reduce the magnification. If you can't see the entire image in the work area, you can click and drag in the work area using the Move View tool (hand).

The Navigator on the right side of the Photomerge dialog box provides the same functionality. The slider under the thumbnail view changes the magnification: drag the slider left to decrease the zoom, or drag it right to increase the zoom. The red box represents your view of the work area. Simply click and drag the red box to change the portion of the work area you can see.

Apply Perspective to the Image

The whole idea of creating a panoramic is to shoot a very wide scene, rotating your camera as you take each shot to photograph the next image in the sequence. Attempting to represent this in a rectangle is actually impossible. The shape must be modified to accurately represent the panoramic. For example, if you focus on the center image of a panoramic, the shape of the image needs to be a "bow-tie"—wider at the ends than in the middle, as shown in Figure 17-3.

Alternatively, if you focus on one of the string of images, the images should get progressively wider toward the other end, as the panoramic gets closer to you, as shown in Figure 17-4.

As you can see from Figures 17-3 and 17-4, one of the images remains undistorted (the center one in Figure 17-3, the left one in Figure 17-4), while the others are distorted to simulate

FIGURE 17-3   Focusing on the center image changes the shape of the panoramic to a "bow-tie."

FIGURE 17-4   Focusing on a string of images changes the shape of the panoramic depending on which image is selected.

perspective. The undistorted image is the *vanishing point* image. To apply this sort of perspective to your panoramic, choose the Perspective option in the Settings section on the right side of the Photomerge dialog box. By default, Photoshop Elements chooses one of the center images as the vanishing point image. However, you can change the vanishing point image. To do so, choose the Set Vanishing Point tool (just below the Rotate Image tool) on the left side of the dialog box and click an image to make it the vanishing point image.

> **TIP** *You can tell which image is the vanishing point image using the Select Image tool. If the displayed border is blue when you click an image, it is the vanishing point image. Images that are not the vanishing point image display red borders when you click them.*

Photoshop Elements has the ability to correct most of the distortion introduced by Perspective. It does this by simulating what the image would look like if you wrapped it around a cylinder. To view this effect, click the Cylindrical Mapping check box in the Composition Settings section. Then click the Preview button to see what the image would look like:

17

While you're viewing the image in Preview mode, you can't make any modifications. When you are done viewing it, click the Exit Preview button to return to the editable version of the Photomerge dialog box.

Once you exit the Photomerge dialog box and start working with the panoramic in the Photoshop Elements main window, you can crop the rounded edges that result from cylindrical mapping, giving you a rectangular image that is easy to print.

Correct Color Differences with Advanced Blending

As mentioned earlier, it can be difficult to get all the images in a panoramic to match in their color, saturation, and brightness. Photoshop Elements can attempt to correct minor differences between images. To activate this feature, check the Advanced Blending check box in the Composition Settings section. The correction is only visible in Preview mode (click the Preview button). Unfortunately, unless the differences are *very* minor, Advanced Blending doesn't really make much difference. You are better off making the corrections yourself using layers.

Panoramics work much better—and have much less distortion—when your subject is a long way off. For example, it is much easier to get a good panoramic of a distant skyline or bridge than your backyard. This is because the perspective distortion in very close objects (like the path and grass in the example photos we saw earlier) is significant, and the amount of distortion changes as objects grow more distant. This makes matching the edges very difficult. It was easy to match the edges of the path near the bottom of the photo (where it was very close to the camera), but the edges of the pool in the background did not match well. Rotating the images helps some, but it is easy to see discontinuities at the edge of a photo, especially in straight lines, such as the reel at the right end of the pool. When you are photographing a distant skyline, the amount of perspective distortion is at a minimum and, more importantly, is roughly the same for all the objects in the panoramic.

Part V

Share Your Images with Others

Chapter 18

Prepare Your Images for the Web and Viewing

How to...

- Choose a format for web publishing
- Reduce the image size
- Optimize the image characteristics
- Create a web photo gallery for posting to a web site
- Create an image slideshow

One of the most popular uses for digital images is to post them on a web site where others can view them. With today's high-quality digital cameras and scanners, it is easy to create images that are huge and impractical to download over a dial-up connection. For example, my Minolta Dimage 7, set to highest quality JPEG, creates images that are between 2.5 and 3.5MB in size. Photoshop Elements enables you to adjust the dimensions and quality of images to reduce the file size.

Once you have the images down to a manageable file size, Photoshop Elements makes it easy to create a photo gallery that you can post on your web site. You can customize many of the features of the gallery, and when you are done, Photoshop Elements creates the HTML (web) page that displays thumbnails of your images and provides links to the images themselves.

Another way to view your images is to create a slideshow—an application that displays your images in the order you specify for a given period of time. Photoshop Elements can create an Adobe Acrobat (PDF) document for just this purpose. Anyone with a copy of Acrobat Reader (downloadable from http://www.adobe.com/products/acrobat/readstep.html) can view the contents of the slideshow.

Change the Picture Size to Keep Transfer Time Down

The simplest way to reduce the file size—and thus reduce the time it takes to transfer an image over the Web—is to change the size of the image itself. To do so, choose Image | Resize | Image Size to open the Image Size dialog box:

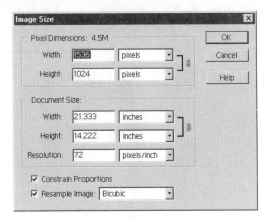

Set the Image Dimensions

Use the fields in the Document Size section of the Image Size dialog box to adjust the dimensions and resolution. To adjust the width or height of the image, type a value into the Width or Height field. You can choose the unit of measure for the width or height from the drop-down list adjacent to each field. Available units include percent, inches, cm, mm, points, picas, and columns.

If you check the Constrain Proportions check box, Photoshop Elements will maintain the original ratio of the width to the height. Adjusting either dimension automatically adjusts the other dimension.

To adjust the resolution of the image, type a value into the Resolution field. You can pick the unit of measure (either pixels/inch or pixels/cm) from the drop-down list adjacent to the Resolution field.

Control Resampling

If you wish to allow Photoshop Elements to resample the image, check the Resample Image check box and pick the algorithm to use for resampling (Bicubic, Bilinear, or Nearest Neighbor) from the drop-down list adjacent to the check box. Resampling enables Photoshop Elements to apply the selected algorithm to either add pixels to or remove pixels from the image in order to produce the combination of width, height, and resolution that you choose.

For continuous-tone images (such as photos), Bicubic works best most of the time.

If you don't allow resampling, the width, height, and resolution are all interdependent and *cannot* be adjusted independently. Changing any of these quantities adjusts the others automatically. Take, for example, an image that measures 21.3 inches (width) by 14.2 inches (height) at 72 pixels/inch. If you resize the width to 6 inches, the height is automatically set to 4 inches, and the resolution is set to 256 pixels/inch *because all pixels are preserved.* If you try to adjust the resolution to 300 pixels/inch, the dimensions are set to a width of 5.1 inches and a height of 3.4 inches.

You can reduce the file size of the image by cropping off the unnecessary portions of the image prior to resizing it.

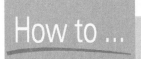

Maintain Image Quality While Resizing

Reducing the file size without impacting the image quality can be tricky. Here are some guidelines to follow:

Keep the ratio of width to height constant   To keep the width-to-height proportions constant, check the Constraint Proportions check box. As you adjust either the width or the height, the other dimension is adjusted automatically. Clearing the Constrain Proportions check box allows you to adjust each dimension independently, which always leads to distortion and is *not* recommended.

Set the width and height to a size that suits your purpose   For example, if the intended purpose is to view or print snapshots of the image, you can set the dimensions to 4 inches by 6 inches (or as close as you can get). If you make the dimensions of the image significantly larger than needed, the file will be larger than necessary.

Set the resolution for the intended purpose   If the intended purpose is simply to view the image, set the resolution to 72 pixels/inch. Realize, however, that if you print an image that is saved at such a low resolution, the results will be unsatisfactory. If the intended purpose is to print the image, set the resolution to between 250 pixels/inch and 300 pixels/inch. A higher resolution does not increase the printed image quality, but does increase the file size.

Avoid resampling if you can   The result of resampling is to add pixels to the image that weren't there before, or to remove pixels that were present. As a result, resampling tends to reduce the quality of the image and so should be avoided. To avoid resampling, clear the Resample Image check box.

Choose a Web Format for Your Photos

Although there are a huge number of possible graphic image formats, only a small subset of these formats are understood by and can be displayed by web browsers. The two most popular are JPEG and GIF.

Use JPEG for Photos

JPEG files use the ending *.jpg*. In general, they are best for continuous-tone images, such as photographs. The JPEG format can support the full range of color visible to the human eye, thus maintaining the broad range and subtle variation of color present in photographs.

Did you know?

Image resolution and printer resolution are completely unrelated. Most high-quality inkjet printers tout resolutions of at least 700 dpi (dots per inch), and many go as high as 2800 dpi. However, these numbers measure how smoothly the printer can reproduce the image on paper. In general, a larger number of small dots (higher dpi) is more effective at producing results indistinguishable from a commercially printed photo.

Image resolution, on the other hand, measures how much detail is present in the image file. Image resolutions higher than about 300 pixels/inch are unnecessary and wasteful. For example, an image resolution of 600 pixels/inch results in a file that is four times as large as an image file with a resolution of 300 pixels/inch—and you can't see the different in the final printed image.

So why do modern flat-bed scanners provide resolutions of 600 dpi, 1200 dpi, and even 2400 dpi? The answer is that you can scan a small photo (for example, 4 inches × 6 inches) at a high resolution (such as 1200 dpi), then print the image at a larger size than the original. In our example, you could reprint the 4 × 6 print at 16 × 24 (provided you had a printer capable of making such a big print, of course). Another reason to scan at high resolution is so that you can crop out portions of the original and still have enough of the image to print it at a reasonable size and 300 pixels/inch.

This information is very helpful if you decide to scan 35mm negatives or slides using a film scanner. Most such scanners tout resolutions of 2400 dpi or higher. However, a 35mm negative or slide measures only about 1 inch by 1.5 inches. Therefore, the resulting scan is approximately 2400 pixels by 3600 pixels. If you want to print at 300 pixels/inch, you could print an 8 × 10 from this slide scan.

JPEG supports compression of the image, which gives a smaller file size than formats such as TIFF or PSD (Photoshop). JPEG compression works by discarding data from the image, and is thus referred to as *lossy compression*. You can choose the balance between file size and the quality of the image by adjusting the JPEG Quality setting. This is a number between 0 and 100, with 0 being the lowest quality (and smallest file size), and 100 being the highest quality (and largest file size). The variation from one end of the range to the other is considerable. For example, Figure 18-1 shows a pair of images displayed in the Save For Web dialog box (discussed later in this chapter). The image on the left is the original (with a quality of 100), the image on the right is the same image with a quality of 0 (the minimum quality). The poor quality of the image on the right is clearly visible, with loss of detail and blockiness in the faces. However, the high-quality image requires a file size of almost 1MB (which will take almost three minutes to download over a 56KB connection), while the low-quality image requires a file size of only 90KB, requiring only 17 seconds to download.

FIGURE 18-1
The difference between a high-quality setting and a low-quality setting for a JPEG is clearly visible.

The size displayed on the left (under the word "Original") is not the JPEG size, it is the size this file would be if saved as a Photoshop Elements file. To see the JPEG file size, you must look at the size displayed under the right-hand image, and adjust the Quality setting in the Settings section of the Save For Web dialog box. Note also that the JPEG quality setting varies between 0 and 100 only in the Save For Web dialog box. If you use File | Save As, the JPEG quality varies between 0 and 10.

JPEG format does not support transparent pixels. Any transparent pixels are filled with the *matte color*, which you can specify using the Save For Web dialog box (the default color is white). Thus, if your image contains transparent pixels and you know the color of the web page on which the image will be placed, you should match the matte color to the background color of the web page.

Did you know?

Each time you edit and save a JPEG image, the quality deteriorates. JPEG compression results in blocky artifacts, which accumulate each time you save the image as a JPEG. This is especially true of images with sharp detail, such as clipart. Thus, if you need to edit a JPEG image, you should save it as a TIFF or PSD file first, make your edits to the TIFF or PSD file, and then, *when you are done editing*, convert it back to a JPEG. To convert a file from one type to another, follow these steps:

1. Open the file for which you want to change the file type.

2. Choose File | Save As to open the Save As dialog box.

3. Choose the type of file from the Format drop-down list.

4. Click Save to save the file in the new format.

Use GIF for Clipart and Vector Images

GIF format is ideal for images with a small number of colors and sharp detail, such as clipart, logos, text, and line art. Unlike JPEG, GIF uses *lossless* compression—no details are discarded when compressing the file. Thus, you don't get the artifacts around sharp details that you would with JPEG files. GIF files also support transparency—you don't have to fill in transparent pixels with a matte color. Instead, you can leave the pixels transparent, and you'll be able to see the background of the web page through the transparent areas. This is especially useful when the web page has a pattern because there is *no* matte color you can use to simulate the pattern in an image.

GIF files only support a maximum of 256 colors. This doesn't sound like much when compared to the 16.7 million colors supported by JPEG, but GIF actually does a pretty good job of representing a photograph. GIF creates a table of the most frequently used colors in the image, and whenever it encounters a color it doesn't have, it substitutes the closest match for that color from the table. When specifying the GIF format, you have the opportunity to customize what is meant by "most frequently used colors." GIF can also simulate colors by combining other colors in a process called *dithering*. For example, a pattern of red and yellow pixels in close proximity can approximate the color orange.

To control the size of a GIF file, you can specify the maximum number of colors allowed, as well as how much dithering is allowed. More colors and additional dithering result in a closer match to the image, but also result in a larger file.

 *For photographs, JPEG almost always results in a smaller file size at a comparable quality. For example, the image shown in Figure 18-1 requires about 250KB in JPEG at a quality of 30% (which actually looks pretty good). To get close to this quality in a GIF file, you must use 256 colors and 100% dithering, resulting in a file size of about 1MB.*

Optimize Your Image with Save For Web

As mentioned earlier, optimizing your image for the Web involves balancing quality against file size. Photoshop Elements provides the Save For Web facility to enable you to change the image properties (such as the JPEG Quality setting) and interactively view the results as well as the estimated file size. Thus, you can experiment until you find the balance you like, then save the result to publish to your web site. To save the results, click OK to exit the Save For Web dialog box. This returns you to the main Photoshop Elements screen with the optimized image displayed. Then save the file just as you would any other file (File | Save As).

 *Save the file with a new name or to a new location to avoid writing over the original (unoptimized) file.*

To optimize your image, choose File | Save For Web. This opens the Save For Web dialog box, shown in Figure 18-2.

The Save For Web dialog box displays two views of the file you are working with. The left-side view shows you the original image, the right-side view shows the optimized version. The general tools in the dialog box provide the following functionality:

Pan both images   Use the Hand tool (upper-left corner) to pan the two versions of the image. Choose the Hand tool, then click and drag either image to change the portion of the image visible in the window. As you pan one image, the other one moves so that both windows display the same portion of the image.

Zoom both images   Use the Zoom tool (the magnifying glass just below the Hand tool) to increase the magnification (click either image) or decrease the magnification (ALT-click either image). The zoom level changes on both images. You can also change the magnification by selecting a value from the Zoom drop-down list in the bottom-left corner of the dialog box.

Select the eyedropper color   The eyedropper color is one of the options you can select when choosing a matte color for GIFs. To pick the eyedropper color, choose the Eyedropper tool just below the Zoom tool, and click the color in the image. The rectangle just below the Eyedropper tool displays the currently selected color. Alternatively, you can click the color square to open the Color Picker and choose your color.

Change zoom.

View original image here.

View adjusted image here.

Adjust image size here.

Adjust image properties here.

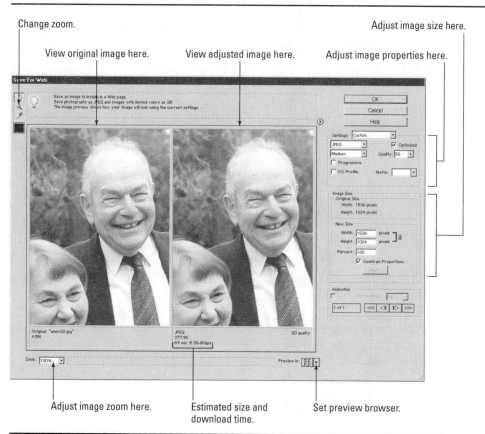

Adjust image zoom here.

Estimated size and download time.

Set preview browser.

Use the Save For Web dialog box to adjust the balance between published quality and file size.

Preview in browser Photoshop Elements can launch your browser and open the image in the browser to enable you to see what the image will look like. To preview the image in the browser, click the Preview In button in the lower-right corner of the dialog box. If you have more than one browser installed on your computer, you can choose the browser to use from the drop-down list alongside the button. Netscape Navigator and Internet Explorer will appear in this list automatically. If you wish to add another browser to the list, click the Other selection in the drop-down list and choose the application file for the browser from the Preview In Other Browser dialog box that appears.

Choose the color profile   Different systems (such as Windows and Macintosh) display images differently. You can choose the color profile—including a standard Windows or Mac system—from the Preview menu. To open the Preview menu, click the arrow button just to the left of the Help button near the upper-right corner of the dialog box:

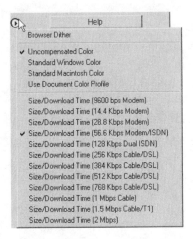

Set the connection speed   Photoshop Elements displays the size and estimated download time under the optimized image. The download time assumes a certain connection speed (the default is 28.8 Kbps). You can change the assumed connection speed from the Preview menu.

Use Predefined Optimization Settings

The easiest way to apply an optimization setting is to select it from the Settings drop-down list:

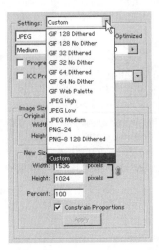

The options in this list combine various file types, quality settings, number of colors, and amount of dithering. As you make a selection from the list, Photoshop Elements recalculates the optimized file size and displays a sample of the file in the right panel.

The options in the Settings drop-down list include two seldom-used web file formats: PNG-8 and PNG-24. PNG-8 supports 256 colors and transparent pixels, like GIF, but not all browsers can display PNG-8. PNG-24 is suitable for continuous-tone images (like photos), but usually results in files that are much larger than JPEG. However, PNG-24 does support transparent pixels, so you can use this file format if you need to preserve transparency.

Set Optimization for JPEG Files

To select a JPEG file, choose JPEG from the file type drop-down list. This displays the optimization fields appropriate for JPEG files:

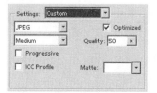

You can use the option selected in the Settings drop-down list as the starting point for further optimization settings. If you change any of the settings in the fields, however, the Settings list displays a value of Custom.

To optimize a JPEG file, set the following fields:

Quality   Set the Quality by choosing a value (Low, Medium, High, or Maximum) from the drop-down list below the file type. Alternatively, you can type a value into the Quality field or use the Quality slider. Remember that lower values of Quality result in higher compression but lower image quality.

Optimized   Check the Optimized check box to create a smaller file for the same quality. Some older browsers (versions 2 and 3) do not support optimized JPEG files.

Progressive   Check the Progressive check box to create an image that displays progressively in a browser. The image displays first as a low resolution version of the image while it completes the download. Using Progressive is considered good manners for large files, so the viewer can get an idea of what the image looks like before it fully loads—and can move on if not interested in that image. Using Progressive does create a slightly bigger file.

ICC Profile   To preserve the color profile of the image with the file, check the ICC Profile check box. Some browsers use the ICC color profile to correct colors.

Matte   Since JPEG doesn't support transparent pixels, Photoshop Elements will fill any transparent pixels with the matte color you choose. Of course, if your original image is a JPEG image, you don't need to worry about the matte color because the image doesn't contain any transparent pixels anyway. To set the matte color, you can choose an option from the drop-down list (Eyedropper Color, White, Black, or Other). Picking Other opens the Color Picker so you can choose the color you want. You can also access the Color Picker by clicking on the Matte field. If you choose None from the Matte drop-down list, the default of White is used.

Set Optimization for GIF Files

To select a GIF file, choose GIF from the file type drop-down list. This displays the optimization field appropriate to GIF files:

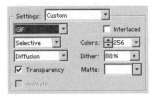

The various fields enable you to fine-tune the optimization of the GIF file.

 *Check the Interlaced check box if you want the GIF file to load as a low resolution image first, giving the viewer an idea of the image content while the rest of the image loads. This works much like Progressive for JPEGs.*

Choose a Color Reduction Algorithm

Use the drop-down list immediately below the file type drop-down list to choose the algorithm to use to generate the color lookup table. The available algorithms are:

Perceptual   Creates a custom color table that gives priority to colors to which the human eye is most sensitive.

Selective   Creates a custom color table similar to Perceptual, but favoring colors that appear in broad areas and attempting to preserve "web safe" colors. This option is the default as it gives the most color integrity.

Adaptive   Creates a custom color table by sampling colors from the color spectrum that appear most frequently in the image.

Web   Uses the standard 216 colors common to Windows and Mac web palettes. In general, this choice produces lower color integrity and larger files (with more dithering requiring), and is really not necessary on modern computer systems capable of handling more than 8-bit color.

Custom   Fixes the current color table and does not adjust the color table when you adjust other parameters that would normally change the color table (such as the number of colors).

Choose the Maximum Number of Colors

Pick the maximum number of colors from the Colors field. You can type in the number of colors, click the up and down spinners to change the number, or choose the number of colors from the drop-down list.

If you choose the Custom color reduction algorithm, you can allow Photoshop Elements to determine the number of colors to use by selecting Auto from the Colors drop-down list.

Choose the Diffusion Algorithm and Amount

Select a dithering algorithm from the field immediately to the left of the Dither field. The Dithering algorithms are:

No Dither   Dithering is not used.

Pattern   Applies a half-tone (square) pattern.

Diffusion   Applies a random pattern that diffuses across adjacent pixels. This is the least noticeable of the dither algorithms and is the default.

Noise   Applies a random pattern similar to Diffusion, but without diffusing across adjacent pixels.

If you chose Diffusion as the Dithering algorithm, you can set the amount of dithering to use by typing a number between 0 and 100 into the Dither field, or by using the slider. Higher dither percentages simulate colors better, but result in larger files.

Set Up Transparency and Matting

GIF files support transparent pixels, so you have several ways you can combine transparency and matting when saving a GIF file for the Web:

Turn on transparency and matte color   If you choose a matte color and check the Transparency check box, partially transparent pixels (like the anti-aliased pixels at the edges of clipart) are matted, and fully transparent pixels left unchanged so that the web page shows through. Provided you choose a matte color that matches the web page background, the edges of the image blend with the background. This prevents the halo effect you get when an anti-aliased image is placed on a background that is a different color than the original background.

No transparency and matte color   If you choose a matte color and clear the Transparency check box, no transparency is preserved. Partially transparent pixels are blended with the matte color, and fully transparent pixels are filled with the matte color.

Transparency and no matte color   If you check the Transparency check box but don't select a matte color, pixels more than 50% transparent are made fully transparent, and pixels less than 50% transparent are made fully opaque. This leaves you with a hard-edged border between the image and the background web page. Use this option if you don't know the background color of the web page on which you are going to place the image.

Modify the Image Size

You can reduce the image size right from within the Save For Web dialog box. To do so, input the new size (in pixels) in the Width or Height field. If you check the Constrain Proportions check box, changing either the width or the height automatically changes the other dimensions to preserve the width-to-height ratio. You can also adjust the size by typing a percentage into the Percent field.

While you can increase the file size by typing in a larger value for width or height, or by typing in a percentage greater than 100%, this is not recommended because it reduces the effective resolution of the result.

Create a Web Photo Gallery

Once you have your photos optimized for the Web, Photoshop Elements makes it easy to create a photo gallery you can include in your web site. The gallery consists of a customizable web page with thumbnails of your images. A visitor to your site can click on a thumbnail to see the full-size image either on a separate page or on another portion of the photo gallery web page. The web page can display the filename, title, author, caption, and copyright notice for each image on the web page.

A *thumbnail* is a shrunken version of an image. Many programs—including Photoshop Elements—can create a thumbnail from a full-size image automatically (I'll tell you how later in this chapter). Thumbnails are very useful on a web page because they give the viewer an idea of what is in the image without taking the time to load the full-size image. In addition, the thumbnail can be a hyperlink to the full-size image; all the viewer has to do is click the thumbnail to see the full-size image.

To begin building a web photo gallery, choose File | Create Web Photo Gallery to open the Web Photo Gallery dialog box:

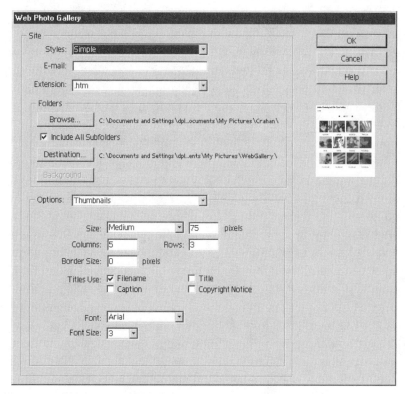

Specify the Site Characteristics

The top portion of the Web Photo Gallery dialog box is used to specify the basic properties of the site. These include your e-mail address (if you want to include it) and the extension to use when naming the web page (.htm or .html).

The most important choice is the overall style of the gallery web page. Select a style from the Styles drop-down list. A sample of the page is displayed just below the buttons in the right border of the dialog box. For example, the previous illustration shows a preview of the Simple style; here is a preview of the Museum style:

If you choose the Table style, you can specify an image background by clicking the Background button in the Folders section of the dialog box. Pick the image from the Select Image dialog box, and click the Open button.

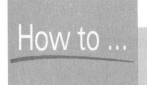

Specify the File Info for a JPEG Image

In order to use file information—such as the title, author, caption, and other data—in your web photo gallery, you must provide that information to Photoshop Elements. To specify the file information, choose File | File Info to open the File Info dialog box:

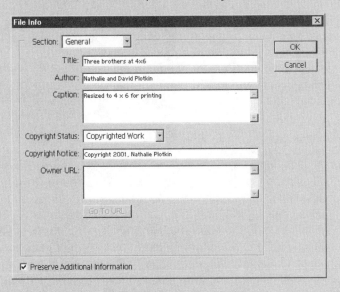

Fill in the fields in the dialog box to make the information available. In the Copyright Status drop-down list, pick either Copyrighted Work or Public Domain to embed a notice in the file data. Alternatively, you can choose Unmarked to leave the copyright status out of the image file. When you are done, click OK to close the dialog box. This information will be saved with the image file the next time you save it, provided it is a JPEG file. You can access the File Info dialog box for a GIF file and fill in the information, but it is not saved, and next time you open the image you'll find that the information has disappeared.

NOTE *Not all the options available in the Options portion of the dialog box apply to every style of gallery web page. For example, the Museum style uses a default font and size for the banner, therefore specifying the font and size for the Banner option is a waste of time.*

Choose a Source for Your Images

All the images you want to include in the web photo gallery must come from a single folder (and optionally, its subfolders). To select the folder containing the images, click the Browse button to open the Browse For Folder dialog box:

Click the folder and click OK to return to the Web Photo Gallery dialog box. If you want to include images in all the subfolders of the selected folder, check the Include All Subfolders check box.

Choose the Destination for Your Web Photo Gallery

Creating a web photo gallery leaves you with a lot of files. These include the large images, the thumbnails, and a variety of web pages (used to display the large images), as well as the web photo gallery page itself (called index.htm). These files are all stored within a destination folder.

To choose this folder, click the Destination button to once again open the Browse For Folder dialog box. Pick the folder by clicking on it. You can also create a new folder to hold the files by clicking the New Folder button. The new folder (called *New Folder*) appears in the directory tree with the name editable. Simply type in the name for the new folder and press ENTER. Then click OK to close the Browse For Folder dialog box.

If you accidentally click elsewhere in the dialog box, the name of the new folder ceases to be editable. To change the name of the folder, right-click it and choose Rename from the context menu. This action makes the folder name editable once again.

Specify the Options

The Options portion of the dialog box enables you to set the properties of the banner, the images, and the thumbnails, as well as set custom colors and specify security. You pick the option to customize from the Options drop-down list, and the lower portion of the Web Photo Gallery dialog box changes to display the properties you can specify for each option.

Set the Banner Properties

Choose Banner from the Options drop-down list to display the banner properties:

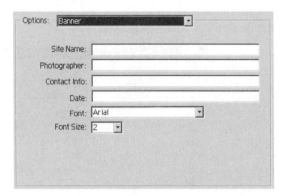

   The banner appears on the web page to provide a title. You can specify the site name, photographer, contact info, date, font, and font size. To choose the font size, select it from the Font Size drop-down list. The sizes correspond to HTML font sizes. For example, a size 3 HTML font corresponds to 12-point text.

Set the Large Images Properties

Choose Large Images from the Options drop-down list to display the properties of the full-size images displayed when you click a thumbnail:

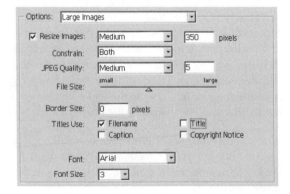

   If you wish, you can resize the images so they are all approximately the same size. To do so, check the Resize Image check box and then set the following values:

   Image Size   To change the size of the image, you can pick a size from the Resize Images drop-down list (Large, Medium, or Small). You can also type a size into the Pixels field. If you do specify the pixel size, the Resize Images drop-down list is reset to Custom.

Constrain   The Constrain drop-down list determines how the size you set is applied to an image. The values are:

> **Both**   Maintains the ratio of the width to the height, and sets the larger dimension to the dimension you set earlier.

> **Width**   Sets the width to the size you set earlier, and scales the height to maintain the ratio of the width to the height.

> **Height**   Sets the height to the size you set earlier, and scales the width to maintain the ratio of the height to the width.

JPEG Quality   You can choose the JPEG compression quality from the JPEG Quality drop-down list. The values range (in order of increasing quality and file size) from Low to Maximum. You can also type a number between 0 and 12 into the field adjacent to the JPEG Quality drop-down list. Finally, you can use the File Size slider to set the file size between small (with low quality) and large (with high quality).

The rest of the options for Large Images are:

Border Size   You can specify a border around each picture. Type the border width (in pixels) into the Border Size field.

Titles   You can add titles to each picture. Options include the Filename, Caption, Title, and Copyright Notice. You can use as many of these fields as you want; simply check the check box for each option you want to include. These fields use the values you specified in the File Info dialog box, discussed earlier in this chapter.

Font and Font Size   If you choose to use titles, they are rendered in the font you choose from the Font drop-down list. The size is set by the Font Size drop-down list. The sizes are HTML font sizes.

Set the Thumbnail Properties

Choose Thumbnails from the Options drop-down list to display the properties of the thumbnail images displayed to give viewers an idea of the content of the image:

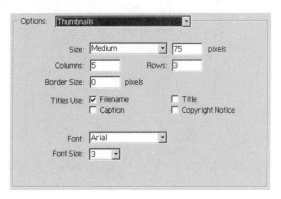

The properties you can set for thumbnails are:

Size   To set the size of the thumbnails, you can either select a value from the Size drop-down list or type a dimension (in pixels) into the field adjacent to the Size drop-down list.

Columns and Rows   Type a value into the Columns field and the Rows field to specify the grid in which the thumbnails will be laid out.

It is possible to specify a number of columns that causes the thumbnails to be too wide to fit on the page. If you do that, Photoshop Elements will render the page as you instruct, forcing anyone viewing the page to scroll to see all the thumbnails. It is best to keep the number of columns small so that horizontal scrolling is not necessary to view all the thumbnails.

Border Size   You can specify a border around each thumbnail. Type the border width (in pixels) into the Border Size field.

Titles   You can add titles to each thumbnail. Options include the Filename, Caption, Title, and Copyright Notice. You can use as many of these fields as you want; simply check the check box for each option you want to include. These fields use the values you specified in the File Info dialog box, discussed earlier in this chapter.

Font and Font Size   If you choose to use titles, they are rendered in the font you choose from the Font drop-down list. The size is set by the Font Size drop-down list. The sizes are HTML font sizes.

Set the Custom Colors

Choose Custom Colors from the Options drop-down list to display the colors you can choose to dress up your web page:

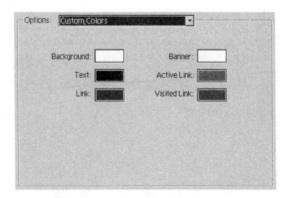

You can specify the background, text, banner, and three kinds of hyperlinks: a standard hyperlink (Link), a link for which the linked page is currently open in another window (Active Link), and a link you have recently visited (Visited Link). Click any of the color rectangles to open the Color Picker so you can choose the color you want.

Specify the Security Properties

If you are concerned about people making unauthorized use of your photos, you can superimpose text on the photo itself, making it easy to spot this unauthorized use. For example, here is an image with a copyright notice superimposed on it:

To specify these security features, choose Security from the Options drop-down list:

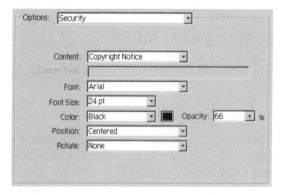

You choose the content from the Content drop-down list. Your content options are:

None   This option (the default) does not embed any text in the image.

Custom Text   This option enables you to type the text you want to embed in the image into the Custom Text field (which is only available for this content option).

Filename This option displays the name of the file.

Copyright Notice, Caption, or Title This option displays the contents of each of these fields from the File Info dialog box.

You can customize the superimposed text with the following fields:

Font Choose the font you want to use from the Font drop-down list.

Font Size Select the size of the font in points from the Font Size drop-down list. Unlike the other fonts in this dialog box, this font is *not* sized using HTML font sizes.

Color Choose Black, White, or Custom from the Color drop-down list. Selecting Custom opens the Color Picker so you can choose a color, as does clicking on the color rectangle adjacent to the Color drop-down list.

Opacity Choose the opacity by typing a value into the Opacity field or using the slider. It is best to keep opacity below 70% so the text won't be too obtrusive.

Position Select a value from the Position drop-down list to specify the position in the text. Options include placing the text in the center of the image (choose Center) or in one of the corners (choose Top Left, Bottom Left, and so on).

Rotate You can rotate the text by making a selection from the Rotate drop-down list. Options include rotating the text so that it runs from top to bottom (choose 90 Degrees CW), from bottom to top (choose 90 Degrees CCW), and two intermediate 45-degree rotations.

Create Your Web Photo Gallery

Once you are done specifying all the options in the Web Photo Gallery dialog box, click OK to build the gallery. This may take a few minutes, especially if you have a lot of photos, and if some are large. If the source folder (the one you chose when you clicked the Browse button) contains any non-graphic files, you'll get a warning about it.

Photoshop Elements automatically converts any image files (such as Photoshop Elements files, TIFF files, and any others it recognizes) in the source directory into JPEG images.

When the web site is fully built, Photoshop Elements opens the web site in your default browser. Figure 18-3 shows the thumbnail page for the Simple style, while Figure 18-4 shows the page that results when you click one of the thumbnails. Notice the navigation controls to move to the previous or next picture, or to return to the thumbnail page.

Some of the styles (such as Museum) show the thumbnails in one part of the page and display the larger image in another part of the page, as shown in Figure 18-5.

FIGURE 18-3

This style of web photo gallery starts with a thumbnail page.

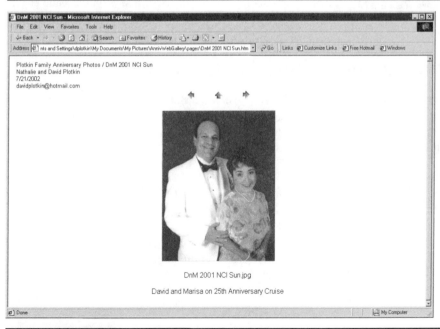

FIGURE 18-4

Clicking a thumbnail presents the large image. Click the up arrow to return to the thumbnail page.

FIGURE 18-5 Click a thumbnail to display the large image on the same page.

Create an Acrobat Photo Presentation

Photoshop Elements provides an easy way to create a slideshow—a presentation of your images, in which you can control which images are included, how long each image is displayed, and the transition effect between images. The result is an Adobe Acrobat file, capable of being viewed by anyone who has the Adobe Acrobat Reader.

 *If you already have Adobe Acrobat Reader, make sure it is version 5 or later. Earlier versions can't open the Acrobat Photo Presentation.*

 *The file extension for an Adobe Acrobat file is .pdf. That is why the Acrobat Photo Presentation is referred to as a PDF Slideshow in Photoshop Elements.*

To build an Acrobat Photo Presentation, select File | Automation Tools | PDF Slideshow. This opens the PDF Slideshow dialog box:

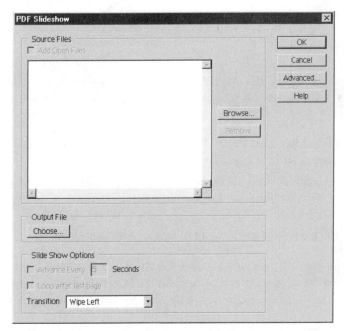

To configure the PDF Slideshow dialog box, follow these steps:

1. Choose the files to include by clicking the Browse button to display the Open dialog box.

2. Select the files to include and click Open to return to the PDF Slideshow dialog box. If you want to include any open files in the slideshow, check the Add Open Files check box.

 To rearrange the files in the list, click and drag a file to a new position. If you change your mind about including a file in the slideshow, select the file in the Source Files list and click Remove.

3. Specify the name of the output file by clicking the Choose button in the Output File section of the dialog box. Type the name of the file into the File Name field, or select an existing file. Click Save to return to the PDF Slideshow dialog box.

 *If you choose an existing filename, your new PDF file will overwrite the existing file.*

4. Set up the options in the Slide Show Options portion of the dialog box. These include the following:

Slide timing To cycle through the slides automatically, check the Advance Every check box. Specify how long each slide remains visible by typing a number into the Seconds field.

If you don't check the Advance Every check box, the slides won't automatically advance. Click the mouse button during the slideshow to advance to the next slide.

Loop After Last Page If you want the slideshow to continue repeating, check the Loop After Last Page check box.

Transition You can specify the transition between slides by selecting it from the Transition drop-down list. For example, the Dissolve transition causes one slide to dissolve into the next.

5. Click OK to generate the PDF Slideshow document.

To run the slideshow, double-click the file you created in Windows Explorer. This runs Adobe Acrobat Reader automatically, loads the PDF document, and displays the slideshow. To terminate the slideshow, press the ESC key on your keyboard to display the PDF document, as shown in Figure 18-6.

While you are creating the PDF Slideshow, you can configure the options by clicking the Advanced button to open the PDF Options dialog box:

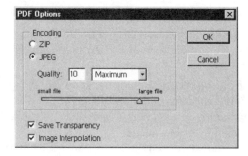

Here are the options you can set:

Compression You can choose to use either Zip compression or JPEG compression when creating the PDF Slideshow. If you choose JPEG compression, you can select the quality by typing a number into the Quality field, selecting a value from the Quality drop-down list, or dragging the slider control.

FIGURE 18-6   Watch your slideshow in Adobe Acrobat Reader.

NOTE   *Unless you have a very good reason to use Zip compression, you should avoid it, as the file is much larger than even a maximum quality JPEG file.*

Save Transparency   If the source images support transparency (such as GIF files), you can preserve the transparent areas by checking the Save Transparency check box.

Image Interpolation   If you want to anti-alias the printed appearance of a low-resolution image, check the Image Interpolation check box.

Chapter 19

Print and Modify Batches of Images

How to...

- Pick options for printing out your image
- Preview the printed image and adjust the size and position
- Print only a selected area of an image
- Optimize a piece of photo paper while printing
- Change the file type, size, and name of batches of images

One of the main reasons to take pictures and modify them in Photoshop Elements is so you can print them out and put them in your family picture album. You can specify all the printing options supported by your printer, as well as scaling and positioning an image for printing using the Print Preview function. Since photo-quality paper is still quite expensive, you can create a page for printing that provides a variety of different sizes of an image, using as much of the page as possible.

Another task that can be a real pain is converting images from one format to another, perhaps changing the size and resolution along the way. While it is certainly possible to do this one image at a time, Photoshop Elements makes it easy to convert a batch of images, and even rename the converted image so you don't overwrite the original.

Set Up and Print Your Image

The most basic way to print an image is to set up the page, select the printing options, and print the picture.

Set Up the Page

To specify the paper size, source, and orientation, choose File | Page Setup to open the Page Setup dialog box:

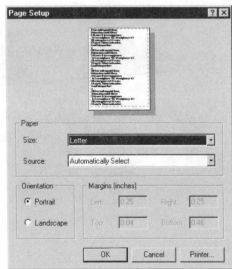

Using this dialog box, you can do the following:

Change printers   If you have more than one printer defined, you should choose the printer you want to use before modifying anything else in the Page Setup dialog box. To do so, click the Printer button to open another version of the Page Setup dialog box, from which you can select the printer from the Name drop-down list and set the printer properties by clicking the Properties button:

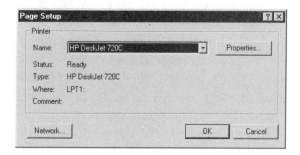

Choose the paper size   Select the paper size from the Size drop-down list. The default size is Letter, which is standard 8.5 × 11-inch paper. Other options include European sizes, envelopes, and index cards.

Choose the paper sources   Many printers have multiple paper sources available. Choose the one that is loaded with the paper you want to use from the Source drop-down list.

Choose the orientation   Select an option from the Orientation portion of the dialog box. Portrait is tall and narrow; Landscape is short and wide.

Print the Image

The simplest way to print an image open in Photoshop Elements is to choose File | Print. This displays the Print dialog box:

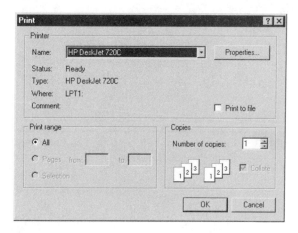

This should be the standard dialog box for your printer. While there are minor differences between printers, most Print dialog boxes enable you to do the following:

Pick a printer   If you have more than one printer attached to your computer, you can select the printer to use from the Name drop-down list.

Set the printer properties   To set the printer-specific properties, click the Properties button. With most inkjet printers, you can set the type of paper (plain, photo, and so on) as well as the quality of the printout you want. You can usually pick from a variety of options designed to optimize the quality of the printout (and use more ink!).

Set the print range   In general, the All option in the Print Range section is all you need to use, as it prints the current image. If you have made a selection before choosing File | Print, you can choose the Selection option to print just the selected portion of the image.

Set the number of copies   Specify the number of copies to print by typing a number into the Number Of Copies field or using the spinner.

Preview Your Print

Given the high cost of photo paper and ink, it is most economical to make sure the image is going to print out the way you want. Photoshop Elements provides the Print Preview function (choose File | Print Preview) to help you with this (see Figure 19-1).

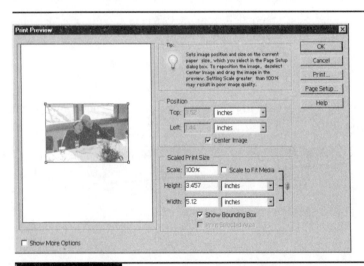

FIGURE 19-1   Get an idea of how your printed image will look on paper with the Print Preview function.

Set the Basic Print Preview Options

Using the Print Preview dialog box, you can set the options and preview the result:

Set the picture position   Use the Position portion of the dialog box to position the image on the page. To center the image, check the Center Image check box. To place the image elsewhere on the page, make sure the Center Image check box is cleared. You can then type a value into the Top and Left fields to specify the location of the top-left corner of the image. You can also click and drag the image to any position on the page.

Scale the picture   You can enlarge or shrink the image. To scale the image by percent, type the percent into the Scale field. To automatically scale the image to fit the paper, check the Scale To Media check box. You can also change the image size by typing a value into either the Height or Width field. Changing either one adjusts the other field so that the ratio of height to width remains constant.

Enlarging the picture so the resolution falls below 300 dpi can result in a poor-quality print. Unfortunately, you can't discern the resolution from the Print Preview dialog box. Instead, you are better off making your size adjustments in the Image Size dialog box, where you can see the resolution. Choose Image | Resize | Image Size to view the Image Size dialog box.

Adjust the picture using click and drag   If you check the Show Bounding Box check box, you can click and drag any of the corners of the image preview to change the size. As with the Height and Width fields, Photoshop Elements constrains the ratio of the height to the width.

Print the selected area   If you selected an area of the image before opening the Print Preview dialog box, you can check the Print Selected Area check box to print only the selected area.

Set Output and Color Management Options

Checking the Show More Options check box opens a new section at the bottom of the Print Preview dialog box to set output and color management options, as shown in Figure 19-2. Select Output from the drop-down list to set the following Output options:

Background color   Click the Background button to open the Color Picker so you can pick a background color. The background color is printed in the leftover sections of the paper (around the edges of the image).

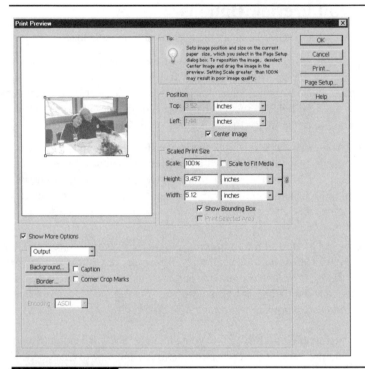

FIGURE 19-2 Customize the printout with Show More Options.

Printing a background color can use a lot of ink, so use this option with care.

Caption If you entered a caption for the image in the File Info dialog box, you can have the caption printed below the image. You have no control over the font and size of the caption—it is printed in 9 pt. Helvetica.

Border If you wish to add a black border around the printed image, click the Border button and type a width into the Width field. You can choose the units (points, inches, or cm) from the drop-down list adjacent to the Width field. Then click OK.

19

Corner Crop Marks Crop marks are short lines that appear at each corner of the image to help you cut the picture out (usually using a paper cutter). You can see what corner crop marks look like in this preview:

Choose Color Management from the drop-down list to set the color profile to use for printing:

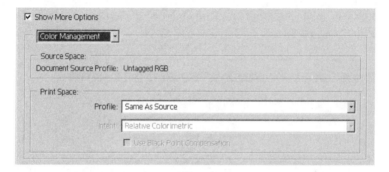

This version of the Print Preview dialog box shows you the Source Space (color management used for the image) and enables you to pick the Print Space options (color management used for the printer). A wide variety of profiles are available by clicking the Profile pop-up list:

Some of the profiles have multiple options, called *intents*, available. If the selected profile has multiple intents, the Intent drop-down list is available, and you can choose an intent from the list. Some profiles also allow the printer to apply black point compensation. If you have this option for the selected profile, the Use Black Point Compensation check box is available.

 *From the Print Preview dialog box you can go straight to the Print dialog box (click the Print button) or to the Page Setup dialog box (click the Page Setup button).*

Optimize a Sheet of Paper with Picture Package

Picture Package is a powerful feature of Photoshop Elements. Using Picture Package, you can print out multiple copies of an image, in multiple sizes, making the best use of a sheet of photo paper. To open the Picture Package dialog box, shown in Figure 19-3, choose File | Print Layouts | Picture Package.

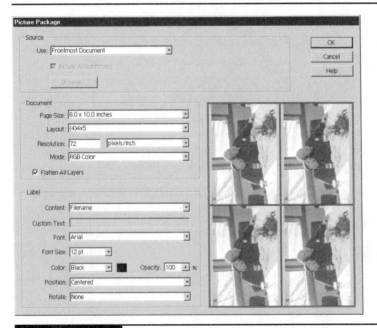

FIGURE 19-3   The Picture Package dialog box

Once you are done specifying the options for the picture package, click OK to create a Photoshop Elements image that reflects all your choices. Then simply print the image (and save it, if you wish). Figure 19-4 shows a sample of the result of using Picture Package.

Pick a Picture Source

To decide what image(s) to create picture packages for, pick a selection from the Use drop-down list. The three selections are:

Frontmost Document   This choice creates a picture package from the top-most open document in Photoshop Elements.

Folder   This choice creates a picture package from every file in a folder. Thus, if a folder contains six image files, you will end up with six picture packages. To include the contents of any subfolders of the selected folder, check the Subfolders check box. To pick the folder, click the Browse button to open the Browse For Folder dialog box. Click the folder you want to use and click OK to return to the Picture Package dialog box.

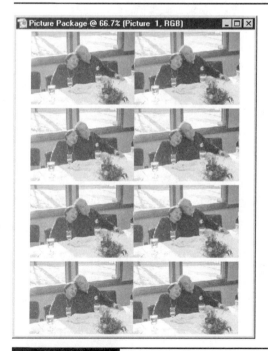

FIGURE 19-4   View the results of using Picture Package before printing the page.

File This choice creates a picture package from a single file. To choose the file, click the Browse button to open the Select An Image dialog box. Pick the image and click Open to return to the Picture Package dialog box.

You can also create a collage from the picture package. In order to do so, click any of the images in the preview section of the picture package. This opens the Select An Image File dialog box. Choose the file you want to use, and click Open. The file is scaled and placed into the picture package, as shown here where I've replaced the upper-left image with a different picture:

Set the Document Options

The real power of Picture Package is in the document options. You can do the following:

Choose the page size Pick a page size from the Page Size drop-down list. Choices include standard photo sizes such as 8 × 10 and 11 × 17.

Pick the layout Picture Package has a large number of predefined layouts available. For example, Figure 19-5 shows a mixture of 4 × 5, small portrait, and wallet-size images. To choose a layout, pick it from the list shown in the graphic on the following page.

19

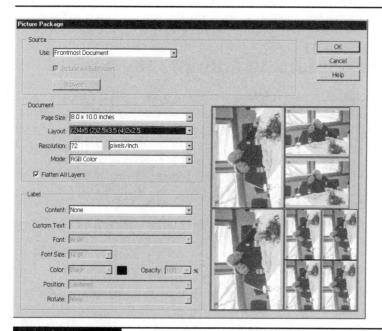

Document
Page Size: 8.0 x 10.0 inches
Layout: (4)4x5
                (1)5x7 (2)2.5x3.5 (4)2x2.5
Resolution: (1)5x7 (2)3.5x5
                (1)5x7 (8)2x2.5
Mode: (1)5x7 (4)2.5x3.25 (2)1.5x2
                (1)5x7 (4)2.5x3.5
☑ Flatten All   (2)5x7
                (4)4x5
Label   (2)4x5 (2)2.5x3.5 (4)2x2.5
                (2)4x5 (8)2x2.5
Content: (2)4x5 (4)2.5x3.5
                (4)3.5x5
Custom Text: (20)2x2
                (16)2x2.5
Font: (8)2.5x3.5
                (4)2.5x3.5 (8)2x2.5
Font Size: (9)2.5x3.25

Color: Black   Opacity: 100 %
Position: Centered
Rotate: None

Picture Package

Source
Use: Frontmost Document
☑ Include All Subfolders
Browse...

Document
Page Size: 8.0 x 10.0 inches
Layout: (2)4x5 (2)2.5x3.5 (4)2x2.5
Resolution: 72   pixels/inch
Mode: RGB Color
☑ Flatten All Layers

Label
Content: None
Custom Text:
Font: Arial
Font Size: 12 pt
Color: Black   Opacity: 100 %
Position: Centered
Rotate: None

OK
Cancel
Help

FIGURE 19-5   The Picture Package dialog box shows a preview of a mixture of picture sizes.

Resolution Type a resolution into the Resolution field, and choose the units from the drop-down list adjacent to the Resolution field. As mentioned earlier, you should select 300 pixels per inch for printing, and make sure that the image will have at least that resolution at the printed size. For example, if you have a 4 × 5 image at 300 pixels per inch and you choose to print it at 5 × 7, the result will be poor quality because you have stretched the image to fit.

Mode Choose either RGB Color or Grayscale from the Mode drop-down list. Only use Grayscale if you are printing to a laser or other monochrome printer.

Flatten All Layers If the image has multiple layers, you can (and should) choose to flatten the layers in the Picture Package file. It isn't likely that you would make adjustments to the Picture Package image. Instead, you would open the original image, make your adjustments, and create a new Picture Package. Flattening layers creates a smaller file than a file in which the layers are preserved.

Set the Label Options

As with the Security options for web photo galleries (covered in Chapter 18), you can superimpose text on the printed images. This works exactly the same way Security options does, with the exception that you can also superimpose the author's name on the image.

Apply Batch Conversions to Multiple Images

One of the recommendations I made early on was *not* to modify JPEG files and save them, because the file degrades each time you do. Instead, you should convert the JPEG files to Photoshop Elements files or TIFF files (or some other file format that does not degrade the image). Then you can modify them and convert them back to JPEG files when you are done. However, what you if you shot a lot of pictures on your last vacation? Converting each one manually can be quite laborious. Photoshop Elements provides the Batch Processing function to automate these types of conversions. Select File | Batch Processing to open the Batch dialog box (shown in Figure 19-6).

Once you have set the options discussed below, click OK to complete the batch conversion.

Set the Files to Convert

To specify the files to convert, make a choice from the Files To Convert drop-down list. The available values are:

Folder Enables you to select the folder containing the files to convert. Click the Source button to open the Browse For Folder dialog box. Choose the folder and click OK. To include the images in any subfolders, check the Include All Subfolders check box.

Import   Enables you to import images from a camera, scanner, and so on. The available options will depend on what hardware (and drivers) you have installed on your computer. Pick the image source from the From drop-down list.

Opened Files   Enables you to convert all files you have open in Photoshop Elements.

Set the Conversion File Type

Regardless of the type of the source files, you can specify only a single type of file as a target. Thus, you can convert a mixture of Photoshop Elements, GIF, and TIFF files to JPEG if you wish. To pick the type file to convert to, choose it from the Convert File Type drop-down list. Your options include various quality JPEG, PSD, and TIFF files:

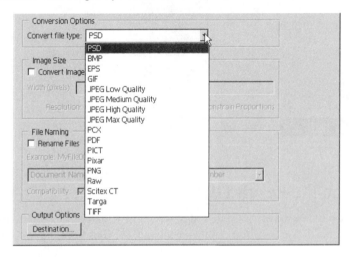

Set the File Size

If you wish to convert all the files to the same dimensions, check the Convert Image Size check box in the Image Size section of the dialog box. To set the dimensions, type a value into the Width (pixels) field or the Height (pixels) field. To maintain the ratio of width to height, check the Constrain Proportions check box. If you do check the Constraint Proportions check box, you can only type a value into either the Width (pixels) or Height (pixels) field—attempting to enter a value in both fields displays a warning.

You can set the resolution by picking it from the Resolution drop-down list. Values include 72 dpi (standard for Windows screens), 96 dpi (standard for Macintosh screens), and 300 dpi (a good value for printing).

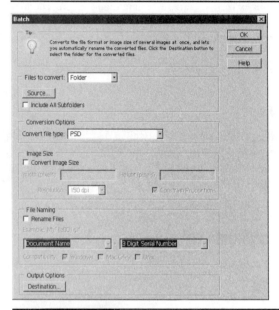

The Batch dialog box

Rename the Result Files

If you want to rename the converted files, check the Rename Files check box in the File Naming section of the dialog box. You can then construct the files from the two lists:

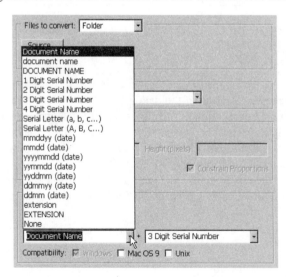

Construct the filename by picking options from the two lists; Photoshop Elements concatenates the results together to create the filename. For example, if you pick mmddyy (date) in the first list and the 3 Digit Serial Number from the second list, you'll end up with filenames like 081402001, 081402002, and so on. You can also type a quantity into either list, and the quantity will be treated as a constant string. For example, if you type *David* into the first list and use 3 Digit Serial Number in the second list, you'll end up with filenames like David001, David002, and so on.

 *Make sure to pick a combination of quantities from the two lists that result in a unique filename (such as Document Name and 3 Digit Serial Number) or the converted files will write over each other. For example, if you combine one of the date formats and the extension, you won't have a filename that is unique.*

You can ensure filenames that are compatible with various operating systems by checking the check boxes for Mac OS 9 and/or Unix (compatibility with Windows is automatic).

Set the Output Options

To set the folder where the converted files will be stored, click the Destination button in the Output Options section. This opens the Browse For Folder dialog box. Choose the folder or click the New Folder button to create a new folder for the converted images.

Index

Numbers and Symbols

(–) minus sign. See plus/minus signs
(+) plus sign. See plus/minus signs
3D Transform filter, 395–404
    aligning shape with underlying layer, 404
    creating/manipulating shapes, 398–399
    cube shapes, 400–401
    cylindrical shapes, 402–404
    options, 397
    overview of, 395–396
    spherical shapes, 399–400
    understanding shapes, 397

A

active layer, 220–221
adaptive algorithm, GIF optimization, 458
Add Anchor Point tool, 3D Transform filter, 402–403
Add Noise filter, 383–385
Add to Selection option, 182
Add to Shape Area tool, 328
Add transparency check box, Gradient Editor dialog box, 212
Adjust Backlighting dialog box, 84–85
Adjustment Layer button, 227, 229–231
Adjustment slider, Hue/Saturation tool, 95
Adobe Acrobat
    creating slideshow, 470–474
    opening, 52–53
    Reader, 472–473
Adobe Color Picker. *See* Color Picker
Advanced Blending, Composition Settings, 444
airbrushing, 121

algorithms, GIF optimization, 458–459
Align with Layer check box, Gradient Fill dialog box, 228
alignment controls, text, 417
ALT key
    creating selected areas from intersections, 184
    grouping layers, 222
    layer visibility and, 218
    moving selections and, 189
    scaling images and, 275
    subtracting areas from selections, 183
    using Free Transform with, 286
    viewing grayscale masks, 242
ambient light, Lighting Effects filter, 389–390
Amount field, Indexed Color dialog box, 68
Amount slider, Unsharp Mask, 87
anchor points, 3D transform filter, 399–403
Angle control, Brush tool, 121
angle gradient, 204
Angled Strokes filter, 347, 349
Animals shape palette, 328
Anti-aliased button, 416
anti-aliasing, 170, 416, 473
Apply button, Filters palette, 340
archival images, compression, 65
arrow keys
    moving insertion points, 412
    moving selections, 188
    selecting text, 413
Artistic filters, 342–347
    Colored Pencil, 344
    Cutout, 344–346
    Fresco, 346–347
    Paint Daub, 347
    Rough Pastels, 343–344
    Underpainting, 342–343
aspect ratios, scaling, 274

INTERNATIONAL CONTACT INFORMATION

AUSTRALIA
McGraw-Hill Book Company Australia Pty. Ltd.
TEL +61-2-9415-9899
FAX +61-2-9415-5687
http://www.mcgraw-hill.com.au
books-it_sydney@mcgraw-hill.com

CANADA
McGraw-Hill Ryerson Ltd.
TEL +905-430-5000
FAX +905-430-5020
http://www.mcgrawhill.ca

**GREECE, MIDDLE EAST,
NORTHERN AFRICA**
McGraw-Hill Hellas
TEL +30-1-656-0990-3-4
FAX +30-1-654-5525

MEXICO (Also serving Latin America)
McGraw-Hill Interamericana Editores S.A. de C.V.
TEL +525-117-1583
FAX +525-117-1589
http://www.mcgraw-hill.com.mx
fernando_castellanos@mcgraw-hill.com

SINGAPORE (Serving Asia)
McGraw-Hill Book Company
TEL +65-863-1580
FAX +65-862-3354
http://www.mcgraw-hill.com.sg
mghasia@mcgraw-hill.com

SOUTH AFRICA
McGraw-Hill South Africa
TEL +27-11-622-7512
FAX +27-11-622-9045
robyn_swanepoel@mcgraw-hill.com

**UNITED KINGDOM & EUROPE
(Excluding Southern Europe)**
McGraw-Hill Education Europe
TEL +44-1-628-502500
FAX +44-1-628-770224
http://www.mcgraw-hill.co.uk
computing_neurope@mcgraw-hill.com

ALL OTHER INQUIRIES Contact:
Osborne/McGraw-Hill
TEL +1-510-549-6600
FAX +1-510-883-7600
http://www.osborne.com
omg_international@mcgraw-hill.com